Prophets and Millennialists

Prophets and Millennialists

The Uses of Biblical Prophecy in England from the 1790s to the 1840s

W. H. Oliver

Auckland University Press
Oxford University Press

First published 1978

Printed in New Zealand
at the University of Auckland Bindery
from type set by Typocrafters
ISBN 0 19 647962 2

For my wife

Contents

		page
Preface		9
I	Biblical Prophecy and Millennialism	11
II	A Sketch of the Tradition	25
III	Responses to Revolution	42
IV	Arguments about Prophecy	68
V	Irving and Drummond	99
VI	The Albury Group and its Context	124
VII	John Ward—the Messiah as Agitator	150
VIII	The Empirically Proven Messiah	175
IX	From the Southcottians to Socialism	197
X	The Mormons—Cosmic America	218
XI	Some Possible Futures	239
References		245
Bibliography		254
Index		266

Preface

This study began as an attempt to find out what Robert Owen meant when he talked about the millennium. It soon became apparent that the answer was to be found in an aspect of the history of religious opinion in early nineteenth-century England, and that this context, in turn, was a part of a tradition many centuries old. The book that has grown from this beginning tries to say something in general about religion in England. I hope it still manages to say something about the socialist and radical milieu with which it was originally concerned.

It is not easy to write English history from New Zealand. It would have been impossible if Massey University had not granted me two considerable periods of leave. During the first I enjoyed the hospitality of Nuffield College, Oxford, and during the second that of the Department of English at the University of Alberta. To these three institutions, to the Association of Universities and Colleges of Canada, which awarded me a Visiting Fellowship, and to my colleagues in the Department of History at Massey University, without whose co-operation I could not have taken leave, I am especially grateful.

In addition, I am grateful to Dr F. B. Smith, of the Australian National University, for a number of detailed comments, to Mr R. D. McEldowney, of the Auckland University Press, for suggesting a number of revisions, to Dr W. S. Broughton, of Massey University, for locating an obscure reference, and to Miss Heather Read and Mrs Delma Reed for typing so many successive drafts.

An earlier version of Chapter VIII appeared in *Robert Owen: Prophet of the Poor*, edited by Sidney Pollard and John Salt and published by Macmillan in 1971.

The conditions under which this book was brought into existence over a lengthy period created another, very considerable, debt. This is acknowledged in the dedication.

Massey University
May 1977

I: Biblical Prophecy and Millennialism

The purpose of this study is to describe some of the ways in which biblical images of the transformation of the world were used in the half-century following the French Revolution. The purpose is, in part, pursued through an examination of the theological writings of men such as Joseph Priestley, Thomas Newton, Samuel Horsley, Claudius Buchanan, Henry Drummond, John Henry Newman and John Keble, who achieved a considerable eminence in their lifetimes and a substantial reputation subsequently for achievements not obviously connected with the uses of biblical prophecy. In part, further, it is pursued through a study of other eminent men—Robert Owen, Richard Carlile, Henry Hetherington, James Morrison and James Smith—whose significance, then and since, would at first appear not to have been primarily theological. These names indicate the context into which the narrower specialists in the exegesis of biblical prophecy and (though they are not a main concern of this study) the more explicit prophetical movements are placed. Such a context should suggest, and the study as a whole will attempt to show, that prophecy, both explicit and implicit, was a normal intellectual activity in early nineteenth-century England.

It may be that such an assertion will, at least initially, appear bizarre to readers more accustomed to meet such ideas in tracts left by Sunday morning callers than to find them between hard covers. Such a response, in itself, provides some measure of the distance between the early nineteenth and the later twentieth centuries. Perhaps the distance is diminishing: a recent *Newsweek* report suggested that some ten per cent of American Christians hold opinions of the kind discussed here. Nor is it any longer the case that the more ecstatic kinds of religious behaviour—a leading aspect of the 'Irvingite' movement—are the preserve of sects which may be readily dismissed as eccentric. Nevertheless, it would not, today, be expected of a handful of leading British churchmen and theologians, or of a handful of leading British radicals and socialists, that they would reveal either a considerable interest in the detailed fulfilment of biblical prophecy, or a readiness to employ prophetic concepts to convey their message. Such, however, can be shown to be perfectly reasonable expectations in early nineteenth-century England.

There is no evidence that Samuel Horsley, still celebrated as the first editor of Sir Isaac Newton's *Works*, felt it to be out of character to reflect and write upon the identity of Antichrist or the bearing of prophecy upon Great Britain's destiny. After all, Newton himself had written upon the prophecies of Daniel. Nor are Joseph Priestley's prophetic sermons out of keeping with his other historical and theological works; he was obviously aware of their relationship, and aware, too, that another great thinker, David Hartley, had used a prophetic approach in sections of *Observations on Man*. Robert Owen, well before spiritualist ideas influenced him, employed prophetic and millennialist vocabulary and images with precision and emphasis. Richard Carlile used the prophetic manner to some effect, responding to his discovery of the vitality of English sectarianism. Here, it is simply urged that if men of this kind did not find such concerns unusual or such concepts obscure, twentieth-century readers who still hold them in respect should accept their guidance.

The scope of this study is restricted to England; this limitation, essentially a convenience of research, has important consequences. Always in the background and often in the foreground is the great fact of the Established Church in intimate alliance with the State. In Ireland and Scotland the Church-State situation was different, a difference which probably affected the kind of prophetical theology produced there. It is readily apparent, from the frequency with which the Irish situation impinges upon the English debate in the 1820s, that such theology had an especial relevance to the clergy of the Church of Ireland, who were in intimate contact with a population which persistently adhered to Antichrist. It is equally apparent that some of the more heterodox forms of behaviour and thought in the 1820s had their origin in Scotland and are related to the intense theological discussions within Scottish Presbyterianism in the early nineteenth century. In this study, however, such situations are discussed only for their bearing upon the prophetic movement in England. The same is true for contemporary developments in Europe and in America. The St Simonians and the Mormons, who had a direct effect upon England, are examined; others, for example Jonathan Edwards and Lammenais, are not. Either a wider or a narrower scope would have been as valid, and might have yielded more satisfactory results. But it was necessary to make a beginning, and the English situation seemed to provide a middle ground between the intensive and the extensive.

The period surveyed was also chosen as a field of research neither too small nor too large. A close study of a few years or a broad survey of many centuries would have thrown up different and perhaps more valid results. But, from the outset, a few general features were evident: that the French Revolution stimulated prophetical publication, that in the 1820s prophecy became a major subject of theological debate, that in the 1830s and 1840s notions derived from prophecy played their part in many interests and causes. It seemed reasonable to conclude that this half-century would provide a reasonable example. Further, because Englishmen did not suddenly discover the uses of prophecy in the 1790s, it was necessary to begin with a tentative survey of the long tradition of prophetical thinking, in order to identify a handful of ideas which were both of ancient origin and of early nineteenth-century relevance. No one, it seems, has tried to see this part of European religious history as a whole; the useful and (at times) brilliant monographs of Norman Cohn and Ernest Tuveson are considerably limited by the special purposes which underlie them.[1] Prophetical theology was normally neither revolutionary nor progressive; it was, for centuries, a normal exegetical activity, a concern of professional scholars, and a respectable way of saying things about God, man and their relationship in society and history.

Of recent years a good deal has been written about seventeenth-century prophetic and millennialist movements, but less about the underlying prophetic and millennialist theology. These studies do not always make it sufficiently clear that biblical prophecy was then, as it had been and as it continued to be, the basis for a wide range of behaviour. Within this range theorizing and mysticism were constant, while efforts to bring about the millennial kingdom were no more than occasional. Because such efforts failed in the mid-century, prophecy did not cease to have its uses. The scholars and the mystics, whose interpretations had briefly helped to shape a programme, continued undeterred by its failure. In particular, because scholarship is more accessible than mysticism, it is very evident that the mid-seventeenth-century failure of the programme of godly rule did not break the academic tradition which stretches (at least) across the century and a half from Joseph Mede to George Faber in the time of the French Revolution; it is this tradition which was drawn upon by many Englishmen to explain the events of their own time.

It is difficult, perhaps impossible, to say what weight, in the history of English opinion in the early nineteenth century, should be given to this traditional theology of the last things. One of the historian's occupational dilemmas is his inability to avoid the use of quantitative terms and his inability to show that he has any clear right to use them. Here the frequent use of vaguely quantitative terms means only that the writer is passing on a guess, and hoping that it is a fair one. In general, three such guesses have been made; first, that in this half-century prophetical theology was a more considerable concern than in either preceding or following decades; second, it was an important aspect of religious thought as a whole; and third, that religious thinking as such contained a good deal of significant thought about society and politics. Perhaps these guesses are too often turned into firm assertions. The weight of received opinions—that prophetical theology is at best quaint and at worst crazy, and that thinking about society is something done by political economists—and the conviction that this conventional wisdom is misleading, may have provided a constant inducement to over-emphasis.

But though quantitative questions are thus constantly raised and constantly begged, it remains demonstrable that a great deal of prophetical theology was produced in this period, that millennial aspirations conveyed the thought of some men about society and politics, that these men were not the wild deluded creatures of popular legend, that even the people reputed to have been wild and deluded appear less so the closer one approaches them, and that these ways of thinking were widely diffused. The ideas here discussed were a real part of the intellectual climate of early nineteenth-century England.

In the light of these considerations one may not confidently draw any firm conclusion as to the social significance of these ideas or the social situation of their propagators. Much of the academic study of prophecy and millennialism has been concerned with present or very recent situations, and has been conducted by sociologists employing techniques which make a search for firm conclusions a more plausible activity. The historian can put questions, but he cannot compel answers. He should be especially reluctant to conclude that prophetic and millennialist theorizing arose from tensions in the lives of individuals and in their society. By the later eighteenth century, prophetical exegesis and social commentary based upon it had become habitual activities. One could write as matter-of-factly about the end of the world as about its beginning, or about what was happening in between. While many writers on prophecy were clearly disturbed by what they took to be gross imperfections in the condition of society, and by the belief that things would get worse before they became better, it is not clear that they were 'disturbed' in the clinical sense of the word. They were attempting to say truthful and useful things about the society they lived in, about everything in its life from parental authority to international relations. Many found their society deplorable and perilous; they could not rest content with the 'orthodox' consolation that all would be set right in eternity. They needed at least the prospect of perfection within history and upon earth. So they were driven to eschatology. In this way eschatological ideas were given a social reference by the men who handled them. For this reason it is necessary to go beyond a simple description of the ideas as a part of the history of religious thought towards a suggestion of the outlines of an underlying historical sociology.

Inevitably, it will seem likely that early nineteenth-century anxieties bear some sort of relationship to the rise of industrial capitalism. Unluckily, such appearances are constantly pressed into service to account for a bewildering variety of phenomena. Writing of late medieval millennialism, Norman Cohn asserted that 'the great social upheavals which accompanied the close of the middle ages' provided the basis for the emergence of 'extremist groups' and further that 'some great revolt or revolution' was necessary to stimulate millennialists into an effort to divert it to their own peculiar ends. He concluded: 'The society which bred them was a society profoundly disoriented by the defection of traditional relationships crumbling under the pressure of the new capitalist economy.'[2] One would be tempted to apply this generalization to the early nineteenth century, were it not for the suspicion that a formula which could be applied equally well to such diverse situations might prove too true to be good. But, even in the early nineteenth century, a period that left more abundant traces behind it than the late middle ages, it is not possible to draw firm conclusions about the social situation of those who heard, read, or heeded the prophetical specialists. Who listened to Joseph Priestley, James Bicheno or Faber in the 1790s? Who were the Southcottians, the Irvingites, John Ward's True Believers, James Smith's readers, or (best-recorded of them all) the British Mormons? At least it is certain that they were not all uprooted by 'the new capitalist economy'. There is no group in which there were not some people with a good deal of money to spend.

The leaders, much more observable than the followers, span the entire social spectrum, from noble to humble, from land to manufacturing, from master to operative, from don to illiterate, from scientist to mystic, from reactionary to agitator. If indeed prophecy and millennialism are related to sharp social disturbance, the information available about leaders and the fugitive hints which remain about followers suggest that disturbance was evenly distributed over

English society as a whole, and was felt by every group, from landed proprietors to out-of-work factory hands.

The view that millennialism and social disturbance go together is derived from the study of modern movements chiefly among non-Europeans.[3] It is used to explain movements among small homogenous populations in the grip of social change affecting nearly all members more or less uniformly and more or less disastrously. A small population abruptly experiencing alien intrusion in the shape of colonization would indeed be profoundly disturbed. Victimhood and total social experience would coincide. There are no precise parallels in the situation of a large and diverse population affected by changes which, however great, came piecemeal and over a lengthy period. There would be no abrupt intrusion; victims and beneficiaries would share a single greater society which kept them together even as they were driven apart. James Morrison, a socialist editor, distressed to find that British workmen were a deprived class, tried to convert their oppressors. One would be surprised to find such behaviour among the leaders of a millennialist adjustment cult. In early nineteenth-century England social disturbance was not total; it did not affect all members of society, and it did not totally affect the lives of all members of a particular group. Though weakened, traditional linkages persisted, religion among them; there was, as well as a millennialism of revolution, a millennialism of counter-revolution.

Nevertheless, the concept of social disturbance is useful. Though industrialization had anything but an instantaneous and uniform effect, by the end of the eighteenth century it had contributed, together with other social changes and political unrest, to a general pattern of apprehension and alarm. These anxieties became a persistent ground-bass during the first half of the nineteenth century. Over the same period, there is a wide dispersion of prophetic and millennialist ideas, and a marked parallelism of response, both socially and geographically. In the 1790s and in the 1820s the upsurge appears to have affected, with similar intensity, all social levels, from the commonroom, the rectory, the country house and the mill-owner's mansion to the city back alley, the labourer's hovel and the operative's tenement. The idea of social disturbance suggests that within each social group some suffered acutely (either in reality or in anticipation), others either benefited greatly or did not despair of their chances of doing so, while the rest (probably the great majority) were distributed between these extremes, available for recruitment to either end of the range according to the situation at a particular time. This is to suppose that there was a 'victim-group' within each larger group, and that a minority of this minority responded in a millennialist manner to the history they were experiencing. Hence the persistence of the millennial mood, its wide social distribution, and its failure ever to amount to a major movement.

Among political radicals and trade unionists one would expect to find a sense of victimhood most apparent. Social millennialism, of which Owenism was the clearest example, reflected that newly-gained class-consciousness which Edward Thompson[4] finds to have evolved by the early 1830s. It was an ingredient in the ideology of the new class; it found non-Owenite expression in the straight millennialism of Ward and the assumed millennialism of Richard Carlile. And yet the very closeness with which Smith's socialism was related to Irving's conservatism, or Ward's libertarianism to Spencer Perceval's reaction, or Owen's new world to Henry Drummond's idea of social duty shows that working-class ideologists were able to construct their explanations from traditional elements in English thought. Even in their revolutionary statements they share a conceptual vocabulary with those they came to recognize as class enemies.

Should this community of ideas prove to occur more widely, a paradox would emerge. The articulation of distinctive class standpoints re-affirmed the relevance of inherited and shared thought-patterns. Perhaps the continuing utility of a common traditional inheritance blunted ideological conflict. The isolation of the working class can be too much insisted upon, whether by its own advocates or by new Tory social reformers or by recent historians. English society consisted of a series of small and overlapping gradations with a constant flow of ideas and information up and down the series.

Or rather, to return from this excursus, it may certainly be concluded that prophetic and millennialist ideas, already widely diffused when the period opened, were significant at all social levels. The scholarly exegete, the self-proclaimed Messiah, the evangelical preacher, the prophet of hope, the prophet of doom, the Mormon missionary, and the restorer of Israel, all employed the same body of religious ideas, spoke the same religious language, pondered the same set of biblical images. This religious inheritance, further, was a useful means of communication for the political radical, the socialist journalist, and the Owenite lecturer. No social group and no intellectual level lacked access to these ideas, concepts and images, should any of its members want to use them. In all groups and at all levels some did; anyone who wanted to adopt a millennialist position could do so without leaving his normal milieu. The millennial dream is simple and infinitely malleable. Millennialism and prophecy were so readily available and useful because they were so entirely traditional and conventional at all social levels.

Because in early nineteenth-century England Christianity remained strong and was largely fundamentalist, millennialism and prophecy were commonplace. Because an explicit biblical frame of reference is lacking, comparable impulses take different shapes in the mid-twentieth century, except in fundamentalist groups which preserve the characteristics of early nineteenth-century Christianity. Today the Bible is not a common frame of reference, and of the minority for whom it remains authoritative by no means all take it to be wholly and literally inspired. Hence twentieth-century apocalyptic and millennialist positions are only remotely if at all biblical. The images and the vocabulary are drawn from a variety of discordant sources—from Marx, Nietzsche, science fiction and astrology. 'When the moon is in the seventh house/And Jupiter aligns with Mars' is the beginning of an apocalyptic and millennialist hymn, but the language is remote from that of biblical prophecy.

Thus the millennialism of the mid-twentieth century, sharing a common impulse with that of the early nineteenth century, is sharply separated by imagery, vocabulary and theology. For the earlier millennialists believed in a venerated book containing passages which had for centuries encouraged men to believe that the present order would end in total change and that this event would illustrate certain theological truths about God, man and their relationship.

If the Bible was all of a piece, then these passages needed explanation, unless it could be admitted (as most could not admit) that God's word was flawed. As these passages had been explained and interpreted for centuries, a rich body of exegesis was available. But they had not, at least until the early eighteenth century and then only occasionally, been explained away. Almost without exception exegetes were literalists in the sense that they believed the Bible to be literally inspired. When they used the term 'literalist' they used it to refer to a literal interpretation of such predictions as the rising of the saints from their graves. Other interpretations, for example the argument that this meant simply the dominance of the beliefs for which the saints had died, were described as allegorical. Both literalists and allegorists could be and were millennialists; both took the promises seriously. As a general rule literalists stressed the discontinuities between the mundane world and the future, and allegorists the continuities, in respect of both the means of change and the result of change. Literalists tend to be pre-millennialists and allegorists post-millennialists.

Millennialism is rooted in theology and specifically in eschatology, the doctrines about the last things, and yet more specifically in apocalyptic, a more limited group of ideas about the last things. Discussion must at least begin at this point, with a situation in which it is accepted that God and man have dealings with each other, and that these dealings occur in a moral God-given order or strategy which incorporates the history of individual, nation, and race. Though within this strategy humanity is constantly subject to providential acts, the three great acts are the creation, the atonement and the end of the world. All three are related to the activity of the second person of the Trinity, the third to his second advent, in glory, as king and judge. Eschatology is the body of teaching about the end of the world through the second advent; it anticipates the winding up of the divine strategy on earth and the translation of all human worth to heaven. Probably most theologians would have preferred an eschatology as general and as unspectacular as this. But many New Testament passages took their colour from earlier Jewish apocalyptic writings which had three troublesome characteristics: first, a set of indications which could be used to predict the time of these events; second, a catastrophic scenario for the last days, so that they become a cosmic morality play in which good and evil meet their just rewards; and third, a notion of a period of earthly felicity between the first victory of good and the final re-emergence of evil at the very end. This is the millennium in which the Messiah rules as king.

The term 'millennialist' is one which it is difficult to use with precision. (Here, for the sake of minimum obscurity, the term 'millenarian' is not used except in quotations.) The millennium is a long ('thousand year') period of felicity on earth which will precede the truly final end. In that period, often described as the 'sabbath' or 'rest' of the world and so as its seventh age, the divine plan will be consummated, the divine purpose in creation fulfilled, and divine justice vindicated. A term is set to the operation of evil; good is shown as the ultimate victor. The vital point is that this consummation, fulfilment and vindication will take place *on earth*; the distinguishing feature of all who look for the millennium is that they cannot rest content with a merely heavenly righting of earthly wrongs. Earth was the scene of the creation and the incarnation; God will be vindicated in the place which he made and in which he became man. Where he once came in obscurity and humility, he will return in majesty and power.

So millennial beliefs emphasize the materialism of Christianity; they were embraced by men who found it impossible to yield up for more than an interval the world and the flesh to the devil. Inevitably then, millennialism had a social character. During the millennium men would live on earth in society; the nature of that society was a proper field for exegesis and for speculation that reflected social ideals. At best, millennialism provided scope for social theory; at the very least, it was a framework for utopianism. The millennium was depicted in contrast, more or less sharp according to the character and situation of the millennialist, to the world as it was. So millennialist social theorizing implied an enquiry into actual society, to identify the evil in it which would be reversed, or (less typically) the good in it which would be preserved. Further, because millennialists learned from the Bible that certain signs would enable them to know when the change from the old to the new was about to take place, and because they believed that these signs were essentially social and political, they had to examine the contemporary situation. Consequently, millennial theories were anything but vague dreams. They were intimately related to the social situation of the theorist by extrapolation, by criticism, by diagnosis. If the theorist was a man of perception and intelligence, his millennialist writings merit serious attention for the sake of the social thought they contain. Naturally this is not always the case, any more than it is with political economists. The use an age makes of millennial ideas is as much part of the history of its social thought as the use it makes of ideas about the nature of wealth.

Millennialism was a mode of social thought; accordingly its images, concepts and vocabulary were relevant well beyond the limited circle of specialist writers and readers. The social and political thinking of men for whom interpreting the scriptures was not a serious occupation, or an occupation at all, was coloured and shaped by prophetic ideas. So, the millennialism of this period included a diffused penumbra of attitudes which were an essential part of its overall character. This aspect may be seen in Robert Owen and the imagery of socialist thought, and among Christians, in Newman, for whom millennialism was not a vital concern, or in those for whom it was transposed into more conventional shapes, such as the 'post-millennialist' advocates of missionary enterprise. These latter exemplify the conventionalization of an inherently radical impulse.

This distinction between pre- and post-millennialists is a good deal more ancient than the terminology; Eusebius was probably the first post-millennialist. The distinction turns, first, upon the continuity or lack of it anticipated between the world as it is and as it shall be, and second upon the character of the events which were expected to accompany the transition from the one to the other. If continuity is stressed, the millennium becomes simply a progressively-achieved improvement upon the present. If discontinuity is stressed, then it becomes its complete reversal. In the former case the transition is smooth, gradual and peaceable; in the latter, it is abrupt, revolutionary and violent. The distinction is focused on the role played by the Christ of the second coming. This role was immediately clear to those who foresaw radical discontinuity. Christ returning in power, first as judge and then as king, would effect the change. So they are 'pre'-millennialists, in the sense that the second coming will precede the millennium. Those who stressed continuity and progressive improvement were embarrassed by the second coming, for it was an event they were not prepared to dismiss. Yet it would introduce such a qualitative change that it would preclude continuity. Their solution was an argument that the second coming would indeed take place, but after the millennium, as the prelude not to a time of earthly felicity but to the final winding up of the earthly experiment. Hence they are 'post'-millennialists.

There is nothing to choose between the two on the score of worldliness—the charge they constantly threw at each other. Each posited a period in which goodness and justice would prevail on earth. The former so despaired of the world as they knew it that they saw the necessity of a miraculous reversal. The latter hoped with such confidence for the world as they knew it that they saw no such necessity. The pre-millennialists are clearly closer to the meaning of the texts both accepted, and nearer to the social situation from which these writings emerged—that of the persecuted and powerless Jews and Christians of the ancient world. Pre-millennialism is the basic stance; post-millennialism a compromise in the form of a metaphor. Accordingly, when the word 'millennialist' is here used without qualification, it refers to pre-millennialism, except in passages where it will be clear from the context that both varieties are being discussed.

These millennialists did more than envisage a desirable future and hope that it would come. The biblical texts and exegetical tradition led men to believe that they could anticipate the change to the new world with some precision. Though it is true that post-millennialists could identify signs, measure historical periods, and predict events, understandably enough, to do so is more characteristic of pre-millennialists. A smooth transition is hard to predict, a crisis very easy. Further, the signs foretold in the texts—tumults, disorders, wars, revolutions and strange sights in the heavens—were all associated with the second coming. If this event is removed to the end of the millennium, the signs lose their urgency. If, however, the second coming precedes the millennium, there is plenty to stimulate speculation and prediction.

The images of disorder were mainly drawn from Luke's gospel but another set of texts, from Daniel and Revelation, were full of such images and were also used to predict the length of Antichrist's reign and so to date the beginning of the millennium at its close. The chief of these was an interpretation of the phrase, 'a time, times and half a time' which led to the conclusion that his reign would last 1260 days, and then converted this period into 1260 years. This view, though arbitrary, was venerable and widely accepted. The majority of millennialists, of either kind, rejected criticisms of this interpretation and were able to use this period to predict the crisis of transition, once they had found a base figure to which to add the 1260 years.

It must be added that not all the people discussed in this book spent much (or in some cases, any) of their time speculating on the nature of the millennium. Some of them, especially professional exegetes, were wholly concerned with the timing and the nature of the events which would lead to the millenium. For example, three of the most industrious, Faber, William Cuninghame of Lainshaw, and Edward Bickersteth, were chiefly interested in the end of the existing order and the critical events which would introduce the new order—the full emergence of Antichrist, the wrath to fall on the nations, the destiny of the Jews and of Great Britain, the second coming and the rising of the saints. They were adventists and commentators on prophecy; often they denounced millennial speculation as a dangerous exercise. Nevertheless, they were in no doubt that these events, which they all located in the fairly near future, would lead to the millennium, and that then total virtue and total power would be joined together. They were still, in spite of their disclaimers, millennialists.

Though it took a multitude of forms, the core of biblical millennialism was simple. It was a flexible predictive mechanism which showed how an existing condition of disorder would move towards a crisis, and how this crisis would bring on a new situation in which old wrong would be set right. The distinguishing millennial and apocalyptical feature is the accomplishment of this change by a miraculous and divine agency, an external power intervening decisively in human affairs. The predicted change is part of an overall transcendental strategy; this strategy confers moral value even upon the most deplorable evidences of evil, war, disease and apostasy. In this way the millennial scheme is marked off from ideas of progress, in which human effort rather than external agency effect the change from bad to good. Accordingly, progressivist programmes are rational rather than apocalyptic in nature, for they require some calculation as to the relation of means and goals. If men are to progress they are to think, to understand, to plan. If, on the other hand, men are simply to be saved (socially as well as individually) they are to hope, to trust, to wait.

However, in the post-millennial compromise the millennialist and the progressive programmes shade into each other. Many post-millennialist writers saved the relevance of Revelation by describing the millennium as the result of human effort in a divine cause. It would, for example, crown the success of the missionary movement and the production of Bibles and tracts. Men who were already influential, often as office-holders in powerful religious societies, were always anxious to marry human effort with divine intervention, rational progressivism with irrational millennialism. And in fact, the content of the two programmes may be identical—evil eradicated and goodness triumphant. Further, the idea of progress is not, in the end, unrelievedly rationalistic; it commonly acquires overtones of inevitability, and takes the form of a supra-human if not an avowedly divine strategy. With Joachim and the Spiritual Franciscans, with St Simon and Marx, it is not easy to say where progress ends and the millennium takes over. The same is the case with some of the humbler prophets of early nineteenth-century England. But the more thorough-going millennialists were abundantly certain that all that passed in their society for progress was a work of Antichrist and an occasion for divine wrath.

That the business of predicting the end, or at least the transformation, of the world had become a tradition is a paradox. Anti-millennialists rehearsed the false predictions of earlier writers, but without dampening the ardour of the latest representatives of the tradition. This paradox suggests that millennialism has an existential validity which is not at all affected by the probability that predictions will be wrong. Although the predictors were sincere when they 'proved' that the world would end, or that some portentous event in the divine timetable would occur, at a certain date, prediction *in itself* did not matter supremely. It was a consequence rather than a motive, an effect rather than a cause. The motive and the cause lay in the necessity felt by some people to live *as if* they were certain that the end was coming very soon. Many preachers, for example, were wholly concerned with the pastoral efficacy of prediction—with its function in shaping character and stimulating correct behaviour. It will be argued later that Irving's fundamental motivation lay in his refusal to accept as final the death of his infant son, which became a compulsion to believe that he would meet him again *on earth* as a risen saint. The *Morning Watch* group, of which Irving was a member, reacted quite as obsessively to social and political change; they needed to feel sure that the things they hated and feared would not last. Owen and the St Simonians, for whom the moment of their speaking was the turning point of history, believed that things could not stay as they were without disaster, and convinced themselves that there would be a quick and total change for the better. This compulsion sometimes led to the assertion that things indeed had changed, whatever the appearances to the contrary. The Catholic and Apostolic Church, in its own view, was the new Church of the new age. Owen in late 1834 closed down a newspaper called the *Crisis* and began another called the *New Moral World*. John Ward dated his publications Year 6, Year 7, and so on, because the millennium had, for him, commenced in 1825. The paradox of a millennial tradition is a good deal more apparent than real: behind it lies a compulsion to live as if the end was near. Behind this compulsion lies a refusal to accept slow and arduous means of survival and salvation. This is the refusal which Augustine, so many centuries earlier, had set out to counter.

II: A Sketch of the Traditions

The history of Christian thinking about the last things has not yet been written, and cannot be attempted here. Nevertheless, some attempt at an outline must be made, simply because the theorists of the period which is the concern of this book were handling ancient arguments, and were aware that they were doing so. They were acquainted with the prophetical theology of the early Christian centuries, and with the arguments used by St Augustine to counter chiliastic excesses. Again, they knew well the uses to which prophecy had been put in the sixteenth and seventeenth centuries, by the Reformers and their heirs. This selectiveness is quite appropriate to Protestants who adhered to the Reformation and appealed to early Christian centuries over the head of the papal centuries.

In the early Christian centuries a cluster of world views contained the promise of quick results effortlessly achieved. No one of them necessarily set a precise and proximate date for the transformation of the world, but each or a combination of them could be used for this purpose. F. E. Manuel[1] identifies four such views, which may be designated triadic, Danielic, sabbatical and meliorist. These four ways of postulating a turning point and a better world are still in use in the early nineteenth century, as is the case which Augustine made against them.

The triadic view, of Jewish origin, divides history into three stages of development; for the Jews before, under and after the law, for St Paul before and under the law, and under grace. Well after Augustine, Joachim and, less ambiguously, some who followed him, built the Trinity into the triad, and so depicted a millennial third age of the Spirit which, if Voegelin[2] is to be heeded, underlies the world views of Comte, Hegel and Marx, the Third Rome of the Russians and the Third Reich of the National Socialists, as well as the more prosaic humanist periodization of history into ancient, medieval and modern epochs. Augustine denounced this scheme, not because it subordinated the Age of the Son to the Age of the Spirit, a development which was yet to come, but because it blurred the frontier between spiritual and secular.

Spiritual and secular are most obviously merged in the historical scheme of four monarchies culminating in the fifth messianic reign, again of Jewish origin and adapted by Christians to forecast the second coming of the Messiah and his earthly kingdom. The cryptic biblical passages (notably Daniel 2 and 7) have been adjusted to meet an infinite variety of political circumstances. The basic interpretative problems have been, first, the identification of the monarchies and the period covered by their succession, and second, the placing of the end of the existing order, which could follow either the fourth or the fifth in the series. Here lay the germ of much disputation. If the fifth monarchy was represented as simply a far-reaching improvement, the millenium became no more than a great quantitative amelioration. If, however, the fifth monarchy (or, in the sabbatarian scheme, the seventh historical day) was taken to result from catastrophic divine intervention, ameliorative views were rejected, the millennium became, literally, the kingdom of Christ on earth, and (as Augustine and his successors would have it) a materialistic vision of a perfect society drove out of men's minds a spiritual concept of heaven.

Daniel's five monarchies became a customary basis for millennialism. Given the identification of the fourth monarchy with the Roman Empire (until recently the conventional opinion), the assumption that the scheme covered all history since the Babylonian Empire, and the belief that the divinely initiated millennium would follow the fourth monarchy, then feverish millennial expectations readily arose from the calamities of the early Christian centuries. The orthodox counter was to accept the Roman identification of the fourth monarchy, to agree that its end would signal the end of the world, but to remove this event to the remote future by stressing the continuities which linked Rome with what are now called the Middle Ages. The protean quality of the millennial impulse can be seen in the way this historical fiction, damaging enough to early Christian millennialists, became grist to the mill of their successors. For if Rome still existed, its demise could still be anticipated, and with it the end of the existing order. Early nineteenth-century British commentators saw Rome in Napoleon's Empire or in Western Europe as a whole, and so foresaw its destruction and the transformation of the world.

Sabbatical millennialism was based upon Revelation's symbolic apparatus of seals, trumpets and vials each grouped in sevens; this, together with the Genesis story of a six-day creation followed by a seventh day of rest, suggested that world history was divided into seven periods or millennia. Here the question of the timing of the second coming—whether it concluded the sixth or seventh millennium—gave rise to the apocalyptic-ameliorative distinction that arose with the fourth and the fifth monarchies. Millennialists drew upon both sources and integrated them by imposing arbitrary values upon the vague time-indications in the sources. They were still doing so in the early nineteenth century. The task of reconciling the five-period pattern of Daniel with the seven-period pattern of Revelation presented no real difficulty to men determined to do just that.

A fourth view identified by Manuel is relevant, though not in a strict sense millennialist. This is the meliorism of Eusebius, briefly flowering in the Indian summer of the Christian Empire, when it was possible, for a little while, to believe that the spiritual kingdom would emerge as human institutions were permeated by the Christian spirit. Such optimists could understand the fifth monarchy or the seventh day as the triumph of goodness through human effort; theirs would be a cool millennium in which divine influences would work through normal channels. This was the millennialism of men at the top, whose vision of felicity was the prospect of the world they managed so well perfected by the removal of enemies who were already on the retreat.

It was easy for some Englishmen, during the eighteenth and nineteenth centuries, to experience a Eusebian mood. The progress of civilization, the expansion of knowledge, the advance of good government, and especially the activity of missionary, Bible, and tract societies (converting as they thought pagan, papist and Jew with equal rapidity), were believed by many to herald the advent of a millennium which would be no more than their own times purged of dross. God would work progressively and peacefully, not abruptly and destructively, through the normal channels of grace and enlightenment, not through a second coming more spectacular and decisive than the first. This 'missionary millennium' was the descendent of the meliorism that seemed tenable before the fall of Rome, just as the apocalyptic mood of its detractors restored the vision of those who had despaired of the world and yet could not forgo it. For the latter divine intervention, destruction and judgement were anxiously anticipated as the prelude to a new earth. For the former these events were indefinitely postponed; they were the epilogue to the new earth which men themselves would build. They usher in nothing at all on earth, for after them there is only heaven.

A catastrophe and a man of genius undercut these theories. The fall of Rome made Eusebian optimism untenable, and (because, after all, the millennium did not begin) apocalyptic millennialism could offer no guidance. Augustine, responding to actual disaster, established an orthodoxy which almost completely drained the secular world of any but an incidental spirituality. His general view of human history as an interim between divine events, spiritually insignificant except as the context in which rival powers competed for souls, made it difficult to hold any theory, meliorist or apocalyptic, which blurred the frontier between secular and spiritual. Society was sharply separated from Church; it could not itself become divine in the millennium. The reign of Christ had in fact begun and was manifested in the life of the Church; the seventh millennium, the Eternal Sabbath, lay quite outside history. To seek to foretell the future with precision was impiously curious; to anticipate the delights of the millennium was sinfully carnal.

More specifically, Augustine denied that the Bible provided any basis for detailed predictions. He did not attempt to deny the relevance of biblical prophecy; much of the Old Testament prefigured the life of Christ. Other passages, the Book of Revelation, Jesus's own words in the Gospels and numerous statements in St Paul's Epistles assuredly pointed to the future of the world. But it was not possible to know what was prefigured until it had taken place. Now that Christ had come, it was possible to see how the Old Testament predicted his coming. When the interim had ended, it would be possible to see how Revelation had predicted the end. Meanwhile unfulfilled prophecy simply assured the faithful that there would be an end, and that good would eventually prevail over evil. To ask for more precision was impiety. Only fulfilled prophecy was useful, for it assured the believer of God's omniscience. It was, to use an eighteenth-century term, among the 'evidences' of Christianity which should comfort the believer and convince the unbeliever.

These arguments remain the stock-in-trade of conservatives in the eighteenth and nineteenth centuries. Anglican divines of this later period used every Augustinian argument against the millennialists, but with one important difference. Many who took his point about unfulfilled prophecy needed arguments against deism and atheism, and devoted themselves to the minute illustration of fulfilled prophecy, seeking and finding its fulfilment in the by now long history of Christianity. Understandably, they ventured across the frontier between the recent past and the immediate future. In this way the Augustinian attitude, in spite of itself, bred its own millennialism.

Both sides of this inheritance reached the nineteenth century by transmission from writer to writer across the centuries. But the Bible itself was the major source of continuity, together with the recurrence of situations which led men to anticipate crisis and look for an explanation. A religion which spoke of a crisis of evil, a second coming, a transformation of the world, a general judgement, a paradise—a religion which, despite Augustine, described history as a process begun, shaped and completed by divine action—would encourage some people to arrange these elements to prove that change would be catastrophic, proximate and desirable. The Bible remained a source-book for revolutionaries without the means of revolution, one which could never be finally closed by theological and social conservatives. Conservatives at most could advance rival interpretations. They might regret that Revelation had been included in the canon; they might note that it was only admitted after misgivings and that it was very opaque. But they could not deny that it was canonical; they had to account for it where (one feels) they would have preferred to exclude it.

The millennial tradition, apparently either in suspense or driven underground during the early middle ages, reappeared in the twelfth century and has been vigorous ever since. But, paradoxically, its later vigour owes nothing to the most subtle and reflective mind ever to use prophetic methods, that of Joachim of Fiore. Recent scholarship[3] has established both Joachim's stature and the magnitude of his influence in the later middle ages. It has also been suggested that his impact was still great in the early sixteenth century.[4] His eclipse thereafter is suggested by the laborious rediscovery of his works and those of his disciples, and by the difficulty of confidently attributing authorship of his reputed works.

Though he may, as is argued by his present-day champions, have kept within the bounds of orthodoxy, his successors, especially among the Spiritual Franciscans and the Fraticelli of the fourteenth century, certainly did not. On the one hand they used his system to attack the papal Church as anti-Christian; this was not likely to commend the Joachite tradition to Catholic exponents of prophecy in later centuries. On the other, they offended against trinitarian orthodoxy by regarding the third Age of the Spirit as superior to the second Age of the Son. Thus Protestant exponents, for whom papal doctrine was in many respects only dubiously Christocentric, would not find him acceptable, for all the anti-papalism associated with his influence. Joachim simply did not match any of the simple polemical necessities of Reformation and post-Reformation Christianity.

Certainly, none of the protagonists in the period covered by this book could have used him to advantage, except those few who stood outside Christianity. The main exponents of prophecy in this later period were too unrelievedly Christocentric, and they had an abundance of prophetic anti-papal arguments from their own sources. In fact, the whole point may well be even less academic; it is unlikely that many writings of Joachim or of his disciples were available by this time.[5]

Although the eschatologies of the sixteenth century anticipated a third age the full impact of Joachism had been left far behind. Reformation salvation-histories, which continue into the nineteenth century and beyond, differed significantly. They were not progressive in that they did not see an Age of the Spirit displacing the Age of the Son. Joachism had been eroded by a simple-minded adventist millennialism and by predictions which depended entirely on Daniel and Revelation. The second age, no longer a step forward to be displaced only by a greater step forward, became a recession. For truer Joachites apostacy was a crisis between ages; after the sixteenth century, for most Protestants, it was an age in itself. The third age became as much a return as a progress, a return to a lost purity. The incarnation of the spirit became the second coming of the son—the second person drove out the third. Not by overt condemnation, but rather by its essential Christocentricity, prophetic Bible Christianity destroyed the idea of a post-gospel and post-Christian dispensation.

Thus the future of millennialism among Christians was not Joachite in character. The quest for a third age became formally Christocentric, though elements of the 'age of the spirit' persist. Such aberrations apart, the extra-Christian implications of the Joachite legacy found a future outside orthodoxy. Well after the Reformation, anti-Christian writers found agreeable the suggestion that the Christian dispensation was merely preparatory and destined to end in corruption and catastrophe. While many eighteenth- and nineteenth-century Christians saw in the corruptions of the Church a sign of the coming crisis, they expected it to restore original purity rather than establish a new truth. By contrast, those, such as the disciples of St Simon, for whom Christianity was a piece of the rejected past, saw in the same phenomena a movement towards a great change which would lead to a new dispensation, one strikingly similar to the Joachite third age of the spirit.

Reformation theologians might well have been drawn to Joachim's successors by their shared animus against the papacy. But they would surely have been repelled by that tradition's ambiguous handling of the relationship between the Age of the Son and the Age of the Spirit. They were unlikely, except in radical instances, to countenance any derogation from the finality of the Gospel dispensation.[6] But within their Christocentric framework, they had every inducement to develop these aspects of the tradition which identified Pope and Antichrist. It is not possible here to attempt to trace the connexions between the Joachite expectation of a future Antichrist who would assume the papal office, and the Reformation identification of the papacy as such with Antichrist. Nor is it possible to set out an account of the Reformation use of this identification. But some effort must be made to indicate those features of sixteenth- and seventeenth-century polemic which are still current coin in the early nineteenth century. The later theologians looked back to the seventeenth century as the great age of prophetical commentary.

The scholars of the sixteenth and seventeenth centuries were obliged by their situation to alter radically the images they had inherited, and their re-emphasis was passed on to their successors. They operated under a polemical obligation to set back into the past one of the two major world-ending events, the emergence of Antichrist. Under the pressure of these necessities some felt a need to incorporate into the life of the Church the other great event, the coming of Christ, and the outcome of these events, the millennium. For, to anticipate, if Antichrist is both past and present in the form of the false Church, so too may the risen Christ and the millennium be both present and future in the true Church, wanting only final perfecting as Antichrist wants only final destruction. So some continued to be millennialists (of a kind) and anti-millennialists, all at once. Such theorists, though they were prone to speculate on times and occasions, were Augustine's true descendants.

The reformers of the sixteenth century and after could hardly avoid attacking the papal Church as anti-Christian. The ambiguity of the biblical phrase permitted its use as meaning no more than 'opposed to Christ'. However, this meaning always carried with it the more complex signification 'he who puts himself in the place of Christ'. This second meaning summed up all the images of quintessential evil, the beast, the dragon, the whore mounted upon the beast, which should emerge at the last times. The papacy became the Antichrist as well as a thing anti-Christian.[7] Joachim's followers, from the thirteenth century onwards, had laid the basis for the complex as well as the simple identification. But the Joachite prophets had attacked a papacy which had recently been corrupted and which would promptly be defeated. They did not consider it necessary to give Antichrist a history; its true history, for Joachites, occurred as the valid Church of the second dispensation was taken over by Antichrist on the eve of its displacement by the Church of the third age. So Antichrist has, as the biblical sources indicate, a crisis role; the theory envisaged the sudden welling up of evil, the victory of good and the inauguration of a new era. These shapely proportions were precluded by the Reformation necessity to attack the papacy as such, all fifteen (or so) centuries of it.

Further, if he took the Reformation with proper seriousness, the polemicist had to hold that the reign of Antichrist had ended or, at least, was in an advanced stage of decline. By this token, the millennium had begun, or was very soon to do so. From this, in turn, two consequences flowed. First in some way the magisterial reformation had to be given millennial lineaments—no easy task in seventeenth- and eighteenth-century England, where the establishment, whatever its virtues, could not without great effort be represented as a condition of near-perfection. Second, the theorists must be post-millennialists. They put such stress upon the activity of Christ in the Church that the second coming had to appear a little superfluous. They set the coming, as a distinct event, into the remote future, and so made it a post-millennial happening. So they could rebut the visionaries of their time who took the second coming too seriously and sometimes too personally. These scholars were, after all, beneficiaries of the *status quo*, and as such were ready-made post-millennialists. As the apologists of the establishments, their tasks made them Augustinians. In fact, Augustine's example must have been very helpful. He had already institutionalized the millennium by identifying it with the Catholic Church; the reformers simply transferred the identification to the their own churches. They found a new identity for the Catholic Church in the figure of Antichrist and thus reduced another cosmic symbol to an institution. They followed him, further, in their concern with fulfilled prophecy, though, of course, they differed in thinking that a good deal more of it had been fulfilled in the anti-Christian history of the papal Church, and in believing that the millennium (without a literal second coming) was so close that it could be safely predicted. They are, in essence, the children of a marriage between Augustine and Eusebius.

It is not surprising that their theories have a contrived air about them. They dealt with images of the cosmic warfare between good and evil, of anguish and joy, of wrath and mercy, of retribution and vindication. Such images, created by men close to despair, would always be ill at ease in the books of comfortable apologists. They were required to make these images credible descriptions of institutions; they had to turn a future crisis into a long history, a sharp struggle into a running fight; they had to remake the present as the millennium. It is to be expected that their theorizing, for all its sincerity of purpose, would lack verisimilitude. This polemical imperative is the basis for the distortions which have been mistaken for the main stream of the millennial tradition.[8]

The symmetry of the true pattern was restored in the early nineteenth century, when (for some) Napoleon gave a more appropriate content to the Antichrist symbol, when (again for some) the fear of social revolution allowed even the most secure to experience alienation; and when even post-millennialists, contemplating British power and virtue, found their prospects infinitely more exhilarating. Irving and the Albury prophets, and the St Simonians in a quite different way, restore the spirit of the Joachites. And with the Southcottians, one at least breathes an authentic air from the seventeenth century; one is in the presence of people who are not defending anything.

The discussion which follows takes a group of earlier writers who were, judged on the evidence of republication or reference, still heeded in the early nineteenth century, so that they contributed to a frenzy most of them would have deplored. Many of these writers are represented in a series of *Prophetical Extracts* published by G. Terry in the early 1790s to show that the revolution in France would lead to the fall of the papacy, and that both events were foretold in Revelation. In these volumes the scholars, even the sober Joseph Mede and the cautious Isaac Newton, rub elbows with the Camissard prophets and their English apologists, with civil war illuminists, with Bohemian prophets, with pre-reformation utterances about the Lion of the North, with Thomas Rymer and Nixon of Cheshire, with the Sybelline oracles, with the tradition of the 'house of Elias', and with a prophecy copied by Jerome which had been inscribed by Enoch on a pillar in Damascus erected by Seth. In these popular forms scholars and visionaries, sober men and wild, rub shoulders, and both are reduced to the status of the folk lore contained in the same publications.

For all their sobriety, even the most scholarly writers had a polemical purpose. None were distinterested investigators; each used prophecy to condemn and justify aspects of his world. Anti-papal polemic is a constant, from John Napier of Merchistoun in the late sixteenth century to Thomas Newton nearly two centuries later. But such polemic could expand into a general attack upon the Church-State establishment: it is so with Brightman in the early seventeenth century and Priestley in the later eighteenth. Further, the events of the reign of Louis XIV encouraged a 'guilt-by-association' condemnation of Bourbon France, at a time when Camissard refugees in London added an ecstatic dimension to the English prophetic tradition by their practice of speaking in tongues. During the same period, it became customary to use prophetical argument to confound enemies rather closer to home—deists and atheists. Demonstrations that prophecy had been fulfilled were regularly employed against unbelief; prophecy pointing to the Messiah was used to counter deism. Not surprisingly, in the early eighteenth century arguments were advanced which concluded that it was not possible to make a case for anything from biblical prophecy, and other arguments which held that reputed prophecy was actually disguised history. Nevertheless, such major intellects as Henry More, Isaac Newton, David Hartley and Joseph Priestley thought the prophetical argument a good one. On another polemical front, prophecy was used to argue the Jews into Christianity, both fulfilled Old Testament prophecy about the Messiah and unfulfilled prophecy about the destiny of the chosen people.

After more than two centuries of theorizing—a little-explored aspect of the history of religious thought in England—the generation which experienced the French revolution was able to draw upon a well-stocked treasury of scholarship. There was an abundance of arguments against Rome, France and infidelity. But there were also, because the tradition was rich and various, arguments against Great Britain and her established Church, and others which gave a providential role to irreligion. Whatever the standpoint defended or the enemy attacked, the explanations looked forward to a crisis, to the wrath and mercy of God, and to the millennium. Why, indeed, the outwardly stable eighteenth century should have bred so many divines who felt that the end was not far off, is a question worth asking. Here no attempt is made to answer it except to suggest that because in this century non-Christianity came of age the faithful were kept in a constant state of anxiety. After the early 1790s the situation of Europe and of Great Britain could only deepen this anxiety and so encourage prophetic and millennial excitement.

From the multitude of Reformation writers on prophecy, a handful may be selected, for the lasting relevance of the particular shape they gave to prophetic arguments. John Foxe taught more than a single generation to see England as an elect nation with a leading role in an imminent drama which would end with the destruction of an Antichrist both papal and Spanish.[9] Towards the end of the sixteenth century, John Napier of Merchistoun, more celebrated for logarithms than for his *A plaine discovery of the whole Revelation of St John*, hurried his commentary out in English to clarify the conflict with Spain, rather than delay for a leisurely Latin translation. This curious work included a very precisely dated historical outline, and a prediction which placed the last judgement between 1688 and 1700. Napier also related his scheme to a rabbinical tradition of three eras each of 2000 years, and to the Sybelline oracles. Thomas Brightman, like Napier, was still remembered in the early nineteenth century for his use of prophecy. He was, without doubt, widely read, but that he was as influential as has recently been asserted is very doubtful.[10] He was second to none in anti-papal polemic, but he was also, as befits a presbyterianizing puritan within the Church of England, sharply anti-episcopal, reckoning the primacy of bishops an episode in the history of Antichrist. If Rome was Antichrist, then Canterbury was lukewarm Laodicea; Brightman's praise was reserved for Scotland and Geneva, the true embodiments of Philadelphia. Napier and Brightman each make a significant extension of the anti-papal theme. Antichrist was seen in a hostile nation as well as in an apostate Church. He was also observed, if in a lesser degree, in churches other than that of Rome. Both extensions were to have great relevance for the eighteenth and nineteenth centuries.

The influence of Joseph Mede, the doyen of seventeenth-century commentators, arose more from his system than from his polemic, though he was as thoroughly anti-papal as any. Mede was the Hooker of the scholarly millennialists; mild, judicious and even-tempered, a polemicist who did not raise his voice, a high churchman with Laudian ideas about the apostolic succession and the respect due to the altar. In his lifetime only Latin works appeared, but the excited early 1640s saw a translation of *Clavis Apocalyptica* (1643), two editions of *The Apostacy of the Latter Times* (1641, 1644), a work on *The Prophecie of Saint Peter* (1642) and *Daniel's Weekes* (1643). His *Works*, which were in Sir Isaac Newton's library, first appeared in 1648, and later in three editions prepared by John Worthington (1663-4, 1672, 1677).

His successors, even when they dissented from his interpretations, wrote of him with great respect, as the first exegete to offer a schematic analysis of the biblical sources. He was, probably, the first writer in English to deal systematically with the basic exegetical problems arising from the symbols and the time-indicators in Revelation and Daniel. Possibly (though the point is speculative) he transmitted and re-ordered the late medieval tradition which was founded by Joachim as exegete, rather than as prophet of the third age. His influence was undoubtedly both great and lasting. His works were constantly cited in the controversies of the 1820s by both sides, and he in fact straddles the points then at issue. Unlike Brightman, he was not an anxious enquirer into future events, but a careful biblical scholar. As a controversialist, he was concerned to identify the papacy with the predicted apostacy and so with Antichrist, the man of sin. This he did in *The Apostacy of the Latter Times*, republished in 1836 by an editor anxious to defend the Church of England's apostolic succession against Roman claims. Here he showed that the apostacy would prevail for 1260 years, and fixed its beginnings as the fall of the Roman Empire, offering a choice of three dates for this event, 365, 410 and 455. But he concluded with the remark that whether God began the 1260 years from one of these events or from any other was entirely God's business and not Mede's. It was as well that his editor of 1836 was quite uninterested in prediction, for this programme would place the beginning of the millennium at 1715 at the latest.

But though Mede refrained from specific prediction, he depicted the future in bold general terms. He thought that the millennium would begin spectacularly, with the raising of the saints, the purification of the world by fire, and the uniting of Jews and Gentiles at Jerusalem. True, he held that the period would be one of great felicity for the Church rather than the personal reign of Christ, but he had given an encouragement to the pre-millennialists which more moderate churchmen would have preferred him to withhold. In the seventeenth century his writings were used to draw conclusions quite unlike his own. Fuller very pertinently remarked: 'I dare boldly say that the furious factors for the Fifth Monarchy hath driven that nail which Master Mead first did enter, farther than he ever intended it, and doing it with such violence that they split the truths round about it. Thus where ignorance begins to build on that foundation which learning hath laid, no wonder if there be no uniformity in such a mongrel fabric.'[11] In 1825 the *Christian Observer*, trying to quell the storm before it had broken, could only recur to this sentiment by wishing that the enthusiastic followers of Mede would temper their zeal with some of his learning.[12]

From the formidable list of later seventeenth- and early eighteenth-century commentators, a handful may be noted here, not because they are necessarily the most important, but because they set out arguments which remained important in the following century. Henry More, Richard Hurd and Thomas Newton provided a set of arguments against enthusiasm, deism, infidelity and popery and entirely in favour of the civil and political establishment. Isaac Newton, David Hartley and Joseph Priestley followed Brightman's hint and went further to include all ecclesiastical establishments within the character of Antichrist; they represent a continuing anti-Anglican tradition. Further, by the end of the seventeenth century, France had succeeded to Spain as the great political support of the papal Antichrist; the two Robert Flemings and Pierre Jurieu gave emphatic expression to this anti-Bourbon animus.

The arguments of these writers had ample relevance in the era of the French Revolution. Their purpose was polemical, and the occasions of controversy were multiplied after 1789. More, in 1680, was anxious to counter such enthusiasts as the Fifth Monarchy men; he believed that the Reformation had inaugurated the millennium. He deployed arguments against atheists from a consideration of fulfilled prophecy, as well as arguments against popery from the character of Antichrist. Hurd and Thomas Newton, nearly a century later, shared these concerns, especially the wish to use prophecy against infidelity.

This anxiety to defend a providential view of history from scepticism and infidelity, one that was shared with the Dissenters, had two consequences. First, the need to use prophecy as demonstration entailed the regular eighteenth-century denial that prophetic language was obscure. Hence the interest of Isaac Newton, William Warburton, and Richard Hurd, in 'the prophetic style'. Hurd took elaborate pains to establish, through an analysis of hieroglyphs and literary conventions, the extraordinary conclusion that 'The prophetic style is . . . *a sober and reasonable* mode of expression.'[13] The writer of Daniel has become an Augustan, and prophecy a rational demonstration.

Second, this polemical purpose required that scrupulous attention be paid to fulfilled prophecy—an activity which Augustine's authority validated. Isaac Newton, Hurd and Thomas Newton are hardly at all concerned with the future. Thomas Newton opened his three-volume *Dissertations* with a clear statement of this purpose. 'One of the strongest evidences for the truth of revealed religion is that series of prophecies which is preserved in the Old and New Testament; and a greater service perhaps could not be done to Christianity than to lay together the several predictions of scripture with their completions, to show how particularly things have been foretold, and how exactly fulfilled.' But he had to meet a sceptical criticism; that the so-called prophecies are really disguised history, written after the events they ostensibly predict. Thus he was required to deal with prophecies which were quite obviously written a long time ago, and link them with events which equally obviously happened quite recently. He had, therefore, to deal with 'instances of things which have confessedly many ages ago been foretold, and here in these later ages been fulfilled, or are fulfilling at this very time'.[14] However, in spite of his declared intention, Newton was unable to keep his eyes exclusively upon the past; from time to time he gave countenance to the opinion that the end was not far off.

The merging of the millennium into the life of the Church, endorsed by both Augustine and Reformation theologians, made it difficult to avoid such an expectation. For Thomas Newton, the Church was in a real if limited way the kingdom, lacking only its final perfection. Hurd, more Augustinian than Newton in his avoidance of speculation about the future, pushed almost everything into the past. The 'latter times' became 'the times subsequent to the introduction of Christianity'. The second advent 'is to be understood of his coming in his kingdom, through all the ages of the Christian Church'. Accordingly his discussion of 'Prophecies concerning Christ's second coming' was wholly taken up with the destruction of Jerusalem, the dispersion of the Jews and the conversion of the Gentiles. Hurd was the Eusebius of the eighteenth century. He conceded that the conversion of the Gentiles lacked '*absolute universality*'; but this, he went on, 'we readily acknowledge; but are in no pain for the event'. Both the present situation and the future completion are accounted for in prophecy.[15]

Against these placid and complacent divines were ranged others of less orthodox persuasion who used prophecy to attack a Church which still maintained its exclusive claims. Isaac Newton held that all nations had corrupted Christianity, and it is anything but surprising to find such an opinion among unitarians. For if, as they hold, the original deposit of faith had been unitarian, then the prevalence of trinitarian establishments argued irresistibly for the conclusion that Rome had no corner on corruption. David Hartley, refreshingly enough in the manner of a philosopher and not that of an exegete, firmly put forward this view in the middle of the eighteenth century. Towards the end of his *Observations on Man* he reflected prophetically upon 'the Expectation of Bodies Politic'. The body politic like the body natural tends 'to Destruction and Dissolution . . . respited for certain Intervals, by partial, imperfect Reformations'. So intimately connected are the civil and the ecclesiastical powers that they will fall together. At this prospect Hartley becomes much more prophetic in tone. 'It is very true, that the Church of Rome is Babylon the Great, and the Mother of Harlots, and of the Abominations of the Earth. But all the rest have copied her Example, more or less. . . . And this Impurity may be considered not only as justifying the Application of the Prophecies to all the Christian Churches, but as a natural Cause for their Downfall. The Corrupt Governors of the several Churches will ever oppose the true Gospel, and in so doing will bring Ruin upon themselves.' He saw the destruction of the temple at Jerusalem as the 'Type and Presage of the Destruction of the Judaical Form of Rites, Ceremonies, and human Ordinances which take place, more or less, in all Christian Countries.'[16] Hartley, though a Dissenter, is almost as placid in tone as Hurd and Thomas Newton. However, very similar arguments were to acquire more urgency in the writings of Joseph Priestley, especially after the Revolution of 1789.

The third theme which retained, and indeed magnified, its relevance in the revolutionary period, was the mobilization of the prophetic symbols against France. The reign of Louis XIV brought France to the centre of the prophetical world picture, and provided another late seventeenth-century influence upon the use of prophecy in the succeeding century. The persecution of the Huguenots, Bourbon interference in English affairs and its connexion with the renewed Catholic threat, the Camissard revolt and the establishment of a Camissard colony in London, and the long wars with Louis XIV whose power, brilliance and religious error invited identification both with the Roman Empire and the Roman Church, all encouraged expositors to find a place for France among the apocalyptic symbols. It became the 'tenth part of the city' whose fall would precede that of the mystic Babylon, the greatest of the ten toes of the Danielic statue, the tenth horn of the beast and the supporter of the little horn. English and Scottish expositors worked on the identifications; Huguenot and Camissard works were read and translated. Friends feared that Isaac Newton, a strong hater of the papacy and a firm believer in miracles, would be infected by the Camissards and their ecstatic practices.[17] Camissard prophecies still had readers in the late eighteenth and early nineteenth centuries; in the revolutionary period because they pointed the finger of wrath at France, and in the late 1820s because they justified miraculous healing and speaking in tongues.

Probably the most influential expositor of the theme that Antichrist was both papal and French was the Scot, Robert Fleming the younger, whose *Apocalyptical Key* (1701) continued to be republished well into the twentieth century. But a work by the notable Huguenot controversialist, Pierre Jurieu, is a good deal more interesting. His *Accomplishment of the Scripture Prophecies* was translated in 1687. It was chiefly devoted to an interpretation of the symbols in Daniel. The ten-horned beast was the Roman

Empire; the ten horns stood for the ten successor kingdoms. Rome-Babylon will fall through the withdrawal of support by these kingdoms; already Sweden, Denmark, England and several German states had withdrawn theirs. France will be next to withdraw and this will lead to its total fall, beginning in 1785 and taking twenty to twenty-five years to accomplish. Christ leading his armies will destroy Babylon, though the sword will be the spiritual power of the gospel. Specifically, three developments may be expected; the preaching of the word, the conversion of those who live in darkness, and the use of governmental authority to sever the links with Rome. Then there will be a commotion of nations (that is, the prophetical earthquake) and a war which will complete the downfall of the papacy. Jurieu, no wild prophesier, added that this was how things appear to him; his location and timing could both be proved wrong by the event.

Jurieu set the millennium before the second coming; still, he saw it as a total renovation. Rome will have fallen, and the Jews and the rest of the Gentiles converted; there will be such an effusion of the Holy Spirit that Pentecost would seem but a lesser prefiguration; it will be a time of holiness and peace. More, it will be '*a kingdom of humility*'; '*Brotherly love* shall make all men *equal*.' Government (probably theocratic) will be without tyranny, insolence, pride and violence; there will be abundant poor relief and no waste on vanity. 'A *community of goods* shall then take place, like that which was seen in the *first years* of the Church at *Jerusalem*.'[18] Robert Owen is not too far away. He was, however, a longish way from the minds of those who published five sets of extracts in the 1790s. These editors added introductory matter, footnotes and appendices linking these predictions to revolutionary events in France.

The prophetic tradition, especially those parts of it shaped by the early Christian centuries and by the Reformation, was an integral part of the intellectual equipment of British Christians at the end of the eighteenth century. From this tradition they derived the belief that history was patterned, that it could be divided into periods, and that, because the pattern of periods was of spiritual and divine significance, history reflected a divine purpose. Prophecy was both an argument for providence, and a way of seeing providence at work. The tradition included warnings against turning a reverent explanation of the past into an impious prediction of the future. But an interest in the future, both a rather trivial preoccupation with dating future events, and a much more significant depiction of future millennial near or actual perfection, remained a part of the tradition.

In a more specific fashion, prophetical theology equipped British Christians with arguments—an important part of a wider apologetic equipment—against enthusiasm, against popery, against established religion, against political enemies, against religious error. By the same token, it also provided them with arguments in favour of the established order in Church and State or in favour of civil and religious liberty. The vague symbols underpinning prophecy, which remained opaque despite the best efforts to turn them into plain speech, permitted a wide variety of emphasis within the tradition. The events of the half-century beginning in 1789 supplied a recurrent inducement to put this tradition to use. Church of England man and Dissenter, trinitarian and unitarian, reactionary and radical, sober scholar and wild calculator, sectarian and socialist, tory and agitator, missionary and messiah, Tractarian and Mormon, all drew water from this well. Each turned the traditional symbols, Antichrist, Messiah, Armageddon and millennium, to uses which arose from their deepest fears and their highest hopes.

III: Responses to Revolution

For British eighteenth-century prophetical exegetes the identification of the papacy with Antichrist was almost axiomatic. Anglicans made a simple identification; Dissenters saw in the papacy the most developed form of ecclesiastical allied with civil oppression, and found anti-Christian features in the Church and State which denied them liberty and status at home. For Dissenters, the events in France after 1789 were the first in a series of clearly marked steps towards the millennium. The papacy's major prop was removed—in prophetic language the greatest of the remaining ten Roman kingdoms had withdrawn its support from the man of sin. The papacy's days were numbered. Religious persecution and civil tyranny would both cease. Their remnants in Great Britain would not survive; a millennium of pure religion and civil liberty was at hand. Or so it could seem in the early 1790s. As time passed, and as Great Britain allied herself with the old order, even becoming the champion and restorer of papal power, millennial joy turned into millennial fear.

In the early 1790s joy at the thought that Bourbon and Pope would fall together was not limited to Dissent. Prophetical interpretations of passing events sprang up on all sides; Anglicans had not, immediately, sufficient reason to keep away. However, George Stanley Faber, their most notable interpreter, significantly enough undertook to show that the new France was Antichrist. James Hatley Frere went further and identified Napoleon as Antichrist; others discovered more devious ways of placing Bonaparte in the picture. Although other Anglican theorists paid more respect to ancient tradition than recent history by maintaining the papal identification, it was important that a secular identification had been made. Behind Napoleon men saw servile revolt and popular tyranny; Antichrist retained this new and more apt symbolic quality. The Albury circle, beginning their series of conferences late in the 1820s, found no difficulty in compressing both popery and democracy into the figure of Antichrist; in the Great Britain of Daniel O'Connell and Catholic Emancipation this was a plausible opinion.

The need to interpret the French Revolution thus gave a new content to one of the central symbols of prophecy. It also stimulated a boom in prophetical publishing. Much of it was republication, which had been going on throughout the century. In the 1790s there was an acceleration of this stream, with many new works added to it. The younger Fleming appeared four times in 1793 (and was to appear twice in 1809), Jurieu once in 1790, twice in 1793 and once in 1797, Christopher Love, a martyr to Cromwell in the interregnum, appeared in 1783, 1792, 1794, 1795, 1800 and 1801; John Owen, the only dissenting Vice Chancellor of the University of Oxford, was brought out twice in 1793 and twice the following year. Archbishop James Usher's alleged prediction had two printings in 1793 and 1797. Most of these re-issues were in the form of extracts; the principle of selection was commonly the linking of the fate of the papacy with that of the French monarchy.

Of all the witnesses summoned from the past to interpret the present, none was more suitable than Pierre Jurieu, who had chanced to predict a date close to the actual revolution as the beginning of the end. It was a profitable influence; Jurieu was no mere soothsayer, but a serious writer on society and politics who used, in some of his works, the prophetic model. So, too, was Joseph Priestley. Priestley, except when arguing against trinitarian doctrine, was not concerned with detailed scriptural interpretation. He, like Hartley but more vigorously, was a reasoner and a controversialist who employed prophecy against the civil and ecclesiastical establishment. The argument of his *History of the Corruptions of Christianity* (1782) had a broadly prophetic shape, but one which did less violence to the past than schemes of dogmatic interpreters. While others sharply divided the three phases of Christian history, primitive purity, degeneration and recovery, Priestley allowed considerable overlap. In tracing the rise of papal power, he pointed to the year 606, for then Phocas had conferred on the Pope the sole right to the anti-Christian title 'universal bishop'. But he also instanced innumerable other steps in the process, from the fourth century to the fourteenth. He was careful, further, to argue that the transitions involved the operation of natural human causes; degeneration had set in because the persisting paganism of the recently converted was too strong for the pure Christianity with which it had to co-exist. Similarly, the shift to a renewed purity will occur because men will wish it to occur.[1]

Priestley had too much respect for history to adopt conventional rigid patterns. Where others organized pre-selected details into a rigid framework, he arranged a fluid body of facts into a flexible pattern. But the two methods are related, and their relationship was emphasized by his use of apocalyptic and millennial images to add a dramatic dimension to an otherwise reflective analysis. So in the preface to *The History of Corruptions* he wrote that the '*night* which has for many centuries obscured our holy religion, we may clearly see, is past; *the morning* is opening upon us; and we cannot doubt but that the light will increase, and extend itself more and more, unto the *perfect day*. Happy are they who contribute to diffuse the true light of this *everlasting gospel.*' He echoed both Revelation and Jurieu in arguing that 'The civil powers of this world, which were formerly the chief supports of *the antichristian systems, who have given their power and strength unto the beast* (Rev. xvii. 13.) now begin to *hate her*, and are ready *to make her* desolate and naked, v.16.'[2]

After the Revolution, in sermon and pamphlet, Priestley became specifically prophetic. On the Fast Day of 1794 he preached on 'The present state of Europe compared with ancient prophecies.'[3] This sermon shows that he fully shared the excited mood of the decade. Though the argument as a whole was his own, its elements were prophetical commonplaces; the literal restoration of the Jews, preceded by a second coming which will be as 'conspicuous' and 'leisurely' as the ascension. The ten toes of the statue, the ten horns of the beast and the little horn were conventionally identified: earthquakes represented revolutions and the heavenly bodies governments; the kingdom of God will come only after convulsions and slaughter. Though there is no precise prediction, he strongly suspected that the prophesied troubles were then beginning. All was conventional except Priestley's standpoint; for the first time in the eighteenth century a major thinker was using these venerable arguments for the purposes of the persecuted.

Thus the restoration of the Jews became more than a piece of prophecy to be fulfilled; it embodied the truly millennial reversal of fortune and of worldly values. 'May God,' Priestley wrote in his *Letters to the Jews* (1794) 'make you the most illustrous [*sic*] as you are now the most despised, of all the nations of the earth.'[4] Further, 'after the destined period for the dispersion and calamities of the Jews, the heaviest of all divine judgements will fall upon those nations by whom they shall have been oppressed.'[5] For the next half-century the Jews were to provide the supreme example of God's values running contrary to those of men. For some, God's standards were most clearly shown by a future in which proud England's noblest destiny would be found in her service to the despised people Priestley had greeted as '*the elder branch* of the family'.[6]

Again, Priestley gave a characteristic shape to his response to events in France. The revolution there may be the earthquake of Revelation 11.3, but it could also be a step towards a very desirable change. In a positive way, pure Christianity was likely to spread from the French philosophers to the French nation and so the world at large. But, negatively, infidelity will probably continue to increase.[7] Here, reflecting upon the beneficial function of infidelity, and elaborating upon the hints he had received from Hartley, and, through Whiston, Isaac Newton, Priestley made his most interesting suggestions.

He saw the increase of infidelity as a major sign that the second coming could be close. For many years, this increase had been remarkable in all countries with anti-Christian establishments, particularly in Italy and France but also in Protestant countries. This infidelity, happily, was destroying the establishments, and so discharging a task for which true Christianity was too weak. 'It seems possible that no Christians, not even the freest, and boldest, would ever have done what was necessary to have done, to the overturning of these corrupt establishments of Christianity, and what unbelievers have lately done in France.'[8]

Priestley reserved the final destruction of 'the great antichristian power' to the second coming. The infidels, one is left to assume, were to deliver a substantial instalment. In the interim between the onset and the fullness of calamity, Protestants should pray 'Come, Lord Jesus', remembering the instruction 'Come out of her, my people' in order to escape the wrath. The hand of God is in everything that happens; therefore Christians should become like the ten men for whose sake, had he found them, God would have spared Sodom. The destruction will come, and it will be morally good, for from it will arise the perfect kingdom. The lineaments of this kingdom also had Priestley's characteristic mark upon them.

Though the kingdom will be the result of supernatural events, it will also arise from 'the gradual improvement of the whole human race . . . to a state of universal peace, virtue and happiness'.[9] Priestley was not explicit about the mechanics of change; probably he thought of gradual improvement miraculously perfected, and this perfection persisting as the condition 'in which we are assured that this world will terminate'. In a general way, the sequence of events is clear enough—a great calamity, the second coming, the resurrection of the dead, the general judgement.[10] Christ as king will then rule with the saints. His kingdom will be 'a proper Kingdom though a kingdom of righteousness, the objects of which will be the happiness of the subjects of it'. 'It is . . . an institution adapted to answer the purposes of them [the kingdoms of the world] but in an much better manner.' If it was to be a purely spiritual kingdom then there would be no need for the destruction of the kingdoms of the world, for it could co-exist with them.[11]

For all Priestley's scholarship, intellect and deliberation, his millennialism is truly a 'religion of the oppressed', of those suffering from a century of discrimination and ill-usage, and from the burst of active persecution which, in the year of this sermon, made Priestley a refugee in America. There is more than exegesis in his affirmation that 'This kingdom . . . will not be established without the greatest convulsions, and the violent overthrow of other kingdoms. Every description, figurative or otherwise, clearly implies violence, and consequently great calamity. The little stone *smiting* the image, and *breaking it in pieces*, is far from giving an idea of peaceable revolution, but one that will be effected with great violence, and in a short time.'[12] The scholar was not too far from the social situation in which the vengeful symbols of Daniel and Revelation had first been forged. The eleventh chapter of Revelation anticipated the destruction of them that have destroyed the earth; Priestley found here a description of the Christian powers destroying each other. 'What had more eminently contributed to destroy the earth, than the anti-christian and idolatrous establishments of Christianity?'[13] He did not merely forsee the smiting of the little stone; he waited impatiently for it to do its work.

Both Priestley and Jurieu influenced James Bicheno, the most interesting prophetical specialist to emerge from the English Dissenters. He was a dissenting minister and schoolmaster at Newbury, Berkshire, and though a radical in outlook was a good deal more moderate than Priestley; Faber considered him a dissenter of the respectable kind. His son became colonial secretary in Van Dieman's Land, and a notable scientific writer. Bicheno's writings began in 1793 and ran through to 1817; the French Revolution, the wars, and England's relationship to them permeated these works; in contemporary events he saw the working out of prophecy, that is, God's dealings with men in societies.

Most of his themes are announced in his first work, *The Signs of the Times*, which was published in five editions in the 1790s. 'Whereever one Christian,' he wrote, 'or sect of Christians, assumes the seat of authority and judgment in the church of Christ, whether they call for fire to destroy those who dissent from them or only exclude them from their communion and affection, there is a portion of that spirit of Antichrist.'[14] The papacy he identified with Antichrist because it was the apotheosis of ecclesiastical allied to civil oppression, and so of persecution, war, intolerance, coercion of conscience, the destruction of Christian unity, free enquiry and civil rights. The relationship between the papacy and the French monarchy perfected this oppressive alliance; he identified Louis XIV with 'the beast which John saw coming up out of the earth . . . which slew the witnesses'.[15] But papacy and monarchy merely expressed evil principles most fully; Bicheno found abundant anti-Christianity in British life.

He cited Jurieu and Christopher Goodwin to show the intimate prophetic link between the papacy and the Bourbons, instancing the long history of persecution in France, from the Waldensians to the Revocation of the Edict of Nantes. The greater number of his somewhat fanciful calculations (e.g. that from the reign of Hugh Capet (987) to what he considered to be the effective beginning of Louis XIV's reign (1653) is, significantly, 666 years) pointed to France, and especially to the events inaugurated in 1789. His juggling with the symbols—the dragon, the beasts, the horns—was designed to show in the papal-Bourbon grouping a combination of ecclesiastical and civil tyranny, originating in the Roman Empire and transmitted to the papacy and the ten successor monarchies, of which France was the most notable. The Bourbon monarchy was oppressive as a civil despotism and as the ally of religious tyranny. Its fall would be a double victory for truth; civil and religious liberty, true religion and a just society, would all triumph.

In this design the revolution in France was of cosmic significance. Bicheno was equally delighted by the proclamation of religious liberty and by the reform of French government. He refused to be disturbed by the terror, ascribing it to the provocation of the enemies of liberty. Further, God could make use of evil instruments to effect the destruction of the papacy and all forms of oppression. Even before the rise of Bonaparte gave this last argument some added force, Bicheno could cite Isaac Newton to show that active infidelity must destroy Antichrist before true Christianity could be restored. Necessarily, Bicheno took a very critical view of Britain's role in these events.

She was courting, perhaps meriting, great danger by joining the side of Antichrist and attempting to restore the political and ecclesiastical *ancien régime*. This situation he described in political, ecclesiastical and prophetical terms—as a desertion of the principles of Locke and of 1688 which were substantially those of 1789 (*Con-*

sequences of Unjust War, 1810); or as a failure to carry through the principles of the Reformation to their true conclusion (*A Glance at the History of Christianity*, 1798); or as a probable demonstration of the truth of the prophecy that all ten Roman Kingdoms would remain sufficiently close to the beast to share in its downfall (*The Fulfilment of Prophecy*, 1817). In whatever way, and Bicheno readily worked in all three modes, great evils could be diagnosed in British life and great fears expressed for Britain's future.

It was, after all, not surprising to Bicheno that Great Britain should enlist upon the side of Antichrist. In *The Signs of the Times* he expressed his fear that Great Britain, by constructing an unholy alliance between papists and protestants, had opted for a share of the wrath to fall on Babylon. He reflected, further, that this was more or less all that could be expected of her; the English establishment would have heartily approved of a Gallican modification in France, but showed its real anti-Christian colours when the French Assembly restored the Church to its true apostolic condition. The establishment's sympathy for distressed French clergy and mounting antipathy to dissenters struck him as a true sign of the times.[16]

In a sermon preached on an official fast day, but with a purpose other than that anticipated by government in proclaiming the fast, Bicheno warned that the end of the fourth Danielic monarchy was approaching and that Great Britain should repent to avoid the wrath which would accompany it: 'We are a guilty people, and it cannot be repeated too often, that nothing but a speedy repentance, personal and national; nothing but a thorough reformation, political and moral, can give us any hope of a long security from calamities most awful.' His list of his country's iniquities was characteristic of the dissenting radical: the slave trade and church patronage, commercial greed and warlike propensities, and the inertia of the movement for political reform. He gave pre-eminence to the unjust war with France; an overmastering zeal for commercial advantage had brought Britain to the championing of 'popery and priestcraft . . . idolatry, persecution, and despotism'.[17]

In his last and lengthiest work, *The Fulfilment of Prophecy Further Illustrated* (1817), he had to cope with a situation in which the war had been won, Napoleon exiled, Pope and despots restored, the world unended and the wrath not yet fallen. This he did in part by an elaborate revision of his former calculations, and in part by a recital of the evidences of continued unrest in Europe: 'all the elements of human society seem to be dissolving', a 'mental ferment . . . agitates all Europe', so that 'it is probable that the Gospel dispensation . . . is fast hastening to its terminations.'[18] The continued and accelerated decline of the Turkish Empire was taken as a clear sign: this long remained a favourite theme with the prognosticators. Earlier hopes that 'the Beast should be slain, Babylon overturned, and the cause of civil and religious freedom obtain the ascendancy', were replaced by a prediction that the true test was yet to come, though very close. The post-war 'revival of the Beast and his coadjutors' was merely a temporary pause between major explosions of divine wrath.[19]

Meanwhile Great Britain's relationship with God continued to inspire misgivings. Compared with the continental nations she was relatively sound, but she had denied both protestantism and liberty by warring upon France and restoring to Europe the apostate Church and the ancient tyrannies. The burden of this unjust war had fallen on her people. Thus she had sinned 'before God, the universal Father; against the industrious classes of society, and against the poor and needy, both whose miseries and vices are thus enormously increased, so that a double cry ascends to Heaven, to call down those judgments which the just and infinitely benevolent Governor of the world dispenses, for the punishment of crimes, and for the remedy of the evils they occasion.'[20] Only by obeying the command 'Come out to her, my people', by withdrawing from pro-Catholic alliances abroad and by reforming abuses at home, could punishment be avoided. For the evils would be ended, either by way of repentance or by way of wrath.

These are the major themes in Bicheno's writing. His calculations —which, by and large, predicted the end of the world in the 1860s— doubtless encouraged many to look around them with fear and hope. For all his diagnosis of current evils, he remained an optimistic post-millennialist with pre-millennial hesitations. In *The Restoration of the Jews* (1800) he speculated briefly on the age to come and the means of its introduction. The millennium would see the end of ignorance, vice and misery, the universal spread of true religion, righteousness, peace and happiness. Swords would be turned into ploughshares, every man would sit under his own vine and none should make him afraid. (These texts, Isaiah 2.4 and Micah 4.4, were to acquire a socialist connotation in the early 1830s.) The millennium would result from 'a mixture of natural and supernatural causes'[21]—God would use a particular nation to restore the Jews, raise up powerful evangelists, and cause a new and greater effusion of the Holy Spirit. Possibly he would intervene directly, to convert the Jews and to defeat the forces of evil at the last battle. Possibly, then, Christ would reign from his throne in Jerusalem. These are possibilities to be entertained—not the certainties they were to become in the minds of later pre-millennialists. Bicheno's main emphasis fell upon progressive means of change—God using usual channels more effectively—and upon a millennium which is a purified *status quo* rather than a total reversal.

This work on the Jews draws attention to a constant concern of commentators during this period. For Bicheno, and for many others, the restoration and conversion of the Jews were vital events in the sequence that would lead to the millennium. The effect of this belief upon attitudes to Jews deserves separate treatment—undoubtedly it caused many Englishmen to be ashamed of their persecuting past, and to regard the Jews with a particular, if patronizing, affection. Many exegetes held that Great Britain had been providentially chosen to effect the restoration, and so to be a prime agent in bringing on the millennium. Bicheno, commenting upon a verse in Isaiah 18 which was thought to point to the means of restoration, could not 'help fearing that we are not the favoured nation. I wish our prospects were more promising.'[22] The French instead were more likely to do it, having already a footing in the Turkish Empire. The opinion of the Bishop of Rochester, Samuel Horsley, that atheistical France was no fit divine instrument, was brushed contemptuously aside. Bicheno was in no way a nationalist; God would use the instrument most ready to his hand, without favouritism. In the double sense of the word, he was a prophet: a diagnostician of present evil as well as a forecaster. He foresaw wrath rather than favour. His mind ran to divine justice rather than to human ambition.

High Churchmen as well as Dissenters could feel gloomy about the future of Britain. A sermon, *The Man of Sin*, preached in 1794 by William Jones of Nayland, Fellow of the Royal Society and a founder of the *British Critic*, a link between the non-jurors and the Tractarians who later earned the praise of both Horsley and Newman, was as reactionary as Bicheno's discourses were radical. Nevertheless, Jones felt quite as strongly that his country deserved punishment, even though she might escape it. The man of sin, significantly, was not the papacy, but 'a particular sort of sinful character, or even the race of mankind, when become sinful in the extreme'. He expounded 2 Thessalonians 2.4 to show that kings and rulers were the ones there called God and that worship was due to them, for they restrained Satan. The sinful nature of man, breaking loose from this restraint, would afford 'a new revelation of sin'; the right of insurrection would displace the right of government, human wisdom would be deified and drive out God's wisdom, the liberty to disobey God would take the place of the liberty to serve him. 'Little did we think twenty years ago, that we should live to see these things fulfilled so nearly as they have been.' In France Christianity had been renounced, government grounded upon the will of men and churches converted to the worship of reason. The second coming would destroy this manifestation of Satan. Great Britain was indeed lucky that she would not be the scene of destruction, for 'the first seeds of all this mischief were sown in Britain. Here it was, that *reason*, now deified in France, was first invested with the right to making its own religion; which, in other words, is a right of being its own God.'[23] The evidence supporting this conclusion has a Young England character: the execution of Charles, the Civil War, the spoliation of the church ('sacrilegious plundering') and the oppression of the people. As Jones was descended from the regicide Colonel John Jones—he is said to have kept 30 January as a day of humiliation—he may have felt personally involved in this record of iniquity. But still, for reasons Jones did not go into, Britain remained a little favoured; the wrath was to fall on France, which brought to their fullness these originally British iniquities. Other Church of England men were to be more anxious about the situation of their church and nation.

Samuel Horsley, bishop and scholar, turned his attention to prophecy in the 1790s. He was near the end of the career that had taken him to high eminence in the Church, the Royal Society and the world of letters. Perhaps Isaac Newton had stimulated an interest in prophecy; in 1785 Horsley completed a ten-volume edition of his works. Certainly, a little later, the Revolution alarmed him; in 1793 his sermon to the House of Lords on the dangers of the revolutionary spirit earned him high praise. Revolutionary France was the great contemporary fact he felt obliged to explain in prophetic terms. In so doing he forcibly denied the papal identification of Antichrist and fixed the label on historical trends then finding vigorous expression in France. Inevitably, as a very patriotic Englishman, he was concerned with the role his country should play in the world-ending events he believed to be at that time beginning. Like G. S. Faber he had no confidence that Great Britain would enjoy immunity from the wrath to come, nor that she would be charged with the providential mission of restoring the Jews. This ultimate gloom about the future of all the Gentile nations, including Great Britain, caused his son to insert the most important of these unpublished writings in the *British Magazine* in 1833 and 1834, when, so it seemed to the son, the Reform Bill and the threat of church reform had renewed their relevance.

In 1798-9 Edward King published his *Remarks on the Signs of the Times*, in which he interpreted the extremely opaque eighteenth chapter of Isaiah to show that the maritime people there described as the restorers of Israel were the French. Horsley replied with his *Critical Disquisitions on the Eighteenth Chapter of Isaiah* (1799), in which he argued that the restoration was connected with the second coming, and that there was no basis in the text for a positive identification of the people to be given this task. Negatively, however, he argued for the conclusion that 'the Atheistical Democracy of France' could not be destined for so high a role, for 'The French Democracy, from its infancy to the present moment, has been a conspicuous and principal branch at least of the western Antichrist.'

Antichrist, he went on, was rising, not falling as would be the case if the second coming was near. The ancestry of 'French Philosophy, Jacobinism and Bavarian Illumination' could be traced to the heretics of the apostolic age; in France could be seen 'the *adolescence* of that man of sin'. The 'son of perdition will be neither papist nor protestant, nor Christian, Jew, nor heathen', but one who 'will claim divine honours to himself exclusively'. So, the fall of the French monarchy should alarm all governments, and that of the Gallican church all churches. Horsley could see 'nothing in the sufferings of the aged Pope, which can be the cause of exultation and joy, in the heart of any Christian; nothing in the indignities and insults which have been put upon him by low-born miscreants, a disgrace to the reformed religion which they profess, but what should incite horror and indignation.'[24] Though such feelings about the Pope and the exiled French priests became more common during the wars, they remain remarkable for their compassion in an Anglican writer on prophecy.

These themes were expanded in the posthumously published essays. In 'On the Prophetic Periods'[25] the historical scheme found in Mede and his successors is rejected; it is based on gratuitous assumptions, arbitrary interpretations and dubious history, 'and, above all, upon that unwarrantable, monstrous supposition, that Christian Rome is Antichrist, and all who have at any time opposed her, however wild and fanatical in their opposition, saints!' The periods of the title are the 1260 days of Revelation, the 'time, times and half a time' and the 2300 days of Daniel. Horsley's calculations are more than usually complicated, but their product is clear enough. The first period concluded with the end of the Roman persecutions (again, a good word for the Christian Empire is implied); the second will run from 1726 ('when the Atheistical Philosophy began to raise its accursed head in France') to 1968 when the reign of Antichrist will begin to end; and the third will extend from 1453 to 1894, from the rise to the fall of the Ottoman Turks. Horsley did not draw the conclusion, but it is plain enough: none of these anti-Christian periods have anything to do with the papacy. Who then is Antichrist? There are two of them in fact, an eastern and a western, which will confederate at the end to embrace the whole territory of the Roman Empire.

This forecast is elaborated in the 'Letters to the Author of Antichrist in the French Convention', written between 1797 and 1801.[26] Here the bishop dwelt upon the symbols in Daniel. France was seen as the little horn of the fourth beast (Daniel 7.8); the Porte as the little horn of the he-goat (Daniel 8.9); the genuine Antichrist was foreseen as a coalition between the two under 'the wilful king' (Daniel 11.36 ff.). The political convulsions to come will be of the greatest imaginable kind, for the natural convulsions which in prophetic language symbolize them describe 'a dissolution of the whole fabric of the external world'. They will be occasioned by the emergence of Antichrist ('a business which, I fear, is begun') and the second coming. The traditional arguments for papal antichristianity are swept aside: forbidding marriage does not mean clerical celibacy but easy divorce, permitted in France and at least demanded in Great Britain. The 'antichristian emperor' (a title which could not at this time point to Napoleon) will be known by his ultimate act of self-deification.

The fifth letter turned to the identity of the two witnesses who will preach in sackcloth, be killed at the height of Antichrist's power, and rise with the second coming (Revelation, 11.3 ff.). Horsley's correspondent had identified them as the Old and the New Testaments, kept in sackcloth for centuries by the papacy. Once again, the bishop had a kind word for the ancient enemy. The papal prohibition of the vernacular scriptures arose from a mistaken and superstitious respect for the Bible; and the debt owed to Catholic biblical scholars was very great. But more, the witnesses are churches, not books: *the* two churches. But which two? The answer is complicated, but in the end clear enough. The growth of the anti-Christian power will bring the disestablishment of existing churches, the pillage of clerical property, the reduction of true Christians to a persecuted remnant. A sham church of nominal Christians will operate as Antichrist's ecclesiastical arm. All this will happen among the Gentiles.

Parallel developments among the Jews will produce a sham church of seduced Jews and a true church of converted Jews. The last days will have two false and two true churches; the latter will preach in sackcloth, be killed and rise again. The true churches 'will not be any two particular churches, of the number of those which now exist, but the two general branches of the church catholic'. Seldom can such an eminent prelate have had such a dark view of the future of his church. A little more hopefully, he adds, their death and the exposure of their carcasses in the market place may be no more than a brief period of extreme tribulation. But that was all the comfort that this sober scholar and ecclesiastical statesman could offer, not one which any church, papal or protestant, could claim as especially its own. Satan and France certainly have a special relationship; God and Great Britain do not.

Or do they? In his Trafalgar Day sermon, *The Watchers and the Holy Ones* (1806), Horsley at least entertained the possibility. (Naval victory was to have a similar effect upon Faber.) Nebuchadnezzar and Napoleon were set side by side, as examples of God raising up and casting down powerful men for his own purposes. The common view that Napoleon *was* Antichrist was neither asserted nor rejected. As the then unpublished 'Letters' show, Horsley thought of Napoleon not as a personification of Antichrist, but as a stage in the process of his emergence. In the 'Letters' Antichrist is both a persecutor and a purifier—the latter because of the former; in this sermon 'the Corsican' is, quite without merit to himself, God's instrument 'to chastise the profaneness, the irreligion, the lukewarmness, the profligacy, the turbulent seditious spirit of the times'. So God allows him, and will allow Antichrist, to exercise a power which will end when men turn to righteousness. Accordingly the opinion (which Horsley says was widespread in the 1790s) that just because Antichrist was to arise in France it was pointless to resist, was impious nonsense. God uses human and natural means. If it be his will that Britain should suffer for her sins through defeat, well; but if 'as we hope and trust, it is the will of God, that the vile Corsican shall never set foot upon our shores; the loyalty and valour of the country, are, we trust, the appointed means of his exclusion.' Patriotism will out; God and Britain may, after all, have a limited special relationship, appropriate to the specific stage of the period of Antichrist the world was then passing through, his 'adolescence'. But even this role was severely limited; the recent victory and the country's preservation since the beginning of the wars are not due to 'any preeminent righteousness of this nation'. 'We owe it, not to ourselves, but to God's unmerited mercy.' 'In the hour of victory, "let us not be highminded, but fear".'[27]

Without doubt, Horsley hoped for his country and believed in her cause. He was sure that to fight France was God's will for her, and he believed that God distributed victories and defeats according to his own purposes. But he did not hold that Britain had a 'chosen nation' role in the prophetic scheme. In this scrupulous caution he was close to the period's one major professional exegete, George

Stanley Faber, an expositor who stands in the great tradition of Mede, More, Isaac Newton, Thomas Newton and Hurd, with a reasonable claim to be considered their equal. His long working life, as fellow and tutor of Lincoln College, rector of Long Newton and prebend of Salisbury Cathedral was uneventful (except, perhaps, for the conversion to Rome of his nephew Frederick William) but immensely productive. Like his great predecessors in prophecy (and unlike William Cuninghame of Lainshaw, the only contemporary who approaches his stature) he was not a narrow prophetical specialist but wrote widely on theological subjects. Like Horsley he inherited the full seventeenth- and eighteenth-century tradition and reshaped it to explain the unprecedented crises of his lifetime. In this tradition he was less an innovator than Horsley, for he retained a sufficient anti-Christian role for the papacy—as befitted a descendent of a Huguenot confessor who had suffered imprisonment, torture, confiscation and exile under Louis XIV.[28] His animus was directed against both the papacy and France, but the atheism and democracy of the latter took pride of place. His revision of the prophetic symbols, while attempting to keep the place of the papacy intact, was designed to find room for infidelity, in politics and religion alike. With Horsley the latter displaced the former; with Faber the two were harnessed together—in a troika, in fact, for room was found for that other ancient enemy, the Turk. He was, again like Horsley, anxious about the destiny of his country, and gave roughly the same answer to this problem. Often, though, Faber cannot entirely avoid the suggestion that Great Britain indeed had a special providential role.

His great output of prophetical writings stretched from 1799 to 1853, the year before his death. He moved among the writers of his time, and sometimes among his illustrious predecessors, like a master among pupils, approving and reproving, correcting and rejecting. He was very considerably read. *A Dissertation on the Prophecies* (1807) went through five editions; his later major work, the three volume *Sacred Calendar of Prophecy* (1828), appeared in a second edition in 1844. His two-volume work on the future of the Jews, *A General and Connected View*, had two editions, in 1808 and 1809. His *Remarks on the Effusion of the Fifth Apocalyptic Vial* was published twice in 1815. After his death *The Revival of the French Emperorship Anticipated* (1853) reached its fifth edition in 1859.

To some extent, though not with the same thoroughness and system, Faber's reshaping of the symbols was anticipated by Henry Kett in 1799. As Kett's purpose was the traditional combating of unbelief by a display of the workings of providence, he gave a prominent anti-Christian character to infidelity. Antichrist was all three of the papal, the Mahometan and infidel powers, and some sort of pre-eminence was given to the third. There was, Kett believed, an eighteenth-century conspiracy to extirpate Christianity inaugurated by Voltaire and the Illuminati. Infidelity was 'first embodied into *a practical system of wickedness* by Voltaire, d'Alembert, Frederic II King of Prussia, Diderot and their confederates in iniquity'. It was the spawn of both Mahometanism and popery.[29] That Faber owed something to Kett is suggested by an acknowledgement in his first major work that Kett was among those who had been prompted by the current crisis to depart from the traditional papal identification. But Faber developed the suggestion much more emphatically.

He first announced his major themes in *Two Sermons* preached and published in Oxford in 1799. Here he argued that the second advent of the Messiah, together with the conversion and restoration of the Jews, could soon be expected. He exhibited a fierce hatred for deism and unitarianism and hoped that a display of providence through prophecy and history would rescue men from these perils. He accepted the Mede-Newton arrangement of the seals and trumpets and vials, but dissented (as the passage of time had made obligatory) from Newton's application of them to modern times. In exegetic terms, his hypothesis was that the seventh trumpet had sounded, that this was the third of the trumpets which announced woe, that the vials of wrath were even then pouring upon the earth, upon France and Catholic Europe in particular. Five of these had been poured, and the fifth had destroyed the papacy. (In later writings he needed to affect a modest revision, so that this vial became current not completed, and the papacy still in the process of destruction.) In the immediate future would be poured the sixth, involving the destruction of the Turks and the restoration of the Jews, and the seventh, which would coincide with the final dissolution. Though he was never to be a millennialist proper, he was later to retreat from this nihilistic vision.

Built in to this pattern are two lines of commentary which persist through his later writings, and find an extremist expression with Drummond and Irving: a hatred of the allied phenomena of democracy and irreligion, and a conviction that the nations, Great Britain included, lie passively in the hand of God. So, in this early sermon, the first vial of wrath is the licentiousness and irreligion most clearly exemplified by Voltaire; the second is the revolution in France, which Faber saw as a form of self-torment and a fit punishment for her past sins; while the third was the spread of revolution to the other persecuting Catholic countries. Divine vengeance would be yet more evident 'should Spain, and the rest of Italy, be doomed to submit to the yoke of democracy'.[30] Again, he is by no means confident that Britain will escape; God will deal with her according to her deserts. Political agitation, irreligion and sensuality suggested a perilous future; repentance, prayer and moral reformation could deflect God's anger. At no point in the future did Faber become fully assured of his country's immunity. His main attention is not upon his country but upon what he took to be the divine plan and its inexorable working out. His Calvinist forebears are not far in the background: he is always concerned with divine sovereignty.

His main work, and the one that bears most clearly the impress of the war, is the *Dissertation on the Prophecies* of 1806. Further books expound specific themes: *A Supplement to the Dissertation* (1806), the *General and Connected View* (1808) and *The Fifth Apocalyptic Vial* (1815). Over this period Faber may be seen revising his identifications, sometimes rather hastily, to catch up with events, a process completed by *The Sacred Calendar of Prophecy* in 1828. There is, however, an underlying consistency; the principles, if not the details, of the 1799 sermon remain.

His analysis has five major foci: the recent history of France, the long history of the papacy, the Ottoman Empire, the future of the Jews, and the role of England. Though Faber was quite immune from the kindly feelings which prompted Horsley, by 1806 he was sure that the papacy was not Antichrist. Into that place he put '*the tremendous infidel power of France*; a power, which . . . I cannot refrain from esteeming *the long-expected Antichrist*'.[31] Accordingly, Antichrist's rise had to be put into the future. This he did by dividing the Christian dispensation into three periods: primitive Christianity, the papal apostacy and the reign of Antichrist. The term of 1260 years applies to the latter two which overlap. Then will follow an 'awful period' of seventy-five years in which Antichrist will rise to the height of his powers and be cast down. 'Unless' Faber concludes, 'I am much mistaken in the preceding remarks upon *the numbers of Daniel* and *St John* we are now removed but little more than *sixty years* from the end of the great period of *the* 1260 prophetic days.'[32] His calculations were as precise as Horsley's; both the papal apostacy and Mahometan power began in 606, so that their term would be complete in 1866 and Antichrist destroyed by 1941. This re-organization of the prophetic periods served a double purpose: first, it conferred on papacy a prominent if subordinate position on the side of evil, and second, it enabled Faber to look with confidence to France to find evidence of explicit anti-Christianity. This he found in abundance.

Unlike some, Faber did not look for a personal Antichrist; he 'was to be *no individual*, but a *power* or *nation* composed of individuals, who should profess and act up to the impious principles of the atheistic scoffers'. In a '*pandemonium of licentious anarchists and determined atheists*' would be found 'the long-expected and late-revealed Antichrist'. 'We can scarcely hesitate to pronounce him to be *revolutionary France*.'[33] In 1815 he engaged in controversy with James Hatley Frere who argued that Napoleon was Revelation's beast from the bottomless pit and ten-horned beast of the sea, as well as Daniel's infidel king. Frere predicted his return to power, first at Rome (so that city would have been successively under the sway of pagan, papist and infidel) and then in Palestine as self-proclaimed Messiah.[34] Frere was obsessed with Napoleon as an individual, but Faber with revolutionary France, and considered Napoleon only as the head of the system of the anti-Christian revolution. Antichrist, an infidel people, was a social not a personal phenomenon.

The leading characteristic of Antichrist as predicted by St John will be his denial of the Father and the Son; this, for Faber, refuted the papal and established the French identification. In revolutionary France could be seen the worship of human liberty and an idolatrous veneration of great men, symbolized by the conversion of the Church of St Genevieve to a Pantheon of heroes. France was also persecutor of Christians and an aggressive proselytizer in the rest of Europe. Catholicism, though not Antichrist, was at least the forerunner; its errors helped Antichrist to grow strong. Fittingly, 'What may in some sense be called the *abortive offspring of Popery* has been made the instrument in the hands of God to visit the iniquities of its parent.'[35]

Faber had no wish to temper the wind to the shorn papal lamb, and no doubt thought he had done all that could be expected of him by erecting a trilogy of enemies—the papal apostacy, the Mahometan 'Imposture' and the infidel Antichrist. Nevertheless, so firmly entrenched was the traditional identification that he was forced to issue a *Supplement* in the same year to defend himself against the charge that he had not been anti-papal enough. He insisted, with equal force, that prophecy did not so identify the papacy and that the papacy was entirely inquitous. But the charge, in spite of Faber's wishes, was not baseless; Antichrist was, in the end, worse than the apostacy; Faber had moved reluctantly to a position close to that of Horsley: 'the abominations even of *the papal superstition* are scarcely visible near the infernal glare of *avowed Antichristianity*.'[36]

The Turkish Empire, the third enemy of the gospel, retained a prominent place. The Empire was in an evident state of disarray;

Anglo-French rivalry was being fought out in the east; and the Turk was sovereign in the region to which the Jews would be restored and where the final battle between Christ and Antichrist would take place. Hence Faber, like his predecessors and contemporaries, took some care in dating and characterizing the history of the followers of the Prophet. This dimension gave symmetry to the prophetic world view. The world of prophecy was the territory of the Roman Empire, the fourth of the Danielic monarchies, still existing through its successor kingdoms and (for Faber) through an ambulatory 'feudal or Carlovingian Emperorship'[37] which had been transferred from Germany to France and Italy by Bonaparte. Over this entire territory Christianity had spread in its primitive purity; in the east it had been persecuted by Saracen and Turk; in the west it had been oppressed by the apostate Church of Rome. Both iniquities began in the seventh century; both would end in the nineteenth—they ran parallel over the magic span of 1260 years. Upon both would fall the vials of God's wrath. But where Horsley had foreseen an alliance between the infidel Antichrist and the Turk (another way, in effect, of exonerating the papacy), Faber's attention was riveted on the west. Here (in accord with his vehement anti-Catholicism) he detected an actual 'union of *Infidelity* and *Popery*'—doubtless Napoleon's Concordat and his coronation—'an union, no doubt preparatory to *the predicted final league* of the beast, the false prophet, and the kings of the papal earth'[38]—the papacy, the Turk and Antichrist. So, indeed, the 'imposture' was given a role in the final events, but it was not one which Faber dwelt upon. His concern with the Jews was much greater, and his interest in the east was probably dependent upon it.

In 1808 Faber published a work, *A General and Connected View*, on the prophecies relating to the Jews, and especially to their future. This exhaustive analysis was required by the apparently contradictory nature of the sources. In brief, he resolved the contradictions by distinguishing between Judah and the Ten Tribes, by supposing that some of the former would be restored by Antichrist and some by a 'great maritime power' only partially converted to Christianity, that the restoration of the converted would be a major blow to Antichrist and that after these conflicts the Ten Tribes would return in peace and tranquillity to the land of their fathers. This complex conclusion—the argument for which occupies the greater part of these two solid volumes—bears testimony to Faber's anxiety to find a significant role for the obscurely depicted messenger-nation of Isaiah 18, the great maritime power. And so, for Faber as for most commentators, the future of the Jews and the destiny of England were inextricably bound together. Without any doubt, Faber and the others had complete respect for the scriptures and a sincere, if distant, concern for the Jews; still, one may suspect that the concern for Great Britain was prior in urgency if not in logic. Further, as Napoleon extended his sway to the Near East and specifically to Palestine, the question of whether Antichrist was to restore the Jews acquired a more than merely exegetical significance.

Though from time to time commentators show concern for the Jews as a persecuted people the centre of their interest lay elsewhere. They saw Jews simply as people to be converted. Priestley apart, the commentators of the eighteenth century saw the history of the Jews as an abstract demonstration of divine purpose, an impersonal argument from prophecy to be used against unbelievers. Faber approvingly quoted Thomas Newton to this effect. 'We see, that after so many ages they are still preserved by a miracle of Providence as a distinct people; and why is such a continual miracle exerted, but for the greater illustration of the divine truth?'[39] During the French wars this use of the Jews remained, and another was added. Granted that the restoration of the Jews was among the last events, granted (both as a matter of inherent probability and as a part of prophecy) that some other people would assist them in the restoration, which other people would have the honour of discharging this divine office? Thus the Jews became a counter in the great game played by infidel France and Christian Britain, a counter which Napoleon took pains to appear to take seriously. For Bicheno the probability that France would be entrusted with this task reinforced his polemic against the British establishment; for Horsley the denial that France would do so was part of his onslaught on anti-Christian democracy. But both were too respectful of the unconditioned divine will to make positive assertions; Horsley, indeed, took pains to insist that no one could say which people would be thus honoured. But his denial was a little disingenuous. *If* the restoration was likely to be soon, *if* it was certain that France did not qualify for the honour, Britain did not have much competition. It is not likely that Horsley took especially seriously a restoration effected by, say, the Dutch or the Americans.

If an ambivalence is implicit in Horsley, it is quite explicit in Faber. Never did he assert that Great Britain will restore the Jews; frequently he took care to say that there was impiety in presuming that this would be so. Such a high honour had to be earned, not appropriated. However, a series of asides and hints cumulatively established at least Faber's great hope that his country would be chosen and his inability to discourage this hope. He balanced uneasily between hope for his country and respect for God's unconditioned will. Conjecture as to the identity of the messenger-people is improper, but 'the more true piety increases among us, the more *likely* will it be that England is *the great maritime power* in question: and, on the other hand, he may no less safely say, without pretending to the gift of prophecy, that, if iniquity increase, and righteousness decrease, among us, we certainly cannot be *that naval power*, which the Lord will delight to honour . . . and it might be well, if, in the present tremendous crisis, we fully considered, how far the buyers and sellers of human flesh are calculated to be the swift messengers of the Most High.'[40]

In the same way the dedication to the *General and Connected View* reflected his concern that Great Britain should earn a safe lodging in the world-ending events, including the restoration of the Jews. Prophecy points to the role of 'some prevailing maritime power of faithful worshippers' as 'chiefly instrumental in converting and restoring a part of the Jewish nation'; but 'we may employ ourselves much more profitably in labouring to diffuse the knowledge of the Gospel and to increase among us the number of the truly pious, than in speculating on the probability or improbability of *our* being the maritime power in question. . . . Our situation peculiarly fits us to be the ark, as it were, of God's Church. We must beware of making *him* our enemy, and then we need not fear what man can do unto us.' So, too, in the conclusion. The future of the Jews is the concern of all men. 'I may add, that *we* of this great protestant maritime nation are *peculiarly* interested; for it certainly is not impossible, that we may be the *messenger-people* described by Isaiah. . . . Hitherto we have been preserved, a column in the midst of surrounding ruins. While mighty empires totter to their base, and while *Antichrist* advances with rapid strides to his predicted sovereignty over the inslaved kings of the Roman earth; *we* through the blessing of divine Providence, have attained to a pitch of naval pre-eminence unknown and unexampled in former ages.'[41] After such an emphasis upon possibility, the routine warning that it is after all but a possibility, carries little conviction. Faber surely thought that Britain's chances of earning the honour, and so of enjoying an especial providential role, were high.

He came nearest to certainty that Great Britain would be saved when, as *A Dissertation on the Prophecies* was going through the press, the great victory at Trafalgar was won, and became the subject of a postscript to the preface. 'The Christian, however, cannot reasonably doubt, that the hand of God is now stretched forth over the earth in a peculiar and remarkable manner; and that all things will assuredly work together to fulfil these prophecies which yet remain unaccomplished, and to prepare a way for the last tremendous manifestations of God's wrath.' He went on: 'in the midst of the awful judgments of the Lord, we may surely be allowed to rejoice with trembling. The signal naval victory, achieved by the great protestant maritime power, interesting as it is to every Englishman, is doubly so to the commentator on prophecy, who thinks there is abundant reason to believe, that the vials full of the last plagues of an offended God will be poured out, not upon those who have come out of the mystic Babylon, but upon those who still adhere to her abominations. May we be preserved to the time of the end, the honoured instruments of fulfilling the counsels of heaven.'[42] But even this guarded approach was uncharacteristically enthusiastic.

The Jews were a counter in another argument, one between rival schools of exegetes. Priestley and Horsley, Bicheno and Faber, were all agreed that prophecies about the Jews should be applied to the Jews. Faber, in spite of the distance which otherwise separated him from Bicheno, highly praised the latter's treatise because it followed this literal approach. Faber condemned the habit of 'spiritualizing' these prophecies by transferring them to the growth and spread of Christianity. Though the language of the prophecies is often symbolic, Israel, literally so, is symbolized. The prophecies do not set forth a vague allegory of general applicability. Faber's treatise of 1808 was a prelude to a scholarly controversy in the 1820s between allegorists and literalists which quickly became a defence of and an attack on the normal kind of missionary enterprise and, generally, upon the worldly and successful Christianity of the great societies. Faber played a part in this controversy (which will be discussed in the next chapter) through his sermon to the London Jewish Society on *The Conversion of the Jews* in 1822. He asked why the missionary success of the first Christian centuries had been followed by so slow an advance, especially by the absence of national and the prevalence of individual conversions. The answer caused a good deal of wrath in missionary societies; it was because '*the converted Jews are destined, in the unsearchable wisdom of God, to be the sole finally successful Missionaries to the Gentile world.*' Their conversion was the necessary prelude to the conversion of the world, a process inaugurated by God acting through such second causes as the Jewish Society, continuing with their restoration through a great maritime nation, and concluding with the direct intervention of Christ to deliver them from their enemies and complete their conversion. Only after all this would the conversion of the Gentiles, through the Jews, take place.

Again the suspicion arises that in every man who chose to deliberate upon the last things, even in a man as comfortable and outwardly secure as Faber, there was a compulsive need to put down the mighty from their seat and exalt the humble and meek. No more eloquent (if implicit) affront could be offered to the great ones than to tell them that their ultimate honour might be, if they were found worthy, to act as servants of the despised Jews, whom God would exalt above them. Neither Faber nor the missionary advocates who disliked his sermon put the argument in these terms, but the reality was probably close to it.

Faber wrote little about the felicity which would follow the great battles; there would indeed be a millennium, but he was more interested in calamity than in happiness. He uttered the routine warnings about the dangers of millennial speculation and, conventionally enough, forgot his own warning from time to time. In the dedication to the *General and Connected View* he made, in a muted manner, the customary millennialist affirmations. Society and the general condition of mankind will be marvellously improved when the great majority of men profess true Christianity, when pagans, Mahometans and nominal Christians have disappeared. 'What the narrow primitive Church was in spirit and practise, the immense millennian Church would likewise be.' There would be no more wars when universal affection took the place of selfishness and 'evil lusts and passions', when 'holiness of conversation' eradicated vice and immorality. 'The world, in a degree, would be brought back to a Paradisaical state'; men would live longer when they no longer suffered from evil dispositions, intemperance and poverty. The change will be effected by God, but by God acting through normal channels in a second and more widespread pentecost. This much he thought to be certain, though he also expected 'a miraculous interference of the Divine Word'.[43] The same possibility was set out in *A Treatise on the . . . Dispensations* (1823). There are three dispensations, the patriarchal, the Levitical and the Christian, which represent a movement from universality to particularity and back to a higher universality (an interesting parallel to the St Simonian characterization of the history of Christianity). The third will end with the general acceptance of the revelation, a period in which, 'there is some reason to believe . . . the Man-Jehovah will preside oracularly, a visible spiritual king, over his obedient people; until the world shall be finally devastated by a deluge of fire, as it was heretofore submerged beneath a deluge of water'.[44] This really final destruction will be preceded by the revolt of 'a race of lawless Titans'. After their destruction and that of the whole earth Jehovah will dwell with men in a new heaven and a new earth—perhaps, as

Faber speculates (in a footnote that reveals the ultimate materialism of all, even the least likely, millennialists) on another celestial body.

When, in 1828, Faber published the large book he had written ten years previously, *The Sacred Calendar of Prophecy*, the vogue for prophecy had reached new heights and proved seriously disturbing to the more sober kind of churchman. Few had done as much as he, by the weight of his scholarship, the respectability of his position, and by the implicitly subversive shape he gave to the prophetic scheme, to encourage this vogue. In the *Sacred Calendar* he altered his method of computation and produced a periodization of sacred history which was new only in details. The conclusion was the same; his scheme showed 'not only the domination of Popery in the West, and the tyranny of Mahommedism in the East, but likewise the prevalence of that modern spirit of Infidelity and Atheism, which exemplified itself in the production of the French Revolution and all its baneful consequences'.[45] In the early 1850s Louis Napoleon was to give him fresh reason for pointing to France as the continuing herald of Antichrist, especially as he had, in 1815, predicted that the Napoleonic-revolutionary regime would be restored. But his main influence was felt in the late 1820s among men whose writings can hardly have pleased him (though he did not condemn them). Irving, Drummond, Hugh McNeile and Lewis Way took two of his themes —the three great enemies with the infidel Antichrist at their head, and the anxious search for signs of England's destiny—and developed them obsessively. He, an elderly man when he put out the *Sacred Calendar*, watched the calendar unfold, with a minimum of exhortation and now no anxiety about divine favouritism among nations. They, in contrast, were full of exhortation and full of concern; between them and him lay a much stronger confidence that Great Britain was the Ark of the Church, a confidence that had been dashed by the events of the later 1820s.

In the early nineteenth century there existed a strenuous millennial nationalism, fostered by reflection on the British role in the struggle with France. In the 1820s George Croly and Edward Cooper showed how Faber's anxiety could turn into an aggressive certainty; an earlier, though vaguer example, occurs in the sermons of Claudius Buchanan, the celebrated Bengal chaplain, writer on Eastern religion and missionary advocate, whose career had been fixed in its evangelical shape by John Newton, Henry Thornton and Charles Simeon.

Buchanan was not a specialist on prophecy; he did not calculate or predict; he simply expressed his conviction that Great Britain's preservation was due to selection by God as his instrument for creating his kingdom on earth. He was confident that this would be so and that the process had begun. Like Bicheno he began from a view of Britain's situation, but drew very different conclusions. In 1810 he preached *Three Sermons on the Jubilee*—the jubilee being the fiftieth anniversary of the King's accession. His confidence matched the patriotic occasion: 'At the present aera Great Britain stands conspicuous in the eyes of the world; she assumes a commanding attitude; and has become, by divine providence, the constituted guardian, in a manner, of the religion and liberties of men.' But her power was not simply for her own security and liberty; it was chiefly 'to carry the principles of moral civilisation and useful knowledge to the remotest nations of the earth, to bring them acquainted with each other as one family, and to impart to them ALL the inestimable benefit of divine revelation'. He called for capitals to proclaim that 'OUR CONSTITUTION IS THE GIFT OF GOD'—in it '*great power* and *pure religion* grew up together.' Great Britain's survival was as directly providential as God's protection of Israel. Her Church was the purest, because the most divinely favoured, of the reformed churches. Indeed it was because of her Church that Great Britain had been chosen: 'whatever honour is assigned to the state for its defence of the rights and liberties of men, is derived ultimately from the duration of the national church.' Her religious condition in the early nineteenth century was, so Buchanan held, purer than it had been since the Reformation, thanks to Sunday Schools, instruction of the poor, benevolent societies, Bible production and missionary activity. So Britain was 'the instrument which God is pleased to use . . . not only to defend the Christian religion at home, but to extend it throughout the world.' Appropriately though, he concluded with a warning: if Great Britain was 'in a certain sense . . . his chosen people', then her betrayal of this trust would cause God to punish her as he punished Israel through the Assyrians. In 1810 it would have been obvious that for 'the Assyrians' one should read 'the French'.[46]

At some points his millennialism became explicit. He told how he had consulted some Jewish scholars in the east on Isaiah 18 and how they had reluctantly agreed that it probably pointed to Great Britain. But Buchanan gave the prophecy a general missionary, rather than a specifically Jewish, interpretation; it meant that a maritime power would use its ships to despatch missionaries and Bibles. In *The Star in the East*, a much reprinted sermon issued in its seventh edition with the *Three Sermons*, he asserted that 'the Time is come for diffusing His religion throughout the world',[47] and concluded with a glowing picture of the prophecies fulfilled by the diffusion of bible

Christianity, especially in the East. For this purpose Britain had been preserved from the hostility of infidels. In Buchanan patriotism fused with religion as did criticism with religion in Bicheno. In both, the social and the sacred intersect and merge, though with a decisively different outcome.

Another who looked anxiously to England's role was Edward Cooper, sometime Fellow of All Souls. His major work *The Crisis* (1825) went rapidly through three editions. He considered Napoleon to have been 'the wilful king' of Daniel (11.36-45), and argued that it was his role to punish Antichrist, not to destroy him, for destruction was reserved for Armageddon. Further, he identified the present with the sixth vial of wrath which was destined to destroy the Turkish Empire. The Greek revolt, the earthquakes at Antioch and Aleppo, and the 'awful mortality in the family of the Sultan' were brought forward as evidence. The papal Antichrist was currently enjoying a respite, between the fifth vial, punishment at the hands of Napoleon, and the seventh, its final destruction. So the current vigour of the papacy—in which Catholic obstruction to Bible circulation in Ireland and the Middle East figured prominently—was a sign of the pending crisis; together with the revival of despotism and infidelity, it showed that the forces of evil were gathering together so that they might be destroyed.

Cooper looked to see where the forces of good were to be found and, rather less unambiguously than Buchanan, found them in England. In an earlier publication, *Letters Addressed to a Serious and Humble Enquirer after Divine Truth* (1817), he had straightforwardly asserted that the British and Foreign Bible Society was the beginning of the conversion of the world, and proof that Great Britain was God's chosen instrument, to be preserved through all the troubles. In *The Crisis* he worked to the same conclusion in a more gingerly fashion, making a good deal of the evils of English life: Sunday newspapers, Sunday travel (especially by the upper classes), the game laws, slavery, dissipation, gambling and (ominously vague) 'promoting the depraved and brutal pleasures of the populace'.[48] But none of this approached Catholic iniquities, such as prayers to the Virgin, the adoration of the host and the continental Sunday.

Positively, too, there was evidence of British virtue triumphing over the pro-slavery, anti-missionary imperialism of the eighteenth century. Pure religion had preserved her from the perils of the recent past: 'The triumph over Jacobinism was, in fact, the triumph of the Bible.'[49] More recently concern for the Jews, both for their just treatment and for their conversion, had reinforced the conclusion that England had indeed effectively separated herself from the papal iniquity in the sixteenth century, and so exempted herself from the wrath due to fall very soon upon Antichrist. In an earlier sermon to the London Society for promoting Christianity among the Jews (1819) he had found in the society's existence a sign of the coming change—adding, rather more humanely, that even if this conjecture proved wrong it was never too soon to reverse the injustice of centuries. Cooper, it should be added, was hardly concerned with the mode of the advent, and not at all with the millennium. He was preoccupied with the fate due to fall upon the papacy and with England's relationship to providence.

George Croly, an Irish clergyman who made a literary career in London (he is better remembered as a contributor to *Blackwood's* and as the author of the Byronic 'Paris in 1815'), supplied these deficiencies in *The Apocalypse of St. John* (1827) and gave the millennial nationalism of Buchanan an explicitly prophetic framework. 'There is the strongest reason for believing,' he announced in his first sentence, 'that as Judea was chosen for the especial guardianship of the original Revelation; so has England been chosen for the especial guardianship of Christianity.' A sketch of English history showed that she had always been weak when either papal or papalizing (e.g. Mary and Charles I) and strong when she returned to Protestant truth (e.g. Elizabeth and Cromwell). The moral for the decade of Catholic emancipation was firmly pointed; if England did equalize popery and Christianity she would get her due punishment. 'But if she faithfully repel this deepest of all crimes . . . there may be no bound to the sacred magnificence of her preservation. Even the coming terrors and tribulations of the earth may but augment her glory; like the prophet on the mount, even in the midst of the thunderings and lightnings that appal the tribes of the earth, she may be led up, only nearer to behold the Eternal Majesty; and when the time of the visitation has past [*sic*], to come forth from the cloud with the light of the divine presence round her brow, and bearing in her hand the law for mankind.'[50]

Some other details of Croly's entirely idiosyncratic analysis of Revelation point directly to the Albury school. He was a pre-millennialist, believing that the fall of Antichrist will be effected by direct divine intervention. He foresaw the saints rising literally in glory at the outset of the millennium. But he is obscure on the question of whether the millennium will be Christ's personal reign; it will be an 'intimate union of the Church with Christ in his manifest glory and sovereignty'.[51] Croly's reaction to Emancipation is unrecorded. The grief which it may be conjectured he felt was abundantly expressed by the Irving-Drummond circle at Albury. In an equation, Croly plus disillusionment equals the Albury school.

IV: Arguments about Prophecy

Faber and Bicheno, the conservative and the radical, were respectable eighteenth-century divines brought up in a tradition which made it reasonable to suppose that prophecy was a way of understanding the present and characterizing the future. They were anxious to persuade others to accept their analyses; prophetical writing was a means of communication, and so of influencing belief and action. Faber sought to turn men from deism, atheism, infidelity, popery and democracy. Bicheno's cause was civil and religious liberty, and his polemic was directed against precisely those values which Faber defended. Early nineteenth-century prophetical writing, in general, had a persuasive and often a polemical purpose. This chapter and the next two examine the variety of these purposes manifested in the 1820s and early 1830s.

All the positions taken in this period had been established in the years of revolution and war. Peace did not dispel the conviction that the times were perilous; on the contrary, distress, agitation and international instability reinforced it. For many, there was a continuing need to appeal from human to divine standards, to reform manners and compel good behaviour, to condemn social ills and prescribe remedies, to display the traditional images of divine power and judgement, wrath and mercy. The pre-conditions for prophetic exposition and millennial yearnings remained intact; by the later 1820s it seemed to some that they were more compelling than they had ever been before.

Not all the expositors of this period were pessimists. There were also optimistic versions for those who looked at their world and found it good and looked to the future and found it better. They too, in the evidences of human progress rather than of human depravity, found plenty to justify their millennial hope. Prophecy, for men of many kinds, but chiefly for pessimists close to despair, remained a conventional way of understanding, of persuasion and exhortation.

That prophetical writing could persuade and so have individual and social results was equally clear to exponents and detractors alike.

Though much that the exponents urged and the detractors rejected was social in character, their basic differences were about theological positions and spiritual goals. As it was man's duty to believe in the Bible, the exponents found sufficient justification in their role as its clarifiers. But their defence proceeded to the assertion that a man's spiritual character and behaviour would be beneficially changed by reflection upon the truths of prophecy: the providential shape of history, the imminence of judgement, and the bliss of the millennium. It was further argued that social and political behaviour would improve under the same influences. More critically the millennium was used as a social and political ideal against which to judge the present. These arguments for prophetical writing lie on the surface of the tracts and pamphlets. There are, in addition, more implicit and deeper individual and social motivations which lie beneath the surface. But both, the explicit and the implicit, begin with an argument about religion.

The vogue for prophetic exposition and preaching in the 1820s prompted controversy on the propriety of this kind of theology. Critics of the accepted prophetical conventions were few in number, though (especially in the case of S. R. Maitland) formidable in controversy. The defenders of moderation and ecclesiastical conservatism typically did not oppose prophetical exposition as such but embraced positions which stressed growth and continuity, the value of social and ecclesiastical institutions and the validity of human effort, against the pessimists' belief in crisis, abrupt change and the vanity of human institutions and achievements. The major controversy was within the prophetic tradition; psychologically, between optimists and pessimists, heuristically between post- and pre-millennialists, and exegetically between allegorists and literalists.

The major charge, then as before, against millennialists was that of de-spiritualizing religion by turning attention away from heaven and towards earth. Pre-millennialists, because they stressed the earthly location of divine action and the necessity of a perfect realization of God's will on earth, had constantly to meet this accusation. Even when they continued their expositions to show that all was taken up into heaven after the millennium, the joys they described on the redeemed earth had a way of making those of heaven seem pallid. From time to time will be found the admission that heaven was too remote and immaterial a goal to satisfy men. Post-millennialists, emphasizing the continuity between a present not too depraved and a future not too disturbingly glorious, were less vulnerable to this charge. Indeed, they often made clear their anxiety to keep heaven intact, both (as it were) for its own sake and for its function as a control on behaviour. Nevertheless, their opponents constantly, and with point, accused them of resting content with a a millennium more human than divine, and so with an earth which God's activity would not, in the end, totally redeem. They were, as always, compromised by their desire to keep heaven intact without foregoing the delights of an earthly millennium.

Despite the charges and counter-charges, the fight was within a conventionally orthodox Christian consensus. There are no striking doctrinal innovations (even Irving's alleged Christological heresy seems to have been largely a matter of semantics); there are variations within an agreed pattern. Writers of either kind warn their readers, perhaps as a half-guilty afterthought, that glorious as the millennium will be, it will not compare with the glories of heaven. Few would have dissented from Faber's aside that death would be each individual's end of the world.[1]

Nevertheless, by the end of the decade the pessimistic literalists had departed perceptibly from the conventional mainstream. Irving's Christology on one side, he and his associates undoubtedly became eccentric in their beliefs about society and politics, church structure and government, and individual Christian behaviour. Among these eccentricities—which are not, however, more strange than those of the Oxford movement—was a millennialism of a distinctly materialistic kind. Indignant orthodox divines used the word 'carnal' with mounting fervour; they also charged that Irving and his kind were weakening social control by turning men's attention away from an afterlife of rewards and punishments. But this accusation was not justified. None of the accused doubted that a secure place in the earthly paradise could be earned by anything except the most arduous rectitude. Irving, Henry Drummond and their more persistent followers saw themselves as a saving remnant whose virtuous lives were to earn God's mercy, perhaps for Britain and certainly for themselves. They believed that in part the value of prophetic teaching lay in its control of behaviour. Drummond is also the author of *Social Duties upon Christian Principles*. This conviction they shared with respectable divines whom no one would have ventured to charge with carnality or subversion. All the expositors, whatever their tendency, exhort their readers to public and private virtue. A clear case is provided by the evangelical pamphleteer and hymn writer James Haldane Stewart, who, interestingly and perhaps significantly, was connected by marriage to Robert Owen.

The title of Stewart's *Practical View of the Redeemer's Advent* announced his intention to expound a theory which would improve behaviour. He took pains to clear away all millennialist associations, as if it were possible to write of the second coming without an implicit millennialism. The redeemer was coming, as Stewart said, to judge; those who survived would enter upon some sort of felicity. Stewart merely declined to describe this felicity, for clear and pertinent reasons. Adventist expectation, normal in the early Church, had been obliterated by the papal apostacy and revived by the reformers; subsequently it had been discredited by 'various crude and fanciful, and indeed carnal and wicked opinions upon the Millennium—a subject quite distinct from the Advent—opinions that tended to overturn civil government, and to introduce worse than heathen licentiousness'.[2] These discourses arose from discussions on the need to pray for a general outpouring of the Holy Spirit. So Stewart looked back to Jurieu's opinion that the last days would be inaugurated by a new and greater pentecost, and forward to the Irvingite belief that the outpouring had occurred in the glossolalia of western Scotland and Regent's Square. Not that Stewart had anything as uncomfortable as glossolalia in mind; but he and those many who prayed in the 1820s for this outpouring were, in spite of themselves, midwives to monstrous children.

Stewart's message was simple: Christians should *always* expect the advent. Yet there were signs that the advent was actually close at hand, events which 'may brighten the hopes of the Redeemer's friends, as well as spread terror amongst his enemies'.[3] He instanced the Turkish decline, the end of Jewish persecution and the beginning of their conversion, and—a sign that evil was increasing—the renewed activity of the papacy. But the most emphatic sign was the widespread preaching of the gospel. Stewart was perhaps the first (but not by any means the last) prophetic writer to use statistics to measure the work of providence: in Protestant countries forty-one societies were spending over £400,000 p.a. on propagation, and doing it in 141 languages. The *Christian Observer* frequently commended Stewart to its readers when other writers went to extremes. For all his acceptance of a fairly imminent end, he deflected millennial yearning into individual and practical channels. He would be more likely to prompt an increased subscription to a missionary society than a restless desire for a new earth.

It was on such grounds that the *Christian Observer* justified the study of prophecy during the 1820s; it kept men aware that they were held in the hands of God, not merely as individuals, but as communities, churches and nations. The traditional religious sanctions for enforcing individual rectitude and social stability appear to have needed, in an age of increasing irreligion and agitation, an injection of apocalyptic fear and hope. The way in which an expectation of the last days was linked with prayer for the greater activity of the Holy Spirit re-emphasizes the 'practical' nature of this millennialism. The evangelical magazines of the 1820s—Anglican, Wesleyan and Dissenting—all show an awareness that vitality had gone out of religious life. Advocates of prayer for the outpouring of the spirit frequently point to American revivals as examples of its occurrence. Evangelicals were uneasy; the great days had departed and must be brought back. At the end of this trans-Atlantic influence lies the mission of the Mormons; again a consequence of little comfort to the orthodox initiators of the movement.

Sincere as these men unquestionably were, it is also clear that they deliberately used prophecy as a revivalistic technique. It was an established opinion that the last days would be inaugurated by a new pentecost. This new pentecost (a remote echo of Joachim in a century that hardly knew him) would be the ultimate revival, and the millennium a prophylactic against the all too familiar post-revival falling away. As a means of revivalism among hearers who had to be stimulated into personal reformation, prophecy and millennialism were more effective stimuli towards serious thought about God, man, and judgement if it was announced that the irreversible last events would take place soon. Thus millennialism became a way in which evangelicals tried to recruit their waning fortunes as the advance of irreligion and the recession of enthusiasm created a need for an intensification of religious sanctions.

In the minds of revivalists and prophetic expositors generally the prime and sometimes the only goal was individual reformation. But a socio-political aspect was also acknowledged. It was accepted that irreligion and disorder went hand in hand and that the threat of disorders was year by year increasing. So prophetic sanctions were applied to social as well as individual behaviour. Writers on prophecy, evangelicals all, constantly stressed the need for Great Britain to purify her life. The desecration of the sabbath, the lottery, prostitution, pornography, individual licentiousness, slavery and child labour, were all offences against God's law, and so existed at the same level of iniquity. It was less urged against them that they did harm to men than that they were an offence to God, and so certain to incur his anger. This argument was the simple stock in trade of the evangelical reformer of manners; the expositor of prophecy who used it simply added what he hoped were additional sanctions—that the wrath so earned might not be far distant, or that it was certainly very close, and sometimes that it could be precisely predicted.

Prophetical writers such as Stewart were particularly alive to the need to stave off wrath by reformation. Their social and political concern was very real, but it was consequential, at least in the logic of their arguments, upon their view of God and his dealings with men and societies. As Stewart put it in a sermon, 'there is no period of a nation's history in which we should not ascribe its state . . . to the unseen but all-directing providence of Almighty God.'[4] Such men wanted a pure society in order to placate a wrathful God; not a wrathful God in order to purify society. So, at any rate, their arguments run; this is the way in which they put it to themselves and their audience. At a deeper level of motivation one may be less sure that their own account is complete or correct. One is tempted to believe that in the order of personal response, whatever the order of the argument, it was social fear which drove them to summon up divine punishment. With some millennialists this temptation became irresistible, for the care with which they delineated the millennium in social and political terms encircled the total argument in a social theory. Irving's revival of divine right theories and Drummond's argument that the authority of Christ could be seen in the power of a master over his servant probably reveal more of their inner motivation than they knew.

Examples of revivalistic justification for prophetic exposition abounded in the religious journals of the 1820s. As early as 1823 a *Christian Observer* correspondent lamented that so useful a study should be discredited by wild men, superficial in scholarship and excitable in temperament. Its real utility lay in confirming the truth of Revelation as prophecy is fulfilled, in depicting a theocentric world view of history, and in stimulating appropriate behaviour, for example the support of missions. The true student of prophecy must cultivate an appropriate spiritual disposition, marked by humility, an absence of idle curiosity, caution, and an intention to apply the results to his own moral improvement.[5] Two years later the same journal reviewed at length twelve recent publications on prophecy, taking pains to separate the wheat from the chaff.[6] 'To some,' the writer conceded, 'and these perhaps the wisest and best of our species, the simple view of the mercies of God as revealed in the Gospel, will have afforded the highest motive and guide to action.' But there remained the vast deposit of biblical prophecy which may not be ignored. The prophecies testifying to the first coming of the Messiah produced a 'glow of expectation previous to his predicted coming'. Prophecies of the future reign of the Messiah 'have awakened, and do still awaken in the hearts of many, the same glow'. The evangelical advantages of prophetic study were set out at some length. 'It tends to raise the mind to heavenly things. It works a separation from earth, and earth-born speculations. It produces a holy disinterestedness as to objects of mere secular worth. It arms the mind against the influence of passing events. It relieves it of many uneasy and doubtful apprehensions. It teaches it reliance on an unseen but infallible Providence, ordering all things in heaven and earth. It both results from and promotes a strength of faith, a brightness of hope, and a fitness of acquiesence in the divine proceedings. It is greatly serviceable in producing a minute attention to the word of God.' The review insisted that prophecy had '*two* proper and intended purposes; one, that of *affording evidence to the sacred and saving doctrines of Divine writ*; the other, *that of furnishing an incentive to present duty, by a consideration of future prospects*'. The first purpose could not, by definition, be served by an exposition of *unfulfilled* prophecy, and such expositors went in danger of becoming obsessed by curiosity and mere virtuosity. They could, however, confer an especial benefit: 'which is timely to warn mankind of their duties, to control their conduct in preparation for the future, and to lead them to circumspection, watchfulness and prayer'.

Drummond and Irving would have assented; they were particularly concerned to move from individual to social discipline, to spell out the considerations implicit in the terms 'ordering', 'acquiescence', and 'duty', and to apply the conclusions to their own times. In this review Stewart was quoted at length and approvingly, to the effect that 'there must be some error' in the widespread belief that though Christians would go to the Lord, the Lord would not come to them in his second coming. Here Stewart and the reviewer implicitly admitted that the traditional sanction for right behaviour, the prospect of rewards and punishments after death, was no longer adequate. Firmer sanctions were needed; the fear of a violent communal death on earth; the hope of a long felicity on earth. The profound secularity of millennialism had a way of catching up with its expositors, the more strikingly because they did not know that it was doing so. The very men who were most anxious to arrest the decline of traditional religion provide evidence of its decline in their correctives. The most heaven-bent of evangelicals were caught up in secularity as agents, not simply as victims.

A work by Gerald Thomas Noel, a celebrated evangelical preacher, showed clearly how prophecy supplemented and reinforced orthodox sanctions. Noel, one of two brothers in the ministry of the Church who achieved eminence in this period, was very well connected (his brother became Earl of Gainsborough in 1841). He was a close friend of Samuel Wilberforce, and was known for his hymns and travel writings as well as for his sermons and theological publications. His *Brief Enquiry into the Prospects of the Church of Christ* (1828) expressed a mood of unrelieved world-hatred, a hatred which fastens with equal ferocity upon papal apostacy, active infidelity and nominal Christianity, with the watered-down official Christianity of his day not too far behind. All that passed for Christianity, except the fidelity of a tiny scorned minority, was a negation of God. 'Once, indeed, his light shone brightly upon our world; but "the darkness comprehended it not", and he soon withdrew his radiance. Idolatry and superstition have maintained their sway over the *Heathen* nations; while a darker gloom of ingratitude and crime has enwrapped the *regions* of *nominal Christianity.*' Though Noel did not say as much, his words suggest that the Christian dispensation had failed. The second coming must make up for the failure of the first: 'Truly the ages which have unfolded their successive eras since the first advent of our Lord, have been ages of night and woe.' He invited his 'fellow Christians to a more distinct recognition of the authority of Christ as the constituted Governor of *this world*', an authority which is not to be manifested until his second advent.[7]

Depravity, so universally prevalent, must be corrected. Is this 'adjustment', as Noel calls it, only to be affected in heaven? Noel has an 'eye for an eye' view of history; the scales must be seen to be balanced on earth as well as known to be balanced in heaven. 'Zion, and Jerusalem, where he will reign, may be literally understood as the chief place of his residence during this state, the spot of ground where he was most despised and ill-treated.' Heaven is the place from which salvation and judgement proceed; earth the place where they are to be enacted. It is an error, though a venerable one, to believe that 'the *scene* and *place* of redemption shall be separated from the persons redeemed'; it arises from an over-spiritualized and over-moralized Christianity. He stressed the manhood of Christ because current orthodoxy diluted this truth, so that 'the *future glory of* the saints is entirely severed from his *human sympathies* and *terrestrial dominion.*' Less strenuously than Irving, but still quite emphatically, Noel wanted to rescue Christianity from error. 'The Image of God has been too exclusively limited to the idea of moral rectitude; but it comprises dominion as well as rectitude; hence, in the renovated world, the saints are described as "kings" equally with "priests unto God".' For all his denunciation of chiliasts and Anabaptists, Noel was very materialistic; the world is destined for renovation, not destruction; the ties linking Christ to the world are not as fragile as 'human theology' supposes. He was concerned with God's power rather than his love; he reasserted the power of God over his world and so over-matched the all too evident power of evil. His discussion of the millennium showed that the world he had in mind was social and political.[8] Two aspects of his exposition revealed its compensatory character; his description of the millennial polity, and his analysis of the immediate and practical benefits of millennialism.

The chief mark of the millennium will be the actual personal monarchy of Christ. However, Noel constantly recalled that the saints will participate in this monarchy. The second coming, an event not too distant, will inaugurate Christ's visible Kingdom. The first resurrection of the saints will literally take place; the Jews will in fact be converted, restored to Palestine, and elevated among the nations of the world. The saints, those rising at the first resurrection together with those living at the time of the advent, will exercise actual power and authority; they will reign and judge and punish. Noel's sense of justice required a nicely calculated turning of the tables. The persecuted and rejected will become 'the redeemed princes of the earth'; rulers will defer to their authority, and 'hold their own authority beneath *their* acknowledged sceptre'. 'These saints of God are surely the ELECT CHURCH of Jew and Gentile . . . *"joint heirs with him"* of the kingdom; even of that kingdom which is to rise out of the ruins of those monarchies which shall so awfully have abused their delegated authority. These monarchies, when smitten by the mysterious STONE, are at the same moment given up to the SAINTS, no longer to be worn down by persecution and scorn!' The reversal of earthly fortunes was made yet more apparent by Noel's identification of the monarchy-shattering stone of Daniel with the stone of Matthew 21.42, the stone which the builders rejected. Noel argued, in effect, that the rulers of the world should honour and defer to the godly; instead they have rejected and persecuted them. In the second coming the rulers will be punished for this; in the millennium the godly will share 'the millennial throne of the Messiah'. Noel, one must suppose, had despaired ever of erecting the kingdom of the saints by normal means, and looked to God to establish 'this wise and harmonious fabric of social order and of religious happiness'.[9]

By retaining certain continuities between this world and the next, Noel underlines the theocratic character of the millennium. It will be like this world; 'human sovereignties' will be preserved so that they may be subordinated. Men will be 'mortal, and subject to occasional ill' but they will be happy and peaceful. Above all, as subjects they will attribute 'all their blessings to the grace and power of Christ'; 'the higher management and control of this world will be in the hands, first of Christ himself, and, under him, in the hands of men —of men, once like the mortal sojourners they govern, but now glorified like their Lord, and living *amidst their mortal kindred* as benefactors, princes, and kings.'[10]

In a lengthy chapter entitled 'Application of the Subject to the Morality of Life', Noel further demonstrated his supreme concern with the affairs of the world. He rehearsed and rejected the arguments levelled against the students of prophecy and proceeded to an elaborate defence. All Christianity is based upon prophecy and upon unfulfilled prophecy at that. The argument of the day was not between prophecy and no prophecy, but between rival interpretations of the body of prophetic statements which all agree will one day be fulfilled. It was between literalists and allegorists, between (as he clearly implied) those who explain prophecy and those who explain it away. Apart from conceding that minute prediction is foolhardy, Noel did not yield an inch to his opponents. He claimed superiority for views unjustly called novel, not upon exegetical grounds, but as judged by practical results. He claimed great and beneficial moral consequences for literal millennialism. Because the so-called orthodox view and his own view coincided in major particulars and primary truths, one could not fairly look for any spectacular moral improvement in those who moved from the first to the second position. But the second is the sharper, more compelling and more efficacious way of presenting the gospel message of 'Salvation by Christ, eternal life, or eternal woe'. His argument showed that *'certain modifications* of these great and essential doctrines of prophecy should give a *coherence* and *symmetry* to the proportions of Christianity'; he went on to use the words light, distinct, vividness, simplicity, beauty, harmony, apparent, attractive, intelligible, familiar, conceivable, bright and clear, to indicate the beneficial results of these modifications.[11] Noel had the pastoral situation in mind; in this whole chapter he judged doctrines solely on a basis of evangelical efficacy.

The word 'familiar' is the key. He wished to present the Christian gospel in images which would compel attention and assent because they related to the world men knew, not the world they could only guess at; they were to relate as descriptive statements, not as metaphors. So to compare a 'purified' earth with a 'polluted' earth 'is to form a *readier* contrast'; it is 'easier' for the mind to contemplate 'an innocent and holy earth'; the traditional sanctions of death and eternity certainly devalue the corrupt world, but 'the same result will more *cheerfully*, and certainly as *efficiently* be produced by the readier contrast between a present and a future dispensation of the *existing* earth.' Noel constantly urged that the concrete imagery of the familiar world will prove a more effective stimulus than the necessarily abstract and 'misty' images of heaven and eternity. 'Heaven is a place, *distant, untried, unknown*.' Millennial views are 'calculated to *reconcile the poorer Christian to the struggles of the present life*' because they present him with a vision of bliss which he can understand. 'Such a solace would still be to him his heaven, but a heaven more palpably reduced to the level of his comprehension and his hopes.'[12] Millennialism became an instrument of social control.

This chapter concluded with a point which will be taken up again shortly. His views, Noel claimed, imply no diminution of moral effort, no idle waiting for the last trump. Rather they should impel every man, just because he is expecting the last trump, to be diligently doing his duty in his appointed place when it sounds. Nor do they down-grade missionary enterprise. This is a duty to be performed whatever might be the times and methods appointed by God for the actual conversion of the world. Missionaries must go as 'heralds', the gospel must be proclaimed 'as a witness'; this is terminology which, in spite of Noel's disclaimers, had an important bearing upon the function of missionary enterprise.

Though Noel was palpably sincere, and held his opinions because he believed them to be biblical, it is profitable to see his argument in a different light. He was an anxious, even a tormented, Christian in an age of emergent irreligion, quite skilfully and resourcefully reshaping the Christian myth to adjust it to new conditions. He advanced no opinion which could not be supported from the Bible. But so could an opposite interpretation, and the question remains: why did he choose to find these views and not other ones? The temper of his times impelled him to seek out the most effective set of religious sanctions available. The result is the usual millennial paradox—to combat secularity the Christian falls into an equally deep secular trap.

Noel and others of his kind were pessimists whose pre-millennialism was closely related to their revulsion from contemporary society. Their approach may be fairly considered as an existential response to the social and individual situation they so pungently criticized. So indeed may the opinions of the optimistic post-millennialists, who differ by looking at men and society and finding them good; however, as firmly as their opponents, they too looked at men and society. The case is the same with those who attacked the whole basis of the current argument; they had an exegetical case but they also offered argument based upon social well-being. The whole debate over prophecy and millennialism in the 1820s, between pre-millennialist, post-millennialist and anti-millennialist, establishmentarian, dissenter and Wesleyan, had its practical, existential and social dimension which was as real as its theological character.

The theological concepts and exegetical principles, undeniably real to the participants, were broad and flexible enough to contain a debate about man in society, which may fairly be evaluated for its own sake. Fairly, because theology and exegesis almost invariably lead towards and never away from an existential situation.

One of the most formidable anti-millennialists, Samuel Roffey Maitland, did not interest himself in social consequences. He was concerned entirely with the harm done by this kind of error to the faith of individuals and of the Church. The opinions on prophecy which passed for *the* Protestant interpretation, particularly the identification of the Catholic Church as Antichrist, were for him 'speculations in which a great many good men, and still more good women, spend their time and thoughts, and too often renounce their common sense, and prostitute their faith'.[13] He published a series of pamphlets and books, full of great learning and bitter polemic, from 1826 to 1834 to combat these speculations. Maitland, one of the leading historians of the age, in general carried too many guns for his enraged opponents. His first large book was directed against Joseph Milner's Church History, taken by evangelicals to be authoritative, especially Milner's high praise for the Waldensians and the Albigensians. He appears to have set his more celebrated grandson, Frederick William, in an historical direction. Maitland believed that the papacy-Antichrist identification had originated in the distortions of reformation controversy, had been propped up over the centuries by dishonest scholarship, and continued by honest ignorance and folly. He set out to show that prophecy referred to a future manifestation of evil of brief but terrible duration. The scholarly shifts of the prophetical specialists arose solely from the need to attack Rome. But Antichrist was no sort of institution at all, least of all the Roman Catholic Church which 'is . . . and always has been, a part of the Catholic Church of Christ; and . . . is viewed in this light by the Church of England . . . notwithstanding her many and great corruptions'.[14]

Maitland had great joy exposing the contradictions of the commentators, who, though fair game, were an easy target. But beneath his polemical zest his purpose was intensely serious. Difference of opinion on minor issues could be tolerated; but was the delivery of the Church 'into the hands of a blasphemous and persecuting power' a minor issue? 'If such an event as this has taken place, is it possible that the church of God can be at a loss to decide *when* and *how* it happened?' 'I cannot', he concluded, 'help again expressing my astonishment at the supposed state of the Church of God. Is it credible, that she has to wander up and down through a period of nearly three centuries, enquiring when she was delivered into the hands of a cruel and blasphemous tyrant? . . . the saints who were thus delivered up knew nothing of the matter. One generation after another passed away, and the secret was not discovered. Centuries rolled on, and the saints knew not, that he to whom they looked as their father, and their head, was making war upon them, and wearing them out.'[15]

But here lies his weakness; his opponents were equally sure that the papal church was no part of the church of God, and Maitland had said nothing to make them change their minds. His purpose was to uphold, in the face of dishonesty and folly, what he considered to be orthodoxy. He was concerned with scholarly honesty, religious truth and their consequences for the lives of individuals and for the Church. He simply believed that Christians would be better off without delusions, especially delusions about the standing of other Christians. It is very likely that he prompted more anger than conviction among those he sought to correct.

The anonymous *Modern Fanaticism Unveiled* (1831) was one of many publications in the early 1830s denouncing the gifts of the spirit supposed to have been manifested in London among the followers of Irving and in West Scotland—gifts which the *Morning Watch*, a quarterly set up specifically to publicize prophecy, and a rival flock of pamphlets welcomed as sure testimony to the approach of the last days. This author, too, saw these extravagances in the context of prophetic religion, and levelled an attack upon the total situation. There were three defects in prophecy as interpreted by 'modern millenarians': 'First, That their theory is carnal in its nature; Secondly, That it fosters arrogance of spirit; and, Thirdly, That it paralyzes exertion for the spiritual benefit of mankind.' To this trilogy of errors, theological, individual and social, were devoted more than thirty unoriginal but eloquent pages. But as with Maitland, one may doubt if this had any effect on the opponents beyond angering them. The case rested upon the assertion that Christianity is spiritual rather than material; that its function is to turn men away from earth towards heaven; and that Christ's kingdom is 'not of this world, not earthly in its principles, nor terrestrial in its character'. This was precisely the point at issue. The writers of the *Morning Watch* and all who took the millennium as more than a metaphor, felt obliged to deny that the kingdom consisted 'not in outward splendour, but in the universal diffusion and intensive operation of divine principles'. When this writer added that 'It matters little to insist that the earth is to be refined and renovated: still it is this identical earth', it was a telling point, according to orthodox lights. To his opponents it would have been no more than a statement of an important and neglected truth. The author went on: 'we cannot possibly look upon it with the same holy indifference if we expect it to be our permanent abode . . . indifference in that case, could not have the attribute of holiness; it would rather be sinful to think lightly of a world, which, instead of being doomed to perish by fire, should be the destined sphere of the Redeemer's personal reign.' Opposing writers would have heartily assented to a conclusion which was given as the ultimate criticism; it was precisely because they held such a belief about the earth and its redemption that they wrote as they did.[16]

For this author the world was a place in which men learned to be good so that they might go to heaven—as far as possible from earth. 'And do we need any incentive to cleave unto the dust? Do we naturally sit so loose in our attachment to this earth, that it may safely be arrayed in such prospective charms as tend to heighten its present attractions?'[17] Sound religion and social well-being depended upon a belief about man which saw him as a pilgrim going somewhere else. Irving, for all his follies, saw clearly that this was a diluted view both of Christianity and human nature.

The suggestion that anti-millennialists were often concerned with the social situation is strengthened by their opinion of the role of women in the movements they disliked. Maitland wrote of the damage done to 'a great many good men, and still more good women' by false opinions; the possibly female author of *Modern Fanaticism* rather archly asserted that 'the followers of our fair visionary consist of young ladies full of ardour, and fond of novelty' as well as unbalanced people in general.[18] Thomas Greenwood, in *The Latest Heresy* (1832), concluded that 'Women, it is observable, are the most numerous and prominent actors in these impious mockeries' and had been since Priscilla and Maxima attended upon Montanus. Ann Lee and Joanna Southcott afforded him prominent examples, but he cast his net wider to include two women in the reign of Urban IV who had a vision about transubstantiation, and Sister Nativity, a French nun whose late eighteenth-century revelations in unknown tongues had been interpreted by her confessor and published in three volumes.[19] 'And women', Greenwood summed up, 'have ever been foremost in the train of almost every false prophet, and pestilent heretic, under the Christian dispensation.' By contrast, the true pentecost happened to men. His explanation for this proneness to error among women was a mixture of ancient prejudice and sharp observation. They are weaker than men, more liable to be imposed upon and more excitable, because of 'the peculiar nature of their virtues and duties'. 'They are formed for the solace of man, and therefore their sensibilities are habitually more on the alert than his. They are required to be, comparatively, keepers at home; and have, therefore, fewer opportunities than he of acquiring that experience which can only be reaped among the more active scenes of life. Their understanding, generally speaking, is more easily deceived than his, and their enthusiasm more readily excited. Add to this, that an atmosphere of persuasiveness floats around them, which belongs not to our sterner mould. Satan has thus a double temptation to exert his skill for their seduction, and a double facility for accomplishing it.'[20] None of this explains the emergence of the prophets and heretics who misled the weak women; it says more about male alarm at the onset of female emancipation than about the nature of women. The Mormons were to use similar arguments against their prophetic rivals, the Irvingites in particular.

These anti-millennialist writers were concerned with the health of the Church and the danger of errors ranging from false scholarship to Satanic possession. This concern made them anti-millennialists, as that term was understood at that time—though Maitland believed that prophecy did point to real events in the future, and *Modern Fanaticism Unveiled* implies an undogmatic post-millennialism. All parties to the controversy were concerned with the good of the Church as they saw it, and of society as dependent upon the Church for its own well-being. However, other defenders of the establishment took up a position within the conventions of prophetic study, not outside them.

Such defensive uses of prophecy, though careful to preserve a modestly glorious future on earth, took greater care to keep intact both the validity of the Church as an institution, and the correctness of opinions about heaven as man's entirely spiritual destiny. Sometimes these defences took the position of Augustine, Grotius, Thomas Newton and Hurd, that the millennium was the age of the Church. Thus another of the many anti-Albury pamphlets, Henry Gipps's *Treatise on 'The First Resurrection'* (1831), argued that there will be no period of universal holiness, that the increase of the Church will not alter the carnal nature of the world, and that the second coming will lead directly to the general judgement and the end of the world.

The more usual defence of the *status quo* kept the millennium in the future while moderating its glories so that it should not outshine either the life of the Church nor the ultimate future, heaven. Thus, though a reviewer of current works on prophecy in the *Christian Observer* in 1825[21] did not hesitate to dismiss views which placed the beginning of the millennium in the past, he did not feel entirely at his ease with theories which set it in the future. The uses of prophecy were to provide evidence about divine providence and an incentive towards doing one's duty. Anticipating the millennium could not serve the first purpose, and though, in the books of sober scholars, it could serve the second, most of the books under review, especially those by Lewis Way, were not by sober scholars. They destroyed the incentive by downgrading heaven.

Where was a good Christian to find solid ground, if not in the answer of Augustine and Grotius? First, he was not to accept any one interpretation as of the faith, which required only a study of prophecy, not the acceptance of any particular conclusion. Second, he was to recall that though there was to be a millennium, it would be earthly and so merely a prefiguration of the glories of heaven. The writer refused to accept as final any interpretation. He handled Augustine roughly for his attacks on the early Christian chiliasts, and treated Papias, Justin Martyr and Tertullian with great respect. Inconsistently, those designated 'allegorists' and believers in a 'figurative' or 'constructive' millennium already begun, were highly praised, both for directing attention to the kingdom of God as it is already set up and for the incentive they offer to effort in building up this low-keyed millennium. The writer was trying to have it both ways, and lacked either the courage or the conviction for the full Augustinian answer to the dangers of millennial speculation.

More vigorous opponents of literal pre-millennialism relied upon the interpretation set out in this review as one of the options; the millennium constructed, under God's direction, by human effort in Church and society. Such post-millennialism is implicitly Augustinian, for if the millennium and the present are continuous, then the former exists in essence in the latter. Thus, these post-millennialists found evidence in present achievements which could be made to point to future near-perfection. They were rooted in the *status quo* of Church and society; they contemplated nothing more than thorough amelioration.

The major controversy of the later 1820s was between those who were rooted in the present and projected a millennium which was its improved continuation, and those whose revulsion from the present led them to posit near-total discontinuity between it and a transfigured future. Because the former anticipated the second coming at the end of their modest millennium, and the latter looked for it to inaugurate their wholly glorious millennium, the two parties may be (as is conventional) designated post- and pre-millennialists. But the timing of the second coming is more a consequence than a cause of differing opinions. The *Christian Observer* reviewer noted that the scriptural texts are anything but plain in meaning. The question remains, why did some men choose to take one interpretation, and some the other? Because, surely, they responded differently to he Church and society in which they found themselves. Satisfaction led to post-millennialism; revulsion to pre-millennialism. This extra-theological dimension is emphasized by the way each side, in arguing for the truth of its own interpretation, made a touchstone of individual and social consequences. Each held that among the criteria which distinguished truth from error was the capacity of a belief to promote correct behaviour in Church, State and society. Accordingly, though these rival expositors were Christians with a veneration for the Bible and a shared horror of tampering with it by what would later be called higher criticism, and though their sincerity is not at all in doubt, it is probable that their hidden springs of action were existentialist, both in reference to individual and social lives; that they were groping towards psychological and social answers through theological questions. It is the case, of course, that they did not believe that this was what they were doing.

The argument between the rival groups was focused upon missions to the heathen, because this activity of the early nineteenth-century churches afforded the most striking evidence to support the post-millennial case, and because rival prophetic interpretations led to opposed opinions about the nature, direction and expectations of missionary enterprise.

As interpreters of prophecy the 'missionary millennialists' were characterized by a resolute, if somewhat perfunctory, identification of papacy and Antichrist, a system of biblical interpretation based upon allegory, a belief that most supernatural events would come at the end of the millennium, a constant concern with the prophecies on the future of the Jews, a tendency to diminish the difference between the millennium and the present world, a belief that God worked among men through men and institutions, and often a lively interest in the role of Great Britain as an agent of providence. They were progressivists and did not, strictly speaking, need a version of the millennium, and it is noteworthy that they regularly deplored an over-great attention to prophecy. An evangelical could be—but it is unlikely that any were, for *all* parts of the Bible were taken seriously—quite without reference to prophecy, intensely opposed to Roman Catholicism, impressed with the vitality of 'ordinary' means of action from printing presses to prayer, impatient of exegetical niceties which impeded practical religion, involved in efforts to convert the Jews, and impressed by the way in which British technology, wealth, and power had accelerated missionary enterprise. Evangelicals, almost as a mass movement, were briskly trying to convert papist, Jew and heathen to the true gospel, by raising funds, printing quantities of Bibles and tracts, and despatching and supporting missionaries. In the early nineteenth century, these activities were commonly, and sometimes quite elaborately, supported by appropriate prophetic systems, though not entirely dependent upon them. In this shape millennialism was at its most utilitarian, and, probably, at its most widespread.

The progressivist character of this version can readily be explained as a reflection of the 'spirit of the age'. Less elusively, it can also be explained within the prophetic tradition. The papacy-Antichrist identification is essential. This Reformation legacy required either the egregious assumption that the papacy had been overcome and the millennium had arrived, or more reasonably, an assumption that the decline of the papacy had set in and that the millennium had commenced. Even this progressive variant was a little incongruous; the exegetes were committed to the search for decisive turning points, and a host of learned volumes bear witness to the difficulty of finding them. Priestley's idea of overlapping developments and the use of prophecy for dramatic highlights had more shape and force about it. Generally the turning points are commonly no more than striking manifestations of long-term trends; Priestley's historical realism is unusual only in being explicit. Most academic interpreters were committed to an historical scheme in which papal power grew slowly to a culminating point and in which its decline was continuous in the face of the progressive increase of true religion. Such writers were bound, because they saw themselves in the van of a progressive movement, to stress divine operations through regular human channels, chiefly preaching and publicity. Thus they related progress to the spread of a certain sort of knowledge. They were not going about looking for the second coming and the resurrection of the saints, and certainly not for Armageddon. These phenomena—which, one feels, they would have been hard pressed to deal with—they either allegorized away, or postponed to the end of the millennium. Thus the millennium became a purified and enlarged version of the world they were accustomed to deal with most efficiently.

The revolutionary era decisively affected the shape and tone of missionary millennialism. In the 1790s the founders of the London Missionary Society, infected by the prophetic excitement of the decade, unhesitatingly located their society among the tremendous events which were bringing on the fullness of times. Appropriately, for this mainly dissenting enterprise, patriotism did not colour the hope held out. The case is quite different with the Church Missionary Society founded early in the same decade. Its advocates linked missionary enterprise to an intensely patriotic view of British religion, history and future prospects, power, wealth and enterprise. These two examples provide a background to the arguments of the early nineteenth century.

However, it must be stressed that in neither instance did missionary apologists rely upon the millennial texts. Conversion remained a duty, whether or not it was part of the chain of events which would bring about the millennium. Very often the millennial hope was exactly that, a hope rather than a certainty. If missionary enterprise should be the means appointed by God to usher in the new world, so much the better; if not, it still remained certain that missionaries were his means of taking the good news to those who lay in darkness. The sober, if intense, founders of great societies did not place entire reliance upon a disputed point of exegesis; they were, however, very ready to add this hope to their techniques of persuasion. The uses of the millennial hope range from a firmly held guess that the last times were near, to the merely rhetorical use of millennial images to reinforce an argument based on other grounds.

The addresses and sermons occasioned by the foundation of the London Missionary Society illustrate the millennialism of respectable dissent very clearly. 'Yet a little while, and the latter-day glory shall shine forth with a reviving splendour' stated an address of 1794 sent to potential supporters. Another preliminary address was yet more explicit: 'May we not indulge the hope that the happy period is approaching, when the Redeemer shall take unto him his great power and reign? . . . And is there not a general apprehension that the Lord is about to produce some great event? Already we have witnessed the most astonishing transactions; and is it not probable that the great Disposer of all is now about, by shaking terribly the nations, to establish that spiritual and extensive kingdom which cannot be shaken? Let us then . . . unite . . . to establish a Missionary Society.'[22]

Of the foundation sermons, that by John Hey of Bristol was the most explicitly millennialist, though none of them lacked at least a rhetorical millennial device. Hey did not use the word millennium, but his title 'The Fulness of Times' meant just that: 'a marvellous season of grace, which has not (at least in the fullest sense of the words) yet taken place'. Christian history has five phases: the early 'golden age of grace'; the pagan Roman persecutions; the Mahometan scourge; the period of the papal beast, and the Reformation, 'that period, referred to in the text' (i.e. Ephesians 1.10). 'What can our apostle intend by this,' Hey asks, 'but the last stage of the gospel dispensation; that epocha of it, in which, the refulgence of sacred truth will burst forth with overwhelming glories, and continue to shine till the gloom of superstition, of error and of sin, is forever banished from the face of the earth.'

The fullness of times had begun, and its completion could be confidently expected. The gospel had gained since the reformation; it was being preached in greater purity and to greater numbers than ever before; it seemed reasonable to hope that it would spread to Europe as well as to foreign and heathen lands. He confidently looked for the fulfilment of the prophecies of the kingdom of God.[23] David Bogue of Gosport, one of Dissent's most learned ministers (in 1815 Yale conferred a D.D. upon him) and also among the founders of the British and Foreign Bible Society and the Religious Tract Society, dealt with objections to the founding of a mission. Even so, he took a millennial text (Micah 4.1, 'But in the last days') and devoted a good deal of attention to the objection that the time for the conversion of the heathen had not yet come because the millennium was still far away. Inevitably, the basic rejoinder was that missionary work did not depend upon the hope of the millennium but on the simple duty to promote true religion. Still, of the options of millennial remoteness which Bogue gave, an elapse of two centuries was the most extreme; he went on to comment with all gravity that the work of converting the world would have to be extremely rapid if it was to begin now and end then. Other pieces of argument revealed a firm if facile millennial attitude. The Church is now pure, popery having been overcome; bigotry is no more, as the formation of the society demonstrates. 'Now when he has restored it to its pristine purity, may we not hope that he will revive its ancient influence in the world?' Further, are not improvements in transport at sea and the discovery of new lands 'the hand of God opening the door, and a loud call to the lovers of the gospel to enter in?'[24]

There seems to have been less explicit millennialism in the circumstances surrounding the birth of the Church Missionary Society, though in his inaugural *Account of a Society for Missions to Africa and the East*, John Venn, Rector of Clapham and one of the society's founders, reflected the same spirit in 'expressing the hope "that since God had so signally defended this Island with His mercy as with a shield, His gracious hand, to which, amidst the wreck of nations, our safety had been owing", would be "acknowledged, and His goodness gratefully recorded, even in distant lands".'[25] One of the founders, Basil Woodd, preacher at Bentinck Chapel, Marylebone, in preaching before the society in 1807, presented a four-fold pattern of historical development not unlike that of Hey—post-pentecostal purity, papal apostacy, Reformation revival, and a time in which the day when all flesh shall see salvation is 'rapidly advancing'. He saw missionary activity as playing a vital part in the fourth and last phase. He did not, however, dazzle his hearers with a vista of inevitability; in the spirit of David Bogue he invited them to fulfil the prophecies. 'All the Holy Prophets look to you Christians, in these latter times, to accomplish the subject of their predictions.'[26] Woodd's mixture of inevitability and exhortation was nicely calculated to enlist support. Nor would it do for a missionary preacher to place the end too soon; Woodd carefully set it in the middle distance.

In the 1790s and in the early nineteenth century missionary enterprise was supported by a range of justifications which included the possibility of realizing the fullness of the Kingdom in the near future. This possibility appears to owe more to the prophetic ferment of the period than to any visible signs of great achievement. The founders of societies, however, were not excited beyond measure; they used the millennial possibility (in which no doubt they sincerely believed) with prudence. Thus the foundation in 1804 of the third great society for conversions, the British and Foreign Bible Society, owed more to a general zeal for true religion than a specific hope for the millennium. Yet John Owen, a secretary of the Society from 1804 to 1822 and its first historian, found in the inter-denominational amity displayed at its first meeting 'the dawn of a new era in Christendom' and something of a return to primitive unity.[27]

Others, however, were ready to use prophecy more explicitly. One of the great prophecies, that of the rising of the witnesses, had often been held to point to the scriptures. A curious discourse published in 1817 added, as its title indicates, a significant development: *An Explanation of the Interesting Prophecy Respecting the Two Apocalyptic Witnesses as Fulfilled by the Institution and Progress of the British and Foreign Bible Society.* The author[28] held that the climax of revolutionary atheism in France had prompted the formation of the Bible Society, 'the most heaven-born Establishment that has taken place', 'the greatest revolution that shall ever take place in the world, till the period of its final dissolution'.[29]

The revolutionary period saw the formation of many societies, not only for missions and Bibles, but also for Sunday Schools, publication of tracts and reform of manners. The organized irreligion of France was countered by the organized religion of the Protestant nation. All these, together with Britain's power, industry and liberty, were woven together into a pattern of progressive millennialism in 1822 by a Baptist preacher, Benjamin Godwin, in *A Discourse on the*

Signs of the Times. His signs of the times were the general progress of civilization, the decline of despotism, the end of the Spanish Inquisition, the increased amity between Christian denominations, and an 'unusual spirit of zeal to enlighten and bless the human race'. This last he exemplified by British missionary enterprise, Bible translation, Sunday Schools and the London Jewish Society. As a true millennialist, he foresaw severe conflict with infidels, papists, and antinomians, but from the conflict there would emerge the universality of true religion, the removal of religious corruptions, the conversion of the Jews. All this would happen soon; prophecy, he argued, can give a firm if general picture of the future. All Christians, he concluded, should adjust their conduct towards what was certainly coming, carrying forward the good work in their personal and public lives. Godwin was an optimist; it is as if Bicheno had cheered up.

Sermons preached to or on behalf of the Society for Propagating Christianity amongst the Jews (usually called the London Society, the Jewish Society, or the London Jewish Society) were especially apt to take a millennial colour. The very existence of this society, and also of those established to convert Catholics in London, Ireland, and on the Continent, indicates an often neglected facet of missionary effort. Though they had little success, these societies bring out an essential aspect of the overall evangelical missionary effort. Their objects sprang directly from the prophetic tradition. Exegetes had to work with a small handful of texts to cover the heathen; when they turned to Jews and papists they found what they would have literally thought to be God's plenty. A great deal of the Bible can be held to refer to the future of Israel and the fate of Antichrist. And though it was far from clear that many of the adherents of Antichrist would obey the invitation to 'Come out of her', it was quite expressly set down that Israel, as a whole, would be converted. The conversion of Israel had been anticipated for centuries. It was left to the early nineteenth century to believe that it was taking place.

David Bogue, preaching on 'The Duty of Christians to seek the Salvation of the Jews' rehearsed the claims Jews have upon the attention of Christians, and added to the unexceptional arguments from gratitude, equity, benevolence and justice, the more striking opinion that they would revive the Church once converted. 'Every friend of the missions, then . . . must be deeply convinced, that in seeking the calling of the Jews we are promoting the conversion of the heathen, and are enlisting fellow labourers to assist us in the work. . . . Nothing is wanting but their conversion, of which *prophecy* has assured us.'[30] Richard Graves, preaching in Dublin in 1811 on behalf of the Jewish Society, listed developments among the Jews as a prominent sign of the coming end, and showed how Napoleon had helped stimulate British activity.[31] Edward Bickersteth, whose interest in the conversion of the Jews began around 1814, possibly under the influence of Cuninghame, was later to claim it to be 'an undoubted fact that more Jews have been converted to Christ during the last twenty years than in any similar space of time since the first ages of the Church'.[32] The conversion of the Jews had a wide appeal. S. R. Maitland inspected Jewish converts in Poland and reported perceptively upon the folly of such conversions when they left a convert still socially dependent upon the group whose religion he had renounced.[33] The Albury prophets, with the help of Joseph Wolff, made the need for the conversion of the Jews a prime argument in their attack upon normal missionary activity, a line of attack which was by no means limited to their own circle.

The assumption that the two sorts of missionary work could go on together and reinforce each other, did not go unchallenged in the 1820s. There was ample scriptural basis for the opinion that Israel would, after its own conversion, bring in 'the fulness of the Gentiles'. Some argued that sending missionaries directly to the heathen was at best wasted effort, and at worst an impious attempt to prime the pump of providence. The evangelical response was prompt and indignant, consisting in a very great deal of Greek and Hebrew scholarship and in the assertion that there was an abundance of heathen. The societies could continue to convert and there would be plenty left for the converted Jews.

All three conversions, of heathen, Jews and Catholics, were held together in a web of prophetic interpretation. All three, in some manner, would accompany the second coming and the millennium. The argument was over priorities, sequences, the manner of divine action and the way in which these signs were related to those of a more socio-political kind: distress of nations, domestic upheavals, the advance of infidelity. The optimistic post-millennial group saw the 'positive' signs (e.g. conversion) and the 'negative' signs (e.g. wars and revolutions) as challenges to a struggle in which human will and effort would co-operate with the divine initiative. The pessimistic pre-millennialists saw the divine initiative operating miraculously: for instance, in the mass conversion of the Jews, and in totally destructive socio-political calamities. There are, of course, gradations between these pure types.

The activist post-millennialism of the establishment men, full of zeal but essentially cool, was challenged in the early 1820s by an upsurge of pre-millennialism, fervent and excitable, passive in that it advised waiting upon God, but strident in its conviction that God was due to act soon. This rose to a climax with the Albury school, who applying this passive approach to regular missionary enterprise, prompted a horrified reaction from the societies and journals which passed for orthodox. Early in the century missionary sermons were cool and moderate; even the soon to be notorious Lewis Way, in 1817 described the prophecies of the conversion of the Jews quite without reference to other missionary goals.[34] The first shots in a drawn-out battle were fired in 1819, when the *British Critic* took aim at the London Jewish Society. References to 'the morbid sensibilities of restless enthusiasts' and the 'prurient fancy of brainsick enthusiasts' brought Way to the defence, with the assertion that 'The Jews are an integral and essential part of Christ's mystical body . . . and their recovery will be life from the dead to the Gentile members thereof . . . but till God shall gather together in one, both Jews and Gentiles in Christ . . . we shall never be *builded together* as a city at unity in itself.'[35] Two years later Way was to move from considerations of Church unity to those of missionary strategy.

Way, a poet as well as a pamphleteer, was an independently wealthy clergyman who founded the Marboeuf Chapel in Paris, and who was reputed to have been regularly robbed by the Jewish converts he sheltered. Iń 1821 he published *The Latter Rain: with Observations on the Important of General Prayer for the Special Outpouring of the Holy Spirit.* Here he objected, at some length and with great vigour, to the exclusive application of the promises to Christians when, literally and primarily, they referred to the Jews. The 'latter rain' of Deuteronomy 11.10-14, meant a special outpouring of the Spirit upon the Jews which will be of supreme significance for the whole Church: 'as the Jews were the seedsmen, so Jews will be the harvestmen of the Gospel.' The prophecies relate to *their* restoration, *their* civil emancipation and *their* conversion. The current appeal for special prayer for a general outpouring of the spirit was misplaced; there should be general prayer for a special outpouring upon the Jews. This (so Way argued, using Horsley as his authority with dubious propriety) is England's special providential task. Once the Jews are converted, a process which has begun, the conversion of the Gentiles will follow. A correspondent in the *Christian Observer* took five pages of close print to rebut this impiety.[36]

But before a year had passed G. S. Faber added the weight of his reputation to Way's argument. His sermon preached to the Jewish Society in 1822, *The Conversion of the Jews*, was a prophetic declaration of war upon the easy-going missionary-oriented versions of prophecy. Throughout the wars with France Faber had shown that the future was calamitous and that no one could feel secure; he was not likely to tolerate a millennialism which depended upon subscriptions, societies and piecemeal conversions. His zeal to defend the untrammelled initiative of God's will was unabated. Why had missionary success been so slight, and limited to the mere conversion of individuals? Because *'the converted Jews were destined, in the unsearchable wisdom of God, to be the sole finally successful Missionaries to the Gentile world'.*

In the same year the Scottish commentator, William Cuninghame of Lainshaw, who had been close to Way in the Jewish Society, set out in *Letters and Essays . . . on . . . Israel* arguments which could be turned against missions to the Gentiles—though, it must be stressed, Cuninghame did not do so. Earlier in his *Dissertation on the Seals and Trumpets* (1812, revised edition 1817) he had argued strongly for a wholly literal interpretation of the prophecies, especially those of the second coming; he went so far as to apply the word 'unbelief' to those who held to a second coming at the end of the millennium.[37] In the *Letters and Essays* he argued that the sixth vial of wrath would be the destruction of the Ottoman Empire and the restoration of Israel, and that the prophecies should be taken in their literal sense; the Jews as a people would go back to Palestine and the Messiah would reign over a kingdom of men from his seat at Jerusalem. Again he had hard words for those who applied these prophecies by allegory to Christians generally. They are practitioners of 'a species of spiritual alchymy', they 'twist and pervert the word of God', they are 'under the influence of the spirit of unbelief', they deal in a kind of 'transubstantiation' in distinguishing between appearance and reality; their refusal to accept God's word in this matter is comparable to a refusal to accept the resurrection of the body. This acerbic Scot probably did a good deal to raise the polemical temperature in the 1820s.[38] The interpretation which he attacked so harshly was exactly that of the missionary post-millennialists; his whole tendency is against them even though he does not specifically attack them. Certainly he believed that 'the final and glorious influx of the Gentiles into the church' would be a consequence of the restoration of Israel. This restoration would be among the apocalyptic events which would end the present dispensation. Cautious asides abound, but Cuninghame hoped and believed that this end was very close. He was emphatic that the conversion of Israel was 'the cause of God' which required an increasing stream of prayers and money.[39]

So, in the early 1820s, the entirely undogmatic millennialism of the missionary advocates met a two-fold pre-millennialist attack. On the one hand pre-millennialists invited people to set their houses in order in the short span of time left to them before the second coming—a span altogether too short for the achievement of the millennium by missionary enterprise. On the other, the role assigned by pre-millennialists to the Jews implied that the societies mistook the ordained order of change: the divine timetable put the conversion of the Jews first, and the conversion of the Gentiles, through the Jews, second. The societies' counter-attack mounted steadily through the 1820s until a firm and successful effort was made to kill the 'modern millenarians' of the Albury School, who, unlike their forerunners, openly declared war upon the societies. Had not these extremists given hostages in the shape of dubious Christological doctrines, alarming views about the activity of the Holy Spirit, a 'high church' ecclesiology and divine right politics, it is by no means certain that they could have been put down so readily.

Until the full horrors of the Albury school were revealed at the end of the decade the leading Anglican journals—the *Christian Observer*, the *Christian Guardian* and the *British Critic*—maintained an ambiguous attitude to prophecy. While they were wholeheartedly on the side of moral exertion, missionary enterprise and the normal channels of grace, they were also hospitable to positions which, as Irving and Drummond made them realize, subverted these goals. The ambiguity of the 1825 review article already discussed was characteristic. When the battle lines were drawn up late in the decade, the journals of the established Church at last knew where they must stand. However, to find a firm and persistent advocacy of the missionary millennium earlier in the 1820s, one must turn to the pan-protestant *Evangelical Magazine*.

Throughout the 1820s the *Evangelical Magazine* championed the cause of prayer for 'a more copious effusion' of the Holy Spirit, often instancing American revivals as a way of resuscitating British religion. The millennium it was asserted, would result from such a second pentecost. This pentecost, however, was seen as nothing more extraordinary than missionary preaching and Bible distribution.[40] In 1822 it printed an indignant attack upon Faber's sermon, *The Conversion of the Jews*, drawing upon David Bogue's progressive millennialism. A pro-Faber reply maintained that the conversion of the Jews would indeed bring the millennium, but conceded that there was plenty of work for missionaries in the interim.[41] To vindicate the cause of human effort, specifically of missionary effort, the editors printed in 1825 extracts from a sermon preached in 1796 at the commencement of the South Sea Mission, which connected the 'throes of kingdoms and states' with 'the widest propagation of Christianity', and used language like that of Buchanan to indicate the British role in this process. In the same year Irving's *For Missionaries after the Apostolical School*—his first attack upon the missionary societies—was reviewed as a piece of mere folly and ignorance.[42] In 1827 Bogue's discourses were drawn upon to identify two erroneous concepts of the millennium—first, mere carnal chiliasm, and second the belief that it would be 'a state nearly equal heaven'. The true view was that the millennium would be a greatly improved gospel dispensation brought about by the Holy Spirit through human exertion: 'Religion will then be the grand business of mankind.'[43] In the following year it published 'A scriptural explanation or exhibition of the millennial reign of Christ'.[44] This essay affords a good example of post-millennialism with a missionary orientation and a distinctly radical political tone.

In this analysis the missionary movement is the instrument of divine power, a sign 'that a great and glorious aera is near at hand' and a means of bringing it about. The 1260 years have concluded: 'Light has broken in upon the Church, and primitive zeal and unanimity have succeeded to the contracted bigotry and spirit of sloth of the times that are past.' No one, even to the end of the last century, imagined that 'the simple mode of sending out missionaries, would become the efficient agency of converting the heathen world.' 'The day-spring from on high has dispelled the mists of ignorance, and knowledge is increasing.' This simple confidence in the power of preaching was as much a delusion as the adventist expectation. But there is a significant difference between a rational delusion of this kind, and the irrational delusion of the pre-millennialists—the difference between an error and an obsession.

The same spirit of optimism pervades the more technical refutation 'of the personal reign of Christ, and of the resurrection of the saints to live and reign with Him a thousand years on earth'. The explanation offered of the text 'And I saw a new heaven and a new earth: for the first heaven and the first earth were passed away; and there was no more sea' (Rev. 21.1), is a good example of allegorical interpretation and shows the linking of civil and religious liberty characteristic of Dissent. Heaven symbolizes rulers; earth, the mass of mankind; sea, wars and tumults. From the beginning 'the political heavens and earth have been filled with disorder'; the scriptures have been perverted; fundamental laws which would infallibly produce good government and a contented society have been ignored. From Nimrod to the present day, most governments have been permitted not ordained by God. Civil despotism and papal usurpation have been propped up by the unscriptural doctrines of passive obedience and non-resistance. A new government and a new-made mankind will mean no more wars and commotions.

The new kind of government will be biblically grounded. Isaiah is quoted: 'the mountain of the Lord's house shall be established in the top of the mountains.' Mountains again stand for the ruling powers; 'it is intended to represent that the political institutions of all nations shall be moulded after the maxims of the Gospel, and the administrations of their laws shall be governed by the righteous and peaceful sceptre of the Kingdom of Christ.' The situation of the Church will be more glorious. The spirit of the martyrs will prevail (the first resurrection), and 'No unbeliever or wicked person shall then have any political power or distinction.' The thousand years will indeed be Christ's reign, but through his triumphant Church. This may seem some distance from missionaries—but not too far for the author. All this will be achieved by 'the dissemination of Divine knowledge. . . . The announcement of the angel Rev. 14.6, is emblematical of the missionary exertions of these times. The various religious societies . . . have all this one grand object in view —*the propagation of* DIVINE TRUTH: before which all idolatry, superstition, darkness, and error of every kind, must ultimately give way. . . . This is *the stone cut out of the mountain without hands*, which is destined to evangelize the earth, and to consummate the triumphs of the Redeemer's cause.'

Similar arguments were more polemically advanced in this journal's lengthy review of G. T. Noel's *Brief Enquiry*.[45] The reviewer drew upon Sir Isaac Newton to show that while only fulfilled prophecy could be relied upon it was highly probable that the last age was approaching. But there are two groups of interpreters: the majority adhering 'to the *ordinary means and influences* of the Gospel dispensation', and a minority introducing 'an extensive apparatus which shall be *extraordinary and miraculous*'. The former took for signs the growth of science and useful knowledge, the increase of peace and liberty, the translation and circulation of the Bible and the sending out of missionaries; these showed the extraordinary use by the Holy Spirit of the ordinary means of grace. This outpouring will lead to the diminishment of papists, heathen and infidels, to the conversion of the Jews and their merging into the Christian body, to peace, liberty, good government and international justice. Thus will the millennial period commence; it will be the spiritual reign of Christ, and it will certainly last for a long period with the power of Satan restrained and the principles of the martyrs triumphant.

A sketch of the 'cool' millennium followed. The period will be less than heavenly, but it will be marked by complete toleration, a spirit of free enquiry and an absence of false religion; literature, science and the arts will be as flourishing as they will be improving; government will be based upon right principles; agriculture, industry and commerce will flourish; perhaps, even, all men will enjoy good health and long life. But the Christian will still need to be on his guard, all the more so because things will be so agreeable. Depravity will still be the human condition, and baptism will still rectify it; men will still sin and so need to seek forgiveness. Eventually there will be a decline. Nominal religion and infidelity will re-emerge; Satan, released, will gather his own for the final conflict. After purification by fire, the earth, rather fancifully, will become a kind of 'resort', a holiday place, for the righteous. This small, quaint detail suggests that the vision of a totally redeemed and paradisal earth to which Irving devoted his descriptive talents was not to be entirely denied even by the most determined of post-millennialists.

Though Noel was praised for his moderation and spirit of devotion, the reviewer had no doubt that, on balance, his views were pernicious and a discouragement to missionary enterprise. The reviewer advanced a series of exegetical and theological arguments against Noel's pre-millennialism, and concluded with a trumpet-blast against the '*baneful practical effect* of the revived millennary doctrine' which 'tends to mislead the hope of Christians, to paralyze or at least miserably to cramp and confine their efforts for the conversion of men, and to substitute a dubious and often false rule of duty, for the plain and ever obligatory precepts of our Lord Jesus Christ.'

The *Evangelical Magazine*'s attitude to Noel is never less than respectfully regretful. It saved its fiercest denunciation for Irving and his fellows, finding antinomianism and something close to Arianism in their views as well as the wrong sort of millennialism. The journal enthusiastically endorsed William Hamilton's hostile *Defence of the Scriptural Doctrine concerning the Second Advent*, quoted Taylor's *Natural History of Enthusiasm* against chiliasm, and commended Maitland's *Second Enquiry*.[46] It urgently recommended a number of dissenting anti-Albury publications, including a series of lectures on prophecy delivered in 1829 to the Monthly Meeting of Ministers: 'When compared with these sound and temperate Discourses, how must the wild effusions of another school dwindle in the estimate of all sensible men.'[47] In contrast, Irving's *The Last Days* stimulated a review which accused him, *inter alia*, of taking a higher church position than that of the Archbishop of Canterbury, of abolishing all human moral responsibility, of holding that the ten commandments were irrelevant to those whom Christ made free, and of explaining the doctrine of the trinity away.[48] It greeted, in 1830, the outbreak of miracles in Scotland and London as 'gross and dangerous instances of superstition', and castigated the 'few pertinacious but talented individuals' who had first propagated wild notions of unfulfilled prophecy and then championed this latest delusion. All this, however, was done in the name of a rival millennialism, that of the progressive dissenters reaching back to Priestley and Bicheno for their vision of a future characterized by civil liberty and religious truth.

Of the major religious reviews, the *Wesleyan-Methodist Magazine* took the least interest in prophecy. Nevertheless, the furore of the later 1820s required a response, and it was mission-oriented and post-millennialist; perhaps significantly, the journal's two major attacks upon the extremists, were written by a Church evangelical, Josiah Pratt, and an American Presbyterian, Lyman Beecher. In 1828, Pratt, a founder and for twenty-one years secretary of the Church Missionary Society, wrote within a broadly post-millennial framework to announce that 'we live in a DAY OF ARDENT AND WELL-GROUNDED HOPES AND EXPECTATIONS'. But he warned against too great a concentration upon the prophecies, a study best left to the learned except as a broad confirmation of Christian grace and hopes. In the same year it reprinted a sermon by the Boston revivalist Lyman Beecher on 'The Resources of the Adversary'—each monthly number of the journal contained a sermon, and this was the first since 1825 on a text from Revelation.[49] Beecher's exposition was appropriately post-millennialist and progressive. His list of 'resources' is interesting: idolatry, imposture (i.e. Mahometanism), papal supersition, political despotism, crime, liberal religion and false religious revivals. The second and the third are subjects of biblical prophecy, and arose at the same time. Popery is 'the masterpiece of that wisdom which cometh from beneath' for it is 'satisfactory to the Pagan, and not alarming to the degenerate Christian'. Liberal religion he defined as accepting infidels without changing them. Thus it comes to resemble popery quite closely, a resemblance in its turn close to Irving's contention that popery and infidelity were twin abominations.

These resources would be overcome by judgements from heaven, by the universal spread of the gospel, by revivals, and eventually by a general revival of religion. Anti-Christian nations can expect 'commotions', which he interpreted as 'moral earthquakes'. One, clearly the French Revolution, has occurred and another is coming. Resistance to Christianity will diminish as the Spirit operates more powerfully through revivals. Throughout this exposition, in a way which recalls Priestley, despotism was linked with the adversary and civil liberty with true religion. This is, perhaps, an unexpected identification to find in a Methodist source; it suggests that Methodism had absorbed a good deal of the spirit of dissent and of American progressivism. This optimism was echoed by an English Methodist, Adam Clarke, in 1830: These are the days of the Son of Man; now is the Holy Ghost given in his plenitude. Never were there times more favourable; never were spiritual advantages more numerous; never was light more abundant; never were the Holy Scriptures more extensively dispersed; and never were their contents better understood. The whole earth is in the way of being filled with the knowledge of God.'[50] This, in its way, is as extreme an expectation as the pre-millennialism of Irving and Drummond; both sides held that God was acting swiftly and decisively, the one hoping to see a good world made better, the other an evil world brought to an end.

V: Irving and Drummond

There is nothing especially original about the explicit content of Edward Irving's ideas. Their implications are another matter; his tendency is more original than his avowed position and readily suggests possibilities which he would not have tolerated. His prophetical theories came from James Hatley Frere, his scholarship from Joseph Wolff, his conservatism from Henry Drummond; even his style was all too frequently that of Milton. His own contribution was his energy; where others annoyed he infuriated. His enemies saw folly in his life, but tragedy too; in his colleagues they saw nothing but foolish wickedness. Much about him is second-hand, derivative, credulous, shallow, conceited and inflated, and yet he contrived to fall only narrowly short of the mark of greatness. His qualities are those of the great popular preacher; a capacity for flamboyant gesture, an ability to hold a multitude of details in a firm generalization, a concentration on the great simple issues—depravity, redemption, death, immortality—which deeply concerned so many of his contemporaries.

His charisma was not a steady light, but a series of fitful flashes. The fashionable preacher who crowded the beau-monde into the tiny Caledonian chapel at Hatton Garden ceased to draw crowds. The new sectaries of the Catholic Apostolic Church turned against him, led by the female prophets he had, at such personal cost, defended. He drew men to him but he did not hold them; it was not in him, as it was in Newman, to alter another's life by his words and example. He is a bizarre figure in the London of the 1820s: a scrappily educated Scot accidentally placed in a London pulpit, there to achieve an unexpected eminence. He was, it is certain, notable as a preacher and a writer. Even this notability is ambiguous; he spoke clearly on the great themes of religion, but he did so in a way which exploited the spurious attractions of an affected seventeenth-century style. He could achieve real eloquence; but one wonders how many of his fashionable hearers went to his chapel as they would go to a concert, or even to a zoo.

His outlandishness may help to account for his persistence in running to extremes. Success in London spoiled him for a humbler Scottish career; and yet, as a member neither of the Church of England nor of Dissent, he had no regular way to lasting success in a religious world dominated by great societies and orthodox journals. He could be a spectacular success, or none at all. He embraced every aberration that occurred among his followers and colleagues: an hysterical response to Catholic emancipation, a horrified assessment of popular democracy, an extreme antipathy to philanthropy, an obsession with prophecy, a credulous acceptance of special gifts of healing and speaking in tongues. No doubt, temperamentally, he had a fatal capacity for extremism. But only within extreme situations could he achieve again the eminence to which he had become accustomed in the mid-1820s. Unlike most of his prophetical colleagues, he had nothing to fall back upon; he was the creature of the aberrations he helped to create.

He alone of the prophetical preachers can be mentioned in the same sentence as Newman without invidiousness. There is, within the inflated image, a man of power: he is angry where others were frightened, horrified where others recoiled, exultant where others gloated. Personally, theologically, politically, there is more humanity than usual in his millennialism. His springs of action were well within the range of ordinary human sympathy. There are three: the death of his first son in infancy, followed by other infant deaths; a conviction that British protestantism had become complacent and inadequate; and a belief that political and social life had become perilous. He was a man of warm domestic affections and of total religious commitment; and if his political alarm was out of all proportion, it was so with many in the later 1820s. There was no eccentricity in his points of departure. His response was extravagant, certainly; the pity and the tragedy of his life is that so soon there is nothing but extravagance, and so quickly thereafter only futility.

One should begin at the point where, by his own account, he began to perceive the full significance of prophecy; by the corpse of his infant son. His own words serve the situation best. This loss was a great grief; his beliefs about death and the last things took shape as

> a meditation . . . with which the Lord did comfort my solitary and sorrowful hours, when that sweet child, who was dear in life and dear also in death, lay near me in shrouded beauty, the daintiest morsell that death did ever feed upon. That was the blessed aera when, to me, the light of this blessed morning star broke through the clouds in which the church is presently shrouded up. I prayed God to avenge me of death. I have sought diligently

ever since to fight against Satan, the Prince of darkness. The Lord hath given me no mean success, blessed be his name. And while I live I will fight against death that so bereft me. And I will conquer him when we come to mortal battle; and I will reign with him under my feet; because I have made the Lord my refuge, and the Holy One my habitation.[1]

This passage identifies the personal crisis which made Irving a millennialist. An important part of his defence of millennialism is, implicitly, an elaboration of this point of departure. For though he was contemptuous of utilitarian questions, which could only be asked in 'a church perverted by usefulness', and asserted that the true question is not 'What is the use of it?' but 'Is it written down?'[2] his main defence centred upon the vitality which prophetic teaching may confer upon the great Christian doctrines. Irving argued, at length and with vehemence, that millennialism was spiritually satisfying, while current Christian orthodoxy was not.

Death and survival played a considerable part in this argument. 'When the great scriptural doctrine of Christ's second advent is thus removed to an indefinite distance of future time, not only is its present influence in keeping alive and awake all the fruits of the spirit, wholly lost; but also most insufficient, and I may say, false views of the doctrine of a future state are introduced, which are attended with the most prejudicial effects upon the soul.' He went on to argue that the reward of the righteous is not a judgement survived, but an actual resurrection, the first resurrection at the second coming. Conventional views had deprived Christians of this great prospective reward, that of rising with the returned Christ. In its place had been put 'a most exaggerated, and . . . erronious idea of the separate state of the soul'. The little to be found in the Bible about the separate state indicates its imperfection. Indeed 'nothing could be said about it which men can understand'. Because such a state is immaterial it is 'ill-defined' and 'undefinable'; the revelation of the future becomes 'indistinct and profitless as a dream'. All that can be said about it is 'guess or conjecture'. Notions of this state, and of the condition of the just after their resurrection, are vitiated by 'the exclusion of materialism, and material actions, and material sufferings'. 'But such views of a material world after the resurrection of the body . . . are looked upon as fanciful though they be the only ones contained in scripture; while any speculation concerning the blessedness of the middle state is entertained as most orthodox and profitable, however unfounded in scripture it may be, or wild in imagination'. Death, commonly held before Christians as an object of contemplation, is really the victory of sin and Satan; its contemplation can only lead to fear, inertia and doubt. Hence missionaries care for security instead of rushing gladly into martyrdom, as they would if they looked steadfastly, not to death, but to resurrection. The paradise said to lie beyond death is no more than the separate state of the soul: 'nothing at all . . . airy . . . shadowy . . . fantastical'.

> It is inert, it is shadowy, it is unworldy. It hath no relation to the present world, that it should lift us above it. It seizeth not hold on the affections . . . upon the understanding . . . upon the feelings . . . upon the interests. . . . It is a mere negation of this evil and that suffering; it hath no positive compensation to any suffering, nor real satisfaction to any desire, nor occupation to any faculty, nor occasion for any function of man; seeing it is not man, but a part of man, concerning which in its severed state nothing can be predicated or understood, hoped or feared . . . the continual turning of the church's eye to this undefined and undefinable estate has paralyzed hope and quenched desire, crippled all the energies of the spiritual man, and impoverished every field of spiritual life.[3]

This viewpoint, at best an aberration and at worst a heresy to most of Irving's contemporaries, will appear less unusual in an age when many theologians reject the other-worldly dimension of Christianity. Not that Irving would have felt at home in their company. But in his insistence that Christianity is intensely earthly and materialistic he shares a common ground with them; he and they require that men should not be put off with abstractions, but drawn into solid human reality. He saw, as they do, the whole Christian drama enacted on an earthly scene, one transformed by divine action. Yet Irving is wholly out of love with the earth, while convinced that beyond its limits there is nothing to seize upon. For one so placed the second coming is necessary; it keeps the action upon the earth while it transfigures the earth. The death of his son, and his attempts to grasp the reality, if any, of the state of his son's soul according to 'the common system' urgently reinforced those conclusions about heaven, which he had already set out in his *Argument for Judgment to Come* in 1823. Whatever the motivation, his theology lowers the barriers between heaven and earth, and confers upon the latter the felicity commonly ascribed to the former. On the transformed earth Christ's presence shall be 'abiding and everlasting'.[4] The person of Christ is radically humanized. The Christ of the first coming was of sinful human nature preserved from actual sin by the operation of grace, not by a nature in itself immune from sin.[5] The Christ of the second coming will rule over the earth personally; Irving saw no incongruity in applying the language of divine right theory to him. He was groping towards a secular Christianity, but his social ideal was monarchical and corporate rather than democratic and individualistic. Drummond's *Social Duties* by a different route also came close to including Christianity within the social structure, in spite of his intention to include the social structure within Christianity.

The biblicist in Irving would have been outraged at the suggestion that he was reducing Christianity to a myth, that he was more concerned with human authenticity than divine sovereignty. Yet his exposition bears this interpretation. He did not consider the situation of Christians who have not had the luck to live near the point of the second coming, except to make the conventional assertion that the dead saints will rise in glory. He rested content with the assertion that it has been 'discovered' that the 1260 years were concluded, that 'We are living amongst the signs of our Lord's coming, we have seen six, and we are waiting for the seventh and last.'[6] He held, further, that this expectation was life itself to the early Christians, and should be the normal condition of all Christians. Two questions are thus rather cavalierly begged. What of these Christians, from the first century to the eighteenth, who (wrongly as it proved) either held or should have held this expectation? And what is left of these doctrines if the second coming is regarded as an effective spur to right living rather than an anticipated historical fact? The short answer to the second question is 'everything', and this is sufficient answer also to the first.

The hope of Christians is to be fixed upon the goal of union with Christ upon a transfigured but still material earth; all that can be known about the soul after death and before that union is that it does not become unconscious and decay, and that it is in a condition of expectancy and unfilled desire. Earlier theologians as intent as Irving upon the joys of the first resurrection had been led to the doctrine that the soul sleeps before rising for judgement. He would have been more consistent if he had followed them. His urgent concern for 'some object and event so glorious as shall carry my eye clean over and beyond this chasm and abyss of being'[7] would have been better served by a period of oblivion between death and resurrection. Mere expectancy, as he himself argues, is a vastly unsatisfying condition. It is only satisfactory, in the terms of this argument, if the Christian really believes that the period of waiting will be brief. A critic could suggest that as some Christian souls have been waiting in this meagre condition for eighteen centuries, the intermediate state, however attentuated, is important enough to be reckoned with, and that theories about Christian expectation should take it into account. If such a period is one of joy, then the need for a millennial vision disappears. If it is not, then the argument from the need to hold out a compelling reward begins to take a curious shape; a reward that has been postponed for eighteen centuries, and could easily be postponed for another eighteen, and yet another, has an uncompelling ring about it. And yet Irving is in quest of a prospect of an immediate reward of an irresistible kind. He has not found it, unless by the strange chance that he and his friends alone of all the prophetic arithmeticians of the Christian era are right. That chance, in its turn, is too slender a hope to rely upon. For all his protestations, Irving has not managed to hold out, within the framework of the theology he accepts, a prospect of reward more satisfying and compelling than conventional views of heaven.

However, he offered an implicit answer to this criticism; it lies behind his opinion that the Christian should always live as if the second coming might occur at any time. Such a situation would endow the Church with boldness and zeal, with spiritual health in abundance. If one takes what he calls materialism and what might be called secularity a little further, ceases to ask if and when there will be a second coming and a millennium, and treats these 'events' as symbols in a myth, validated by their impact upon situation, character and conduct, then one can suggest an answer; but it is not one which Irving actually gave. However, the fact that he came quite close to giving it, that the logic of his argument could have taken him there and indeed should have taken him there, that the tone and colour of his argument does take him there, makes him a rather more significant figure than his scandalized critics. Some have speculated that had Irving avoided the eccentricities of tongues and healing, he could have revived orthodox Christianity. More likely, he would have proved a true contemporary of Arnold and Carlyle. His concern for individual regeneration and social discipline found, perhaps adventitiously, a millennial framework, and for a time it proved adequate. A longer life and a more fruitful milieu than the sect he helped to found, could have shaped one of the most significant secularizers of the mid-nineteenth century.

This will appear a paradox only if too much attention is paid to his inherited thought-categories, and too little to the ends he made them serve. For him, beyond a shadow of a doubt, Christ was the second person of the trinity, Satan a cosmic enemy, the incarnation a divine act, and the resurrection a past and future miracle. But though the struggle is cosmic, the battlefield and the victory are earthly. The Old Testament promised 'an inheritance upon the earth', and the New 'a kingdom and a crown'; in the millennium the saints will be 'for ever with the Lord, partakers of his throne, partakers of his crown, and partakers of his government; his assessors in judgment, his deputies in power, ruling over the cities of his dominion and judging the tribes of the sojourners of the earth'. Then will 'Nature [be] repossessed of all her original beauty, and society of all its proper blessedness, peace, gentleness, and meekness restored on every hand, all men blessed in Jesus and calling him blessed.' The man troubled in his flesh can look forward to the possession of 'a glorious body'; the oppressed to 'power over the world'. 'There is no middle state, quietism or vacuity in the delineations which Scripture giveth of these Christ's honoured members; who come to share his kingdom, to take part in the judgment, to advance righteousness, to glorify God with every faculty, and command the earth with what [*sic*] noble vicegerency Adam heretofore commanded it. The expectation, and hope, and assurance of this, doth raise the soul to a compass and pitch of endurance and exertion which nothing else can.'[8]

Irving was overwhelmingly concerned with the ideas carried in the phrases 'restoration', 'command the earth', and 'endurance and exertion', and also with 'the lameness and inertness of the church in these latter times' due to the neglect of true doctrine.[9] He faced a degenerate world, perverted from its original purity, in which evil prevailed, in which the Church was powerless and betrayed, and in which impiety and vice grew daily. His response was not to leave the earth to evil and locate good in an unassailable heaven, but to insist that the earth must be restored to its original goodness. Such a response made reformers of some men; Irving it made a prophet. He was preoccupied with the world. He was also preoccupied with God and his sovereignty, and in his own view the latter concern was primary. But it is a delicately balanced equation. The sovereignty of God requires a purified earth. Equally, a purified earth requires a sovereign God. For Irving and for many socially conscious millennialists, God's apocalyptic role was a necessity of argument as well as an objective belief; perhaps it became an objective belief because it was a necessity of argument. For without an external agency, God for Irving, reason for some, and history for others, the world could not be purified. It is not that the external agency was invented to guarantee this consequence; it is rather that the millennialist's God, the myth-maker's God, the rationalist's reason and the historicist's history share a common human necessity and function. It is not unlikely that this human necessity was psychologically and existentially prior, though not logically and argumentatively. Irving did not invent God in order to impose a sanction upon human action, but the result would have been the same if he had.

If one wishes to speculate about the way he might have developed had he lived, one must not ignore this profound if implicit secularity, nor the emphasis with which critics pronounced him heretical for over-stressing the humanity of Jesus. Had he lived through the 1830s and 1840s it is very improbable that he would have become the Newman of the evangelicals, warming up with the fires of his energy an orthodoxy to which he had become a stranger in the 1820s. It is more likely that his path would have run parallel to that of his friend Carlyle. Had he become a secular prophet, the millennial framework could have served him well, as it served Robert Owen.

The ideas which will bear this interpretation were certainly not brought from Scotland by the young and ambitious preacher who took over the near-empty Caledonian Church near Hatton Garden in 1822. Three fresh influences shaped the thought of a very young and impressionable man—a concern for social welfare and justice, a conservative and organic view of political obligation, and a pre-millennialist approach to prophecy. He preached often upon the decay of traditional social virtues. He attacked the gentry's neglect of their duty to protect their dependents, the industrial employers' indifference to the welfare of their hands, and the viciousness of a social system which rewarded greed. He discovered a different seventeenth century; Milton, the puritan hero, became 'the archangel of Radicalism' while 'the fathers of the English Church and literature' taught him to think of society and politics in terms of hierarchy and obligation.[10] Basil Montagu, who introduced him to London society and also (more profitably) to Coleridge, helped bring about this re-orientation. Irving became enthusiastic about Bishop Overall's anti-contractarian *Convocation Book*, the probable source of his divine right political opinions and his identification of Church and commonwealth. At the same time his conventional expectation of a progressively achieved millennium was replaced by an extreme pre-millennialism. James Hatley Frere helped shape the details of the interpretation he accepted, but, on his own account, it was in conversations with Coleridge that he learned to discard 'That error under which the whole of the Church is lying, that the present world is to be converted unto the Lord, and so slide by a natural inclination into the Church—the present reign of Satan hastening, of its own accord, into the millennial reign of Christ.'[11] From Coleridge, too, as well as from the divines of the seventeenth century, he would have absorbed the high church opinions which marked his doctrine of the Church and his pastoral practice.

By the end of the 1820s other and much less stable influences had been added. The first conference on prophecy was held at Henry

Drummond's Albury Park house in 1826; from the series of conferences so commenced were to proceed the three-volume *Dialogues on Prophecy* which constitute the high point of pre-millennial excitement. At Albury Irving met, among others, the missionary to the Jews, Joseph Wolff, the adventist J. H. Stewart, the prophetic calculator J. H. Frere, the fanatical anti-liberal William Cuninghame, as well as the mercurial Drummond. Further, in identifying the author of *The Coming of the Messiah*, Irving had the assistance of Lewis Way. None of these were moderate men. Wolff and Way would have directed his attention to that extreme version of the millennial upset which ascribed world power to the despised Jews. Did Irving, lampooned, ridiculed and attacked as a dangerous fool, see his own situation as in essence that of the Jews?

In 1823 his first hopeful publication was greeted by the *Trial of the Rev. Edward Irving*, in which Doctor Squintum was arraigned before the Court of Commonsense by Jacob Oldstyle, Clerk. This lampoon went through five editions in one year, hardly the sort of fame Irving was seeking. A year later he called a fresh storm about his head by preaching to the London Missionary Society a sermon demanding that missionaries throw prudence to the winds, go out without scrip or staff, and seek martyrdom. In publishing *For Missionaries after the Apostolical School* Irving announced that profits would go to the widow of a Demerara missionary who had died after being imprisoned by the settlers for allegedly stirring up the slaves, a gesture which did little to endear him to the influential. Each successive publication was reviewed with scorn and contempt. Like the Jews he championed, Irving was an outcast. All his attitudes were those of an outsider attacking an alien establishment; his ideas of social justice attacked the socially and economically powerful, his divine right politics the rulers of the State, his high ecclesiology the rulers of the churches. His pre-millennialism was an onslaught upon society as a whole. The men with whom he became intimate were all, very self-consciously, voices crying in the wilderness.

Henry Drummond provided a more immediate political influence than Bishop Overall. This son-in-law to Henry Melville, Earl of Dundas, exercised a persistent but erratic influence on many early nineteenth-century developments in religion; for example, upon the Bible Society, upon efforts to convert the Jews, upon the Continental Society, which aimed at Catholic conversion, and upon the early history of the Catholic Apostolic Church. He was also a politician and his social and political ideals dominate his religious writings. He emphasized the need for authority in Church and State, the duty of superiors to protect their dependants, the well-being of inferiors as a function of their obedience. Drummond forcibly expressed traditional notions of social hierarchy, of organic links holding the strata in the hierarchy together, and of society as a religious phenomenon. The social content of Albury millennialism is more explicit in Drummond's systematic presentation than in Irving's similar but fragmentary reflections.

Drummond's theology and politics cohere in a concept which may be called that of the 'apostate nation'. The apostate nation is that people which has been chosen by God, but has rejected the duties imposed upon it by that choice. Foxe's 'elect nation' has betrayed its election. The very evidence used by millennial nationalists to show that Great Britain had been chosen brought Drummond to the contrary conclusion. He agreed that Great Britain was 'more favoured than any spot on the whole earth with the number of preachers of God's word' and that she was 'selected by Jehovah to be his witness against the Popish Apostacy'. But this past election, set alongside the Lord's saying about Sodom and Gommorah, made Drummond's heart sink within him 'at the thought of how many talents Britain has to answer for'.[12]

Earlier in this pamphlet he had suggested a comparison between apostate Britain and apostate Rome. Each had committed apostacy by putting the things of man in the place of the things of God. The early Christians did this when they permitted the Roman Empire to succour them, forgetting that that Empire was the Beast of St John; papists continued the displacement by according to the Pope a power, that of prophet, priest and king, which belongs only to the returned Christ. The 'Evangelicals of Britain, assuming that their Bible and Missionary Societies are going to convert the world, can never believe that the Churches of England and Scotland, and this Pharasaic and Infidel nation, will, because she has been most highly favoured, be the first to feel the weighty hand of the Lord's vengeance'.[13] Great Britain had been displaced from the divine favour because her Church had succumbed to the world. The '*peril* of the *last days*' was not caused by 'the openly profane' but by 'those who are lovers of their own institutions, and of wealth; boasters of their charitable, and missionary exploits; lovers of expediency rather than of principle; laying false accusations; speaking against the plain letter of God's word; and yet having the form, circumstance, and profession of godliness'.[14] Irving, smarting under their censure, had compared the reviewers in the religious journals with the Inquisition; he and Drummond were entirely serious in believing that popery and 'official' protestantism were twin apostacies. Catholic Emancipation, passed by bishops' and ministers' votes, urged by Dissent and accepted by the established Church, reinforced this conclusion.

Papists and evangelicals, on this reasoning, had displaced God with the merely human. Each apostacy had constructed an apologetic by falsely interpreting the gospel and especially the prophecies. The parallel is not exactly drawn, but it is clear that Drummond saw in the Augustinian identification of the millennium with the Church a sin identical with the post-millennialism of the evangelical activists. Each theory denied the divine initiative; in each Christ's kingdom was 'spiritualized' into a merely human regime. So the Papacy and 'the religious world' of Great Britain were equally opposed to the students of prophecy. 'You speak', he addressed William Hamilton whose attack upon the millennialists he was answering in this pamphlet, 'of those who spiritualise, as it is called, the plainest passages of the Old Testament, as if they were the Orthodox in every age. Surely, Sir, you must know . . . that the spiritualizers are the Papists, that the system began with them.'[15]

Rome retained her place as *the* great apostate, but Britain joined her just because she had turned aside from the divinely appointed function of opposing Rome. The first of the judgements that will usher in the millennium will fall upon the Protestant nations because they had been the most highly favoured: 'Query? is Tyre the type of Britain?'[16] Britain, then, had degenerated from the elect nation to the apostate nation, from the divinely appointed to the divinely condemned. This degeneration was evident in her religious error, most clearly in the persecution of the students of prophecy. It also characterized her political evolution, a parallel falling away from the divinely established condition, from authority and hierarchy to liberty and equality. Drummond did not systematically relate these two themes, but that they in fact co-existed in his mind as twin appearances of a single error is suggested by a passage in his *Social Duties upon Christian Principles* (1830). He found in the remnant of God's true people among the British not only true religion but also true politics. These 'reverence the vicegerent of the only King of kings'; they 'will be found to have a place in that kingdom on this earth, which shall be under One absolute autocrat; with a church and state inseparably united; with a Priest on a throne; where there shall be no toleration, no republicanism, no liberalism; and where those who say that the people are the only source of legitimate power, shall be held accursed; while many who have been worshipping idols set up in their own hearts, are refusing to have this man rule over them, and trying by societies to establish a millennium without him, shall be cast out.'[17] Drummond was not especially systematic in his exposition; he juxtaposed ideas rather than related them. However, the juxtaposition in this passage encourages the assumption that he saw, in recent English history, parallel religious and political declensions which together amounted to a total socio-religious apostacy. The apostate nation is also the disordered nation.

Drummond's social and political views were set out in an extended and rather abstract manner in *Social Duties*. This is a genre work, a book of advice to servants on how to conduct themselves in their allotted station. But it develops into an exposition of the reciprocity of obligations and benefits, duties and rights, which should obtain in an authoritarian social hierarchy. Little is said to justify the hierarchical model, other than frequent assertions that it is in accord with the Bible, and that it leads to stability and contentment. People are happy, in Drummond's view, when they know where they are and when they are sheltered from temptations to seek to be anywhere else. Individualism has infidelity as its religious consequence and liberalism as its political consequence, and leads to disorder in both Church and State. These twin consequences of individualism are identical with the apostacy described in his polemical writings. In each case men are putting their own wishes and wilfulness in the place of God's will and his explicit directives. This total decline is itself a sign of the coming end.

Earlier in this chapter it was suggested that Irving came close to giving religion an entirely this-worldly orientation, and that, in part, he judged religious doctrines according to their capacity to shape character and stimulate action. Drummond, with his main emphasis upon society where Irving's is upon the individual, echoed this pre-occupation. He attacked the insufficiency of a religion limited to the affirmation of beliefs and the performance of actions. 'Religion means a system of obligations; of bindings of man to God, and of man to man: the bonds which hold are the ordinances of God's appointment; and every individual is religious or other wise, according as he sees God in the sphere in which he is moving, and fulfils to him the purpose for which he was placed in it.' The Bible 'gives an account' of God, of Christ, and of the divine purpose; and it declares 'the various relationships assumed by God towards man, and various institutions appointed by God, in order to keep these relationships ever in man's remembrance'. The traditional reverence for the Bible as the record of God's saving acts and so itself a vehicle of salvation has been muted. No doubt Drummond held this to be true of the Bible—there is no evidence to the contrary—but he went some way towards making such a belief superfluous. He asserted that 'the graces of God are not scattered abroad promiscuously, but ordained to flow in certain channels; first to Christ as head, then to the members of Christ; yet not direct to them indefinitely, but through the channels and ordinances of His appointment; to nations, through their Sovereign; to churches, through their Ministers; to children, through their Parents; to families, through their Heads; to individuals, through Preachers.'[18]

Just as one may subtract from Irving his belief in traditional Christian doctrines, and leave one of his defences of millennialism intact, so one may subtract from Drummond the same beliefs quite without affecting his identification of religion and social order. If religious correctness lies in the due discharge of social duties, it is difficult to see why the usual religious questions about God and man should be asked. Certainly debate over the answers to these questions is precisely the sort of distraction from the clear path of duty which Drummond deplored. These ultimate questions did not become irrelevancies for Drummond, but he would not have written very differently if they had. He, too, is to be accounted among the proto-secularists of the early nineteenth century—the writers who, in spite of themselves, prepared the way for the thorough-going secularizers of the next generation.

Much of the book was devoted to depicting an ideal social order which had irrevocably departed. Drummond denounced the rapacity of employers, the betrayal of the aristocracy, the breakdown of parental authority, the iniquity of public school education, the sinfulness of lay influence upon the Church and the depravity of doctrines of popular sovereignty. The true polity is patriarchal; the relationship of master and servant extends to 'every situation where degrees of superior and inferior are found'—farm, factory, regiment, ship, province, kingdom. Thus he advanced, against the temper of the age, 'the Christian doctrine of the Divine right of kings', citing with approval the refusal of Louis XVIII to yield up any of his prerogatives. He did not go beyond denunciation, for there was no prospect of reform: 'every lofty feeling has withered under the chilling grasp of expediency, and nothing is now estimated either with regard to God, to king, to parents, to children, to wife, or to friend.' He went on: 'The principles and meaning of every ordinance of God has departed from the ken of men. They are become like the day-dreams of times long gone by. It is not in the power of individuals to revive them; but we may observe their decline, and thence learn to know the hour in the world's chronology at which we are arrived.' That hour is the hour of the last things, the eve of a millennium in which true political and social principles will be permanently established. The millennium is a device for restoring a social order seen as otherwise quite beyond recall.[19] Nostalgia is an important element in this picture. For Drummond there had been a time, glowingly described, when most domestic servants were born and bred on the estates of the noblemen for whom they later worked, when chaplains controlled the religious training of the extended noble household, when apprentices were treated as members of their masters' families, when labourers lived in the farm houses and there were few cottages.

As hierarchy is the mark of an ordered society, so it is a characteristic of the Church. The Church is part of the divinely given order. Its welfare should be the first object of the Christian king. Indeed it is impossible to conceive 'a state to exist without a religion of some sort being united to it'. Drummond's doctrine of ministry was, if less than high, a good deal more than low. 'A Minister of God's word in Christ's Church, is one who has a right to speak with authority in the name of his Master.' He foreshadows the hierarchy of the Catholic Apostolic Church in speaking of ministers, pastors, bishops and angels and their functions. These brief passages, together with the fuller treatment in *Dialogues on Prophecy*, suggest that the movement of the Apostolic Church into hierarchy and ritualism was no mere aping of Tractarianism, but a parallel development. In the 1820s this ecclesiology enabled Drummond and his friends to attack lay presentation in the Church of England, and the lay control of chapels, whether Anglican or Dissenting. Further, echoing his belief in the equal apostacy of papist and evangelical, Drummond compared the veneration of the individual preacher to the popish veneration for the priest. Both were priestcraft: 'that is . . . an assumption of authority to themselves, as individuals, which is only due to their office'.[20]

Drummond's (and Irving's) revulsion from the secularization and demoralization of the Church is comparable to the attitude of the Tractarians, though with two crucial differences. The latter still saw the true Church behind the unprepossessing face of the establishment; Drummond saw it in the post-adventist Church of the millennium and in the contemporary remnant which would be its nucleus. Human society, he argued, is not autonomous but a 'scaffolding' which enables 'the spiritual temple' to be built. 'God upholds Christendom only until the number of His elect shall be accomplished. As soon as that has taken place, the whole fabric will be taken down, and the pure and beautiful church and city of the New Jerusalem alone appear.'[21] The second difference is implicit in the phrase 'church and city'. For the early tractarians salvation occurred within a Church which was in but not of human society, and it led to fulfilment which was other-worldly. Drummond saw 'church and city' as always interpenetrating; first, according to the true form of God's ordinances; second, in the contemporary decline from these ordinances; and third, in their observance during the millennium. For all his conventional belief in the subservient role of society as the scaffolding of the temple, it was not, after all, a scaffolding he was ready to dismantle. The scaffolding, as much as the temple, reflected God's will; the new Jerusalem would be a true city as well as a true Church. The goal did not lie in heaven, but on a new earth. Like Irving, Drummond set the entire cosmic battle upon earth, and related (though he did not limit) its causes, nature and consequences to the social order.

This ecclesiology was fully set out in the three-volume *Dialogues on Prophecy* (1828-9). This work recorded in a heavily edited form, the discussions held at Albury in three annual week-long conferences. It is anything but a verbatim report; the participants are disguised by classical pseudonyms, and the style throughout is fairly uniform. An effort to penetrate the pseudonyms would probably be unrewarding, for the publication was Drummond's responsibility and he was not a man to make room for the opinions of others. Irving is occasionally severely criticized and Drummond from time to time is highly praised—a detail which anticipates the elimination of Irving's influence from the Catholic Apostolic Church in 1833 and 1834. The work may not represent precisely Drummond's viewpoint, but it is certainly his version of the consensus of the conferences.

Though it examines all aspects of prophecy, a major and recurrent theme is the nature of the Church and of its relation to the State. The dialogue form did not lead to systematic presentation, but a consistent ecclesiology can be constructed from a series of separate discussions. This ecclesiology, with echoes and anticipations of Hooker, Andrewes, Keble and the Tractarians, stresses the identity of Church and nation. The State had betrayed the trust basic to this identification. It was necessary to rediscover and proclaim the true nature of the Church. The *Dialogues* advanced a high concept of the Church as the continuation of the incarnation, an apostolic view of the role of the ministry, a distinction between the true and the nominal, the invisible and the visible Church, and the elements, at least, of a sacramental, a sacerdotal and a quasi-monastic approach. The ecclesiology ended with a diagnosis of contemporary ills in the Church and a prescription for their correction, together with a world-view which identified the present crisis and related it to earlier critical moments in the life of the Church. It is, in all, a consistent and sophisticated theology of Church and State; it is permeated by rather than wholly dependent upon the prophetic tradition; in many respects it anticipates and parallels the Tractarian development of the mid-1830s. The *Dialogues*, too, appeal to a neglected but vital norm, but to a biblicist and Calvinist norm. It is a high church statement, but the touchstone is the early Reformation rather than the Middle Ages. Though the different model led to a different result the ground common to the two movements is as significant as the points at which they diverge.

The correspondence is sometimes striking in detail: for example, the use of the terms bishop and priest, the notion of a daily 'regimen of prayer', an emphasis upon the sacramental life, a partiality for emotionally warm, even ecstatic, states of mind. What took place in Drummond's Albury chapel is unrecorded, but there is an instance of Irving hearing a woman parishioner's confession in London. Further, he advocated seeking the intercession of departed saints, whom he called 'interveners'.[22] But the true common ground is the conviction that 'The church must rise; the state and she are no longer one', a motto which would have served John Keble well in 1834. The Church is a perfect society in itself; it is prior to and not dependent upon the nation. Though it should be State established and supported, this 'is not an act on its part, but on the part of the kingdom who [*sic*] establishes it; the kingdom comes into the church, but the church does not go forth to take the kingdom.' It has its own unity through its sacraments; its members, the elect, are scattered throughout the world; they continue the sacrificial work of Christ in full union with him. 'Thus there is a full union with Christ, without being on a level with Christ. The suffering church is supplying that which is lacking in the sufferings of Christ, Col. 1.24, that is, is wanting in continuation and purpose of God, not in propitation.'[23]

However, the *Dialogues* are frequently Erastian in spirit; the role of lay protectors, especially in rescuing the Church from error, is a very high one. Drummond (this indicates how seriously the students of prophecy took their historical role or at least how seriously Drummond took his), is compared with Moses, Nehemiah, John of Gaunt and Frederick of Saxony.[24] But in essence the doctrine is that of *Unam Sanctam*: the State is legitimate because it protects the Church. If it destroys where it should preserve, then the Church should reassert her independence and her faithful members should recall the State to its proper duty. The betrayal, if persisted in, will bring down divine judgement. This judgement will fall upon the State and the visible Church equally; the true Church of the elect will be separated out, will suffer, but will be saved.

A doctrine which would, in other times and in other minds, have led either to a theory of rebellion or a theory of deposition, to a Huguenot or to a papal solution, led to neither in an apocalyptic context, for the notion that vengeance belonged to the Lord was taken quite literally. God will destroy and God will depose. Though his instruments may be such calamities as servile revolt and war, they will merely serve his over-riding will, which is to gather the true Church, both Gentile and Jewish, and set it over the nations in a perfect theocracy.

The identity of Church and nation is asserted, but in a relationship conferring all rights upon the Church and all obligations upon the State. The relationship is really between two churches and the State. At the centre is the invisible Church of the elect; incapsulating it is the visible Church of the nation; standing guardian to both is the State. The basic theological doctrine is that of election, for thus men become members of the true Church. If a national Church had freed itself from Rome it was authentic, for then it could shelter the elect. It did not need further validation, for instance, by way of episcopal continuity. Within the visible Church the elect preached in obedience to the apostolic commission, and celebrated the sacraments according to their dominical institution. The betrayal of the elect Church, and so the defiance of God's will, occurred when these two activities were frustrated; when, that is, the doctrine and sacraments of the true Church were perverted or overlaid with error. Most clearly this had occurred in the papal Church, and Rome was 'one form of Antichrist'. But equally it had occurred in the protestant churches of England and Scotland; this other apostacy, this second form of Antichrist, could be seen in the laxity and error of the visible, national and established churches, and in the betrayal of its obligations to religion by the State. 'The cause of Protestantism is betrayed by those whom the secular authority has placed as watchmen in our Zion.' Echoes from previous prophetical writings are clear, especially of the millennial nationalists who saw England as chosen and all British power and wealth as providentially conferred and to be providentially removed should the chosen nation turn from God.[25]

Thus the oneness of Church and nation is as likely to be a source of doom for the nation (the visible Church and the State) and trial for the elect (the invisible Church) as of joy for either. Both will suffer in the judgements, but the sufferings of the elect will lead to resurrection and those of the nation to total disaster. This is so in theory; in fact the possibility that Great Britain will be finally spared for the sake of her elect is sometimes anxiously explored.

In the Church-State theory of the *Dialogues* primacy rested with the Church, though some ambiguity results from the significant role which is preserved for the State. According to polemical need, the Erastian emphasis could be used against the papacy and the Dissenters, and the theocratic emphasis against the Establishment and the State. The divine right of kings and the divine right of the Church could be used in turn against appropriate enemies. On the one hand, duly constituted authority in Church and State was upheld; on the other, the salvific role of a remnant was exalted, with all the self-regarding rectitude of a sect. This was not quite running with the hare and hunting with the hounds. The two extremes were held together by an eschatology within which the nation both receives and betrays its trust, the visible Church both shelters and persecutes the invisible Church, and the elect both suffers as a scattered remnant and shall reign as the glorified visible Church in the millennium. Before the betrayal Church and nation are one, and from their unity flows authoritarianism; during the betrayal Church and nation cease to be one, and from this severance flows the polemic against the Establishment; after the betrayal Church and State will be perfectly one in the millennium. This ideal-type provides the measuring stick both for the normal relations of the pre-betrayal era, and the disruption of the betrayal period in which Drummond and his fellows believed themselves to be living.

Accordingly, in the evidences of papal apostacy, the assertion that it was divinely ordained that the Church should 'submit to the temporal rulers of the land' is prominent; in fact papacy 'has carried on one unceasing struggle, to make both princes and people her slaves'. In England this anti-Christian programme was reversed by Henry VIII, a wicked king but still an instrument of God. British Dissent, for all its original high moral qualities, became an impious opposition to the ordained union of Church and State. Until the 1820s Church and State in Britain remained true to their alliance, but Catholic Emancipation was a double betrayal. Both the nation and the visible Church betrayed the elect Church by flouting the principles of the alliance, principles that required protection and orthodoxy from the State and the established Church.[26]

It is hard to avoid the suspicion that the history of the early nineteenth-century Church is one of over-reaction. The horror of the Albury school at Catholic Emancipation, an extreme form of a widespread Tory response, seems now to be quite disproportionate to its occasion. But lack of proportion was common enough, for example, the evangelical attitude to pornographic books, the lottery, Sunday trading and travelling, making these equal with slavery as abominations. The Oxford campaign to unseat Peel in 1828, and especially Newman's part in it, was a comparable over-reaction to Catholic Emancipation. Newman again, hurrying through Paris in 1833 and averting his eyes from the Republican tricolor, illustrated a revulsion no less absurd than Irving's and Drummond's. Again, as a starting point for a movement to reform the Church, Catholic Emancipation was a larger event than the Whig threat of ecclesiastical reform and redistribution of episcopal incomes which prompted Keble's *National Apostacy.* If judged by the seriousness of the underlying occasion, the Irvingite movement rested upon a rather more solid base than the Oxford movement. But either was a solid enough base for a nineteenth-century British Christian. Neither was eccentric in an age which was to see Gladstone resigning over the Maynooth grant on the strength of convictions he no longer held, and Shaftesbury seeing a special providence in the appointment of a British vice-consul to Jerusalem. Reactions of this kind do not seem over-strenuous in a century which had room for Henry Phillpotts, Pius IX, the Wilberforce-Huxley confrontation, and the storm over *Essays and Reviews.*

There was, then, less eccentricity than might at first appear in the response to the repeal of the Test Acts and to Catholic Emancipation in the *Dialogues.* 'The principle', it is laid down, 'of these restrictive statutes is clearly that the nation and the church are one, and that the unity of the individual with the nation is to be attested by his unity with the church; which unity again is itself attested by that Sacrament, the habitual reception of which, according to the forms which the church prescribes, is the only possible outward and distinguishing sign of a continued adherence to the communion of the church.' The repeal of these statutes implied the separation of Church and State; it sanctioned the opinion that government rests upon the people, not upon God. In truth, however, government rests upon God alone: 'the king is Christ's Vicegerent during the whole time-state of the church . . . the representative of Him in His kingly office, even as the church is the representative of Him in His Priestly Office.' By repeal Parliament 'formally renounced' God by opening 'the highest offices of the State to men who have no God'; the State will no longer know nor care whether a magistrate be a Christian, a deist or an atheist.[27]

Not only the State but also the national Church had betrayed its trust. The declaration required of non-Anglican office holders 'relates merely to the temporal wealth of the Church, which she thinks to preserve by this compromise of her principles, and abandonment of her doctrines.' 'In this', the passage goes on, 'she will be deceived; for this is but the first of a series of measures which will strip her as bare as she will deserve to be stripped, for not having raised her loudest protest against this repeal.'[28] Again a comparison with the Oxford Movement is instructive. The Tractarians were concerned to protect the property of the Church from the impious hands of the State. The State should endow the Church, but never take away or even redistribute its property. The early Tracts summon bishops and priests to martyrdom in defence of the Church against an attack upon ecclesiastical control of property. The students of prophecy, too, talked of martyrdom under the figure of the suffering Church. The two movements share a zest for martyrdom, but there the resemblance ends. The Tractarians placed visible and invisible Church in a much closer relationship: for working purposes the institutional Church was both. Its wealth was sacred wealth; Lord Melbourne was bent upon sacrilege. Nor were they, except in mood and tone, apocalyptic. The institutional Church would continue and would need its wealth for its everyday functioning. For the Albury school visible and invisible Church were more loosely joined; the former had betrayed the latter, and the time had come for the elect to stand alone. The end was close, so that property became an ecclesiastical irrelevance, except that its loss would manifest the divine wrath the Church deserved. Persecution and martyrdom would come to the elect, but total destruction to their persecutors: a State made victim to the turmoils of popular sovereignty, a false Church pillaged by an anti-Christian State.

This is the theoretical basis of a discussion which was never far from a concrete consideration of Church and State in Great Britain. The past character and future prospects of British Christianity supplied the impetus behind the argument. Protestant Christianity as it had been most perfectly expressed in the religion and history of Great Britain was judged and found guilty. The British were *the* Protestant people, a chosen and elect nation. Britain was the Israel of the Christian era; the enormity of her betrayal may be measured by the dignity of her rejected destiny. Her apostacy was terrible because her choosing was divine. These prophets pronounced God's judgement on the elect nation turned into the apostate nation. Even their insatiable imaginations recoiled from the full horror of the implications of this reversal.

Great Britain was the first and the greatest nation to come out of papal bondage and apostacy, and remained great while she held true to her Reformation history. The French Revolution and Napoleon were powerless against 'our modern Judah'. 'While he [Napoleon] confined himself to the papal nations, against whom Jehovah had raised him up, his sword was invulnerable; but when he turned it against the shield of England, God's witness, he found it had no edge.' The beginning of her apostacy followed quickly upon her preservation; instead of ascribing it to divine favour, she attributed it to her own merits. She denied both her past and her God, and earned the wrath which will fall upon her. This analysis was followed by a prolonged apostrophe to England, made up largely of Old Testament sentences, appropriately adjusted for time and place, which recounted the history of the winning and losing of divine favour by the modern Judah. 'Behold I will fill all the inhabitants of this land, even the kings that sit upon the throne of the House of Brunswick, and the priests, and the prophets, and all the inhabitants of London with drunkenness; they shall be as insensible to sound reason as drunkards are; and all their desire shall be for an increase of that with which they are already intoxicated. And I will dash them one against another, even the fathers and sons together, saith the Lord; they shall see whether religion has nothing to do with politics, and whether it is possible to preserve the bonds of society together when all fear of me is removed. I will not pity nor spare, nor have mercy, but destroy them.' The device is clumsy, the effect incongruous, but the parallel is clear: two chosen peoples have betrayed the conditions of their choosing; each will deserve and receive its doom. And further, just as Jehovah repented him of his anger for the sake of the few just men, so too might England, in the end and after great suffering, be spared for the sake of the remnant of the faithful. Israel, in spite of its apostacy, remained chosen and still destined for greatness; so, hopefully, it might prove to be with Britain.[29]

The wrath will initially take the shape of servile revolt: 'when two millions of starving labourers are stalking up and down the land, who have been taught by their rulers that religion has nothing to do with politics, from which lesson they will not be slow to draw the fair deduction, that religion has nothing to do with any other social tie; will political sagacity save the land from being one universal scene of pillage and confusion?'[30] But the major wrath will be the manifestation, in Great Britain, of Antichrist. Servile revolt is integrated neatly into the symbols of Daniel and Revelation: the result is a theory of a triple Antichrist, papal, protestant and future, which completes the re-adjustment begun by Horsley and Faber. This revision of the traditional doctrine occurs in three places, and though the three expositions are not systematically built together, this is not difficult to do.

In the first volume it was conceded that 'the opinion of Ben Ezra, Mr Maitland, and others, is not to be overlooked, which considers that the greater part of the Apocalypse is yet to be fulfilled in a literal period of 1260 days.'[31] Prophecy may have a double fulfilment, during the Christian dispensation and in a brief future calamity. Maitland's interpretation, which was also the Catholic one, was that the prophecies point unambiguously to a future brief era in which Antichrist would arise and be defeated by the returned Christ. Faber and Horsley had described a future Antichrist then beginning to appear in France. Drummond and his colleagues retained Faber's characterization of Rome as the apostacy, but they continued to insist that Rome was 'one form of Antichrist'.

The second form was a worse manifestation for it was the apostacy of the chosen people. 'Hence observe too the wickedness of man, who, with all the advantages of the grace of Christ Jesus, and all the ordinances of his visible church, could so far forsake him, and fall away unto Satan, in both ways of apostacy, and over all the extent of Christendom.' The first apostacy is papal; the second is protestant: 'Bigotry and superstition were the handmaids of Popery; while self-conceit and scepticism have accompanied Protestantism.' Because the protestant apostacy is the worse, to it will fall the unenviable distinction of bringing forth the third form of Antichrist, 'this last monster of infidel apostacy'.[32]

The three forms were identified prophetically in the final volume.[33] The dragon was identified with the Roman Empire, and so with 'the spirit of arbitrary and bloody power'; the false prophet with the little horn of Daniel, and so with the papacy and with 'superstition and delusion'; while the beast 'must mean the infidel spirit of savage cruelty which arose at the French Revolution and raged for a quarter of a century'. The three evils work together but in a spiritual alliance with infidelity at its head. Out of the dual apostacy, papal and protestant, would emerge mankind's near-total turning away from God, the third and greatest Antichrist. Superstition and rationalism, respectively bred by popery and protestantism, each nourish infidelity, the final Antichrist, to whom the other two forms stand as progenitors. The dramatic shape of the biblical symbols was restored; Antichrist was no longer the history of an institution, but a terrible and sudden eruption of evil, a fit enemy for an avenging Christ. The sub-Antichrists, papal and protestant, preserved intact one ancient enmity and gave a place to a new one. The students of prophecy attacked protestant apostacy at home and (in part also at home) the rising fortunes of popery. These two, evil in themselves, were the more evil as the breeding grounds of the final apostacy of complete infidelity. Given the relevance of a biblical vocabulary, Drummond and his circle had forged no mean polemical instrument for frightened men in alarming times. So far, the *Dialogues* have diagnosed evils and foretold disaster.

But no apocalyptic world view is complete without a promise of felicity to comfort the good while its vision of evil disconcerts the wicked. This promise had two aspects—the discovery of assurances that Britain will, in spite of everything, be eventually exempted from the final wrath, and the confident anticipation of the bliss of the reign of Christ and his saints in the millennium. The two aspects were joined by the notion of the saving remnant, both the probable occasion of mercy and the nucleus of the new age. This dual awareness of destiny surely prompted the separation of the 'Irvingite' or Catholic Apostolic Church.

England had involved herself in the fate of the papal kingdoms by rejoining them; this was a prophetic commonplace, though, curiously for these rigid establishmentarians, it was a theme they could have derived from Priestley and Bicheno. In the first volume of the *Dialogues*, which recorded discussions held in 1826, it was suggested that she might, after all, reject Catholic Emancipation and apostacy; and in the second (when this faint hope had passed) a reversal of the traditional harsh policy towards the Jews was held out as a possible way of escape not from wrath itself but from its totality. But in the third the sole hope of Britain derived from the activity of the students of prophecy. Wrath will indeed fall upon Great Britain; nevertheless, she was 'set apart from extermination', thanks to the spread of belief in the second coming and the revival of prophetic preaching. 'There is a work of God proceeding in the land, of another kind than the evangelical revival. The Lord is teaching unto his people the foundations of Zion, that when the shock comes, they may know whereon their feet do rest.'[34]

God still intends that Britain shall 'do great things for his people Israel'. Britain will be saved, in the end and from the worst, for the sake of the remnant which faithfully awaited the end—the utter end for the infidel and apostate majority. The struggle within the hearts of the students of prophecy between their hatred of modern Britain and their veneration for the essential Britain found, in this way, a wholly satisfactory resolution. The punishment of the wicked was not one whit abated, and their own role was magnified as they became the occasion of national salvation.

They were confident of their membership of the elect Church, and convinced that they were 'a generation which shall arise out of the present professing churches'. They believed that they were among those who would rise with the dead saints and reign with the returned Christ over a regenerated earth. The wicked, by contrast, would be twice punished: first, by the wrath of the second coming, and second at the re-emergence of evil when Satan is loosed at the end of the millennium. 'Speechless, without excuse, self-condemned, and condemned of God, the millions who have not Christ dwelling in them, and walking in them, that is energizing in them, are cast into the lake of fire.' The true character of the second coming is contained in its definition as 'an exterminative and beatific process' —death and life are dealt out with equal totality to the unregenerate and to the elect.[35]

During the millennium the elect will enjoy a transfigured material existence. The 'blessed dead' will rise at the second coming, and 'the bodies of the blessed living' will be changed; together they will constitute the saints who 'shall *reign* as well as *serve* with him'. But their life will be unlike that of ordinary mortals. 'They shall not justle [*sic*] with men in the flesh, and though intermixing when need be, individually, shall be visible only by special operation and appointment.'[36] Here as with Irving's future-life materialism earth discharges the function of heaven. On heaven, the *Dialogues* are significantly silent; the total stress is upon what happens *on earth*. Here the saints will reign visiting, like Christian Olympians, the rest of mortal men. Here, too, the divine drama will be fully enacted and the divine victory finally won. Satan, like heaven, has a very attenuated role in this system; Christ is responsible for the torment of the damned in the lake of fire, and Satan has little more to do than appear from time to time to lead the wicked to destruction.

The second coming of Christ is second only in order of time; in dignity it is superior to his sitting at the right hand of God in heaven. 'With respect to its dignity, it is the chief step in the act of God, for it is the exhibition to the world of the manifester, upholder, and doer of all his works from beginning to end'. In a couple of cryptic remarks, the earth itself appears to be vested with immortality. The final (i.e. post-millennial) judgement 'puts a last end to the present *form* of this earth, though not to its *material*, and gives commencement to a new era, and to a new scene, of which we know no particulars, but know assuredly that there shall be such, in which the saints [are?] erect for ever round the throne of God and of the Lamb, and the wicked prostrate for ever as their footstool, in the impenetrable, impassable, and indissoluble enclosure of hell fire, a new heaven and a new earth.'[37] It is a little hard to say what all this is about (though reasonably sure that it is a picture of unrelieved unpleasantness) except that the eternity of the earth is clearly stated. Such, indeed, should be the case: if earth sees the complete playing out of the divine drama, then it is rightly beyond time and destruction. Irving's and Drummond's materialism and secularism have a full, if more abstract, expression in this imagery of the future.

VI: The Albury Group and its Context

The theory just outlined was, for some, a guide to strenuous activity. The students of prophecy saw themselves as prophets, warning the nation to put on sackcloth while there was yet time. This, indeed, had been their regular function since the time of Thomas Brightman. Further, Irving, Drummond and their colleagues believed that they occupied a vital position in the history of the Christian Church. In the early centuries the major theological task had been to establish correct ideas about the second person of the trinity; in the Reformation it had been to vindicate the doctrine of election; now, and equally important, it was to advance the true interpretation of unfulfilled prophecy, because false interpretations were eroding the solid core of truth about God and man. They were, they believed, reclaiming man and the earth for God, as the successors to Athanasius, Luther and Calvin.

Understandably they tried to mobilize opinion, both to save Great Britain from the wrath of God and to carry through a religious revolution. Their activity can be broadly called political, though it was not chiefly directed towards the State. The first duty of these (as they saw it) faithful ministers and laymen was towards their own churches, especially the Church of England. Reformation in doctrine would be the first and crucial step towards recalling the nation to a sense of its true destiny. The way to reform civil government was 'to look to the church as the kernel within the shell'.[1]

Some of the men who conferred at Albury behaved as a pressure group within the established churches, waging an intensive pamphlet and periodical warfare against the conventional 'religious world'. Excepting Irving and Drummond, it it is difficult to say who was active in this campaign. But they were formidably energetic, and they had a numerous audience of receptive readers. Prophecy was in fashion; Bickersteth, writing in 1831 and commenting on a lack of zeal for missions, noted that 'Things are in a most dead and cold state here [a midlands county]: may the Lord revive his work! . . . the good men are all afloat on prophesying, and the immediate work of the Lord is disregarded for the uncertain future. These things ought not to be so. But I think anyone who has known this place for the last seven or eight years might have foreboded all we now see.'[2] Well might Bickersteth feel uneasy, for he was at that time beginning to embrace the interpretation which had helped bring the change about. A few years earlier the *British Critic*, in the course of a hostile review of books by Frere, Croly and Irving[3] had referred, pityingly, to 'a numerous class of religionists, whose minds are peculiarly apt to be perplexed and harassed by the portentous system of Apocalyptical Divinity'. In 1830, reviewing Taylor's *Natural History of Enthusiasm*[4] it referred to 'This madness, which was for a while epidemical among a certain class of religionists' and which had since nearly died away. A little later the editor of the *Evangelical Review* was not so sure that it had. In the preface to the 1830 volume he found the combination of millennialist propaganda and miraculous claims 'truly alarming'. He went on: 'In Scotland, England and Ireland, a spirit of daring speculation obtains, to a most painful extent, on subjects connected with the study of unfulfilled prophecy;—so that the predictions of the infallible Spirit are put out to pawn, in certain quarters, upon all the political and passing events of the times. This unhealthy state of a portion of the public mind, which owes its existence to a few pertinacious but talented individuals, has, of late, associated itself with the doctrine of *modern miracles*; so that every one who has reached the proper pitch of enthusiasm now vests himself in the garb of apostolic authority, and calls upon the victims of nervous debility, in the name of the Lord Jesus, to arise and walk.'[5] Simply because this witness is testifying to the spread of opinions he would sooner not have observed, a good deal of reliance may be placed upon him—and, in general, upon the energy with which all the orthodox journals set out to extirpate the error.

The pressure group made only one effort to seize control of a major religious body. The pamphlet warfare culminated in an attack upon the British and Foreign Bible Society in 1831. The challenge to the society—demands that membership be limited to trinitarians and that meetings be opened with prayer—arose from an internal difference in the society. Drummond, Irving, Spencer Perceval and the *Morning Watch* threw themselves into the campaign, adding to the indictment the publication of Bibles containing the apocrypha for continental Catholics. This was poorly chosen ground; the society's defenders were able to show that in the 1820s Drummond had paid for a printing of the Bible with the apocrypha as part of his work in the Continental Society, and that Irving had drawn heavily upon the books of Esdras in some of his exegetical writings.

Though Drummond and Irving did not begin the attack, they had reason to think that it gave them an opening they could exploit. Prominent among the attackers were the Noel brothers, of whom Gerald T. Noel had expounded prophecy in a way very similar to their own. The *Christian Observer* took the Albury element among the attackers very seriously, and was delighted when the manifestations of the spirit at Regent Square provided additional ammunition. In the event the resolutions of the trinitarians were rejected by large majorities. The minority formed a breakaway Trinitarian Bible Society, in which the Albury group was prominent, but still a minority in a wider group that could, for a time, attract the support of so eminent a figure as Bickersteth. The new society itself split; the party now called 'Irvingites' were expelled by the rest. Speaking in tongues at Regent Square again helped to drive the minority out of the minority.

In this manner, an opportunity became an abject defeat. But the defeat owed more to glossolalia than to a particular prophetical position. Had not the tongues manifested themselves at this very time, it is possible that the Albury group could have applied pressure to more purpose and found satisfaction in the impact they were making upon the general ecclesiastical situation. As it was, defeat showed that they could not rally churchmen to their standard; they were not about to become leaders of a significant movement. If the pressure group was not to become a movement, there was only one thing left for it to do, other than disappear. It could become a sect—another way of disappearing, but a more consoling one.

The chief element in the life of the future sect began when the *Morning Watch* accepted the authenticity of the miracles at Port Glasgow in 1830. By contagion, some of Irving's parishioners at Regent Square began to speak in tongues and to be cured of their illnesses early in 1831. The *Christian Observer*, while it was defending the Bible Society and attacking the modern millennialists, was critically examining the case of Miss Fancourt's miraculous cure and reporting resignedly on the extraordinary happenings at Regent Square. The Irvingites, it believed, were destroying themselves by their own excesses. That would be one way of describing what was about to happen. But from an Irvingite point of view, the picture was very different. The tongues and the healings were clear signs of a new pentecost, an effusion of the Holy Ghost which would usher in a new dispensation. The miracles confirmed the imminence of the last days; they were a sign of divine favour and the spiritual baptism of the new Church of the elect gathering out of the old churches. The remnant drew together to await the end, confident that they were the nucleus of the saints who should rule with Christ. They were, by and large, an eminently respectable lot, but in all except social status they were like those humbler Englishmen who were soon to cross the Atlantic to await the Messiah on the banks of the Mississippi.

The movement into a sect was again that of a minority within a minority. In London most of the Regent Square congregation held fast to the London Presbytery and forced Irving to take his faithful few into the wilderness. At Albury Park Drummond presided over services in his private chapel while the rector, Hugh McNeile, held firm to orthodoxy in the parish Church. In this diminished way the sect that was to be the Catholic Apostolic Church took shape. The unworking leaven became an organized remnant, a tiny Zion awaiting the Lord's coming. In the process Drummond rose to first place, Irving sank into humiliation, and McNeile passed over into bitter and significant opposition.

Drummond and Irving, in forming a pressure group to influence their churches, did not behave unreasonably. They expected, not without reason, the support of great numbers of Anglican clergy. There was a large body of opinion, perhaps only in the late 1820s and before the miracles came to obscure the issue, to which they could appeal with some confidence. There were many perplexed, frightened (and, perhaps, simply vengeful) Christians, who looked for the judgement and the millennium. Because of this, Irving and Drummond had for a time the satisfaction of setting the tone and subject of much current theological debate. Arguments over prophecy took up an increasing share of the pages of the journals. Their writings were accorded reviews as lengthy as they were hostile; the *Morning Watch* was regularly attacked by the other journals, and as often it attacked them.

The contest was more than a squabble between ill-tempered exegetes. Rival exegetical positions corresponded to rival theologies, almost to rival Christianities. In the world order depicted by prophetic literalism the initiative was always with God; men could obey or disobey but never act decisively. The divine will sanctioned a socio-ecclesiastical order which men could ignore if they chose, but which would be restored and indeed eternalized by divine acts of wrath and mercy. Though the 'religious world' agreed that all was in the hand of God, it rejected the use of a God-dominated world view to condemn the laborious human constructs of religious and political life. As the orthodox were unable to treat the prophetic parts of scripture as less than inspired, they had to accept the progressivist post-millennialism also contained in the prophetic tradition.

On the surface, then, the contention was an argument about the interpretation of the Bible and the meaning of prophecy; at bottom, however, it was an argument about how God acts and how man responds.

In holding such opinions, Drummond and Irving were far from isolated. They shared a considerable common ground with theorists either loosely or not at all connected with their immediate circles. Further, people who stood apart from the whole argument and put little or no stress upon prophetical theology, shared many basic positions, especially revulsion from a complacent society and Church. To set Irving and Drummond in context, the ideological correspondence with the opinions of three other groups must be examined —those who were closely related, those whose connexion was solely a matter of similar ideas, and those who, on the face of it, were wholly unrelated in ideas and in organization. The discussion will centre upon Hugh McNeile, J. H. Frere, and William Cuninghame; Edward Bickersteth and Henry Gauntlett; John Keble and J. H. Newman.

McNeile described his break from Irving and Drummond in a pamphlet published in 1834, *Letters to a Friend.* Two earlier publications, *The Times of the Gentiles* (1828) and *Popular Lectures on the Prophecies relative to the Jewish Nation* (delivered in 1827 and published in 1830) had been in substantial agreement with the men he came to denounce. The three works, taken together, show how a very closely related set of beliefs could be held by an eminent clergyman without affecting his eminence because never drastically acted upon. McNeile's breakaway seems especially significant, for he owed his opening in the Church to Drummond, who presented this obscure young Irish clergyman to the rectory of Albury in 1822 after hearing him preach in London. In later years he became a celebrated preacher and controversialist, a strenuous anti-Romanist who retained his interest in prophecy and in the Jews. Later in his life he became Dean of Ripon.

In the 1820s his chief interest was in the future of the Jews, a concern shared by Irving and Drummond, Frere, Cuninghame, Way and a host of others. The suspicion that Englishmen championed the Jews because they saw their own combination of rectitude and powerlessness reflected in the Jewish situation, is strengthened by the terms in which McNeile dedicated his *Time of the Gentiles* to Drummond. He did this 'Because . . . you are evil spoken of' and 'because . . . you . . . are also a diligent student of all that is revealed concerning the approaching advent and glory of the King of the

Jews.'[6] Quite literally, McNeile meant the king *of the Jews* as a restored people. The Jewish theme had absorbed much attention at the Albury conferences, where it was symbolized in person by that erratic convert (first to Rome and then to Canterbury—a double shift which must have seemed to fulfil, in microcosm, two major aspects of prophecy) Joseph Wolff.

The basic contention of *Times of the Gentiles* was that in the incarnation 'the accomplishment of the promise made to Abraham was partly brought to pass, and partly delayed.' The salient characteristic of Christian era, the preaching to the Gentiles, is not as missionary apologists suppose a cumulative process leading inevitably to the fullness of the kingdom. The history of the Church is not progressive; it is characterized, rather, by loss and by mere survival: 'Her course resembles the emigrations of a pilgrim rather than the triumphant establishments of a conqueror.' Even in Great Britain Christianity has 'subsided into a goodnatured quietness, a plausible profession of individual humility slily praising itself'. 'The church . . . occupies a lower and a broader platform than is meet.' High civilization, again to anticipate Newman, is not the same as true Christianity.

Far from being final, the Christian dispensation has the limited purpose of gathering out of the Gentiles a small, persecuted, world-shunning 'elect church', a 'remnant'. The total conversion of the world is to be accomplished in the millennium. In the meantime the recruitment of the elect will be accompanied by the individual conversion of an equivalent remnant among the Jews. The faithful will be isolated in an ocean of unbelief. The times of the Gentiles will end with the separation of the saints from the ungodly; 'the termination of the times of the Gentiles . . . will synchronise with the restoration of the Jewish church, and precede the introduction of millennial blessedness.' Faber's sermon of 1822 is fittingly cited at this point.[7]

McNeile's *Popular Lectures on the Prophecies relative to the Jewish Nation* expand the argument at one or two points. He foresaw the restoration and conversion of the Jews being effected directly by the returned Christ, who would be not some mysterious manifestation of the divine, but 'plainly a man, with risen flesh and bones, in figure as a man, and beaming in the glory of God'. But his central theme was that 'The Jews shall have national pre-eminence in the earth; and shall prove a blessing to all nations'—the title of the seventh lecture. As he discussed the character of national pre-eminence, Great Britain was obviously in his mind. The millennial superiority of the Jews will not be based upon power, commerce, culture, prosperity and liberality, for such pre-eminence is the fruit of self-interest, envy, hatred, malice, war, death and sorrow. It will be typified by righteousness and peace. Further, British pre-eminence 'may consist with *infidelity*'—'Men of any creed or of no creed are alike eligible to national honour and glory.' The Jews, on the contrary will have the eminence of a 'nation of true worshippers'. McNeile did not take further his criticism of contemporary Britain; in the hands of Irving and Drummond the same national sins led to the concept of the apostate nation.[8]

McNeile's 'elect nation' was the Jewish nation, and Britain simply a country, possibly the most Christian but still not Christian enough, from which some of the elect were being recruited. Perhaps this saved him from sectarianism. As he did not look upon the British as a chosen people, he did not need to despair when it became clear that they were set in their evil ways. A theological detail confirms this impression of moderation. While the extremists (e.g. Lewis Way, and Drummond in the *Dialogues*) talked of the millennial condition of man as a return beyond mere imputation to the original innocence of Adam, McNeile expressly limited it to the righteousness of the converted sinner; not inherent righteousness but still righteousness through Christ. McNeile was not a radical pre-millennialist. It is readily understandable that he should have declined secession and found a useful future in the Church of England.

He explained his refusal in a pamphlet addressed to Spencer Perceval: *Letters to a Friend, who has felt it his duty to secede from the Church of England, and who imagines that the miraculous gifts of the Holy Ghost are revived among the seceders.* The nucleus of the new Church, in McNeile's account, was a group of people who had left Scotland believing that the tongues had missionary utility. Mary Campbell, who was probably among them, had let it be known that she spoke in the language of the Pelew Islanders, a safe assertion, as Mrs Oliphant wryly remarks. They spent two years at Albury, where they exchanged the vestigially rational missionary intention for a thorough-going voice of the spirit explanation. They attracted about two hundred persons from the neighbourhood. Their pretensions may be judged from the title of a printed but unpublished pamphlet cited by McNeile, 'A narrative of the circumstances which led to the setting up of the Church of Christ at Albury', which assailed McNeile for his failure to co-operate. Clearly, while Irving was going ahead with some residual caution at Regent Square, Drummond was pressing impetuously forward at Albury. Here no doubt he acquired his ordination as 'angel' and also the pre-eminence which enabled him to put Irving down when the two groups came together.

Because he had been so close to the new sectarians, McNeile felt able to explain their secession very precisely. The seceders, 'filled with admiration of the predicted holiness and beauty of the *perfected* church of Christ, at the second advent of her Lord, and looking at this truth alone, to the neglect of present duties arising out of other portions of holy scripture, have become impatient of human infirmity, and determined to have a holy company even now. Forgetful of what manner of spirit they are themselves, they have hastily seceded from the militant and imperfect church in which they were baptized, gone into diverse excesses of extravagant excitement, and denounce all who will not go with them.' At Albury ministers of the Church of England were held up to reprobation as ministers of Antichrist—this, indeed, was no more than the logic of the Albury conferences over which McNeile had recently 'moderated'. On the last page of the book McNeile quoted a letter from 'our friend M——' (probably Lord Mandeville, a participant in the Albury conferences) to much the same effect. The Lord will undoubtedly come to destroy the man of sin, whether he be papal or infidel, 'and there will *then* be a pure church, and miracles will attend *that period*. Irving, and his followers have anticipated the event. The enemy has caught them in that snare. It is not so? They will soon find, in their new assembly, that tares and wheat will grow together till the harvest. And then, wherein are they better than others?'[9]

The Jewish theme was explored in the eighth letter. The phrase, the latter rain, had been taken by the new sectaries to mean 'the revival of miraculous gifts of the Holy Ghost in the christian church, in this the latter portion of her history'. Lewis Way had fathered, in a significantly different form, this kind of interpretation. In the pamphlet of this name, he had epitomized sacred history in the imagery of rain: a shower after seedtime, a drought, and a shower before harvest to swell the grain. This, as McNeile was able to show, was Drummond's view when (in 1832) he wrote his preface to the pro-Camissard tract *The General Delusion of Christians*. Way, however, had made the imagery point to the conversion of the Jews; the Irving-Drummond group had applied it to themselves. McNeile insisted that the promises to the Jews are promises *to the Jews*, and adds something of Maitland's destructive literalism: 'it is abundantly evident, that the expression *latter rain* signifies literally, the vernal rain upon the land of Canaan, and nothing else.' He noted with some relish how the very men who had been strict advocates of a literal interpretation had fallen into the allegorical errors they once denounced. McNeile denied that the promises to the Jews were to allegorized and spiritualized Israelites. It is clear that in the new sect the Jewish fixation had been cast off, and that the promises were wholly applied to a Gentile remnant.[10]

There is nothing surprising in such a development. The radical dissatisfaction underlying the expectation that a new world will come soon is a condition which may have other remedies. There were none for Irving, who dragged out the small remainder of his days in dejection and illness; it does not appear that he either gave up the hope of the coming end or contented himself with the raptures of sectarianism. Drummond, irrepressible and unreliable, was a man of a different order; it is easy to imagine him busying himself with tasks which Irving would have found a shade contemptible, ordering the ritual, ceremony and hierarchy of the new sect. Drummond was born to be a man to hasten the process from sect to denomination. Within a very short time nearly all passed away from the wrongly called Irvingites except the fancy dress of an isolated high church group; self-contained and content to remain so, the tongues as institutionalized as in a modern pentecostalist assembly in a respectable suburb. Dropping the improbable talk about the future of the Jews was simply the first step towards normalizing the life of a small denomination.

Others who had taken part in the Albury conferences avoided McNeile's embarrassing proximity to the proto-sect. Frere and Cuninghame, who had been publishing commentaries when Irving was a schoolboy, appear to have remained contented with the satisfactions of the professional exegete. Frere, possibly irked by the constant iteration of the names of Frere and Irving, coupled together as if they were twin heresiarchs, gently dissociated himself in 1831, rather in the manner of an old prophetical hand correcting the hot-headed excesses of youth. He needed to do so; Irving had taken up the ideas of his *Combined View* (1815) and when this work was re-issued in a 'corrected' edition in 1826 (*On the General Structure of the Apocalypse*) Frere had a word of praise for Irving's *Discourse on the Prophecies*. In *Eight Letters on the Prophecies* (1831) he took up a position distinct from that of his one-time disciple, but on a question of application rather than on principles.

Frere held that Great Britain was the favoured nation whose 'sacred character' was firmly established by the prophecies. However, 'through our authorised infidel amalgamation with the Papacy' the favoured nation had merited punishment. Frere was much more hopeful than the Albury prophets that God would remember to be merciful, as he had been to Israel. The signs of divine favour were still plentiful: the Bible Society, the missionary societies and the prophetic movement. This listing showed Frere to be a long way from condemning the ordinary operations of providence through human institutions.

Nevertheless, he was equally certain that a change was coming. In the *Combined View* he had argued for a Bonapartist restoration at Rome as a prelude to Armageddon; the 1830 revolutions, he now thought, made this imminent. In Great Britain, Catholic Emancipation (so a very obscure passage should probably be understood) effectively separated Church and State, so that the true servants of Christ were separating themselves from their enemies, again a prelude to Armageddon. The wrath was coming soon, and it would fall on Great Britain.

All these arguments (except the Bonapartist restoration) matched the theory of the *Dialogues*. But at two other points Frere significantly diverged. He defended the Bible Society, while conceding that the participation of non-trinitarians was among those developments 'fatal as far as the interests of this country are concerned'. Nor, he added, should the Bible Society object to the prophetic writers because some of them were shaky on doctrine. Frere, in fact, did not care especially much if the Bible Society had made a bad mistake, nor if Irving and Drummond were less than orthodox, nor if the 'interests' of his country were to suffer. For he, like McNeile and Cuninghame, had turned his attention away from Britain to the Jews. The only interesting question left about Great Britain was whether pious individuals would be saved from the wrath, for 'the time of our preservation as the Protestant nation, standing in the situation of the ancient Israel, the peculiarly favoured people of God, is drawing to its close; and the re-establishment of the literal Israel in their former Supremacy is at hand; while we have already begun to cast off our Protestant character, which had hitherto been our shield and protection; and blasphemous acts of impiety, and open defiances of Christ, are perpetrated in our metropolis, surpassing even those which distinguished the first period of revolutionary and infidel impiety in France.'[11]

This analysis of the state of Britain ran parallel to that of Drummond and Irving. They, however, by applying the prophecies to the Gentile Israel, could do nothing but despair of the nation and rest their hopes upon a saving remnant. Frere, light-heartedly announcing the doom of Britain, looked to the still-future and therefore re-assuring restoration of the Jews, and (for all one may know to the contrary) was contented by the prospect. The same object of hope kept Cuninghame busy on prophecy for another two decades.

William Cuninghame of Lainshaw, Scottish layman, early contributor to the *Christian Observer*, polemical opponent of Faber, close friend of Edward Bickersteth, held ideas on prophecy very similar to those of Irving and Drummond. But he was a professional expositor with a reputation and a satisfying occupation. Though he came to the Albury discussions, that was the limit of his relationship with the more extreme spirits. In stature and scope he resembles Faber, and was also moved to expound prophecy by the French Revolution, the Napoleonic Empire and the wars. His overall scheme, locating the probable period of the end between 1792 and 1867, is similar to Faber's, though the two experts disputed learnedly over details. Both wrote on the future of the Jews; both were absorbed by the disasters that would accompany the second coming and hardly at all by the millennial joys that would follow it. Again, both were exercised by the prophetic role and fate of Great Britain. On this issue, Cuninghame pretty evenly balanced the profit and loss account, concluding that there was no ground for confidence. Every individual should set himself right with God, in case the last days were upon him and in case Great Britain was due for an adverse judgement.

Cuninghame and Faber, finally, were at one in seeing a relationship between revolution in France and British political reform, intellectual pride and creeping infidelity. Especially in the additions he made in 1817 to the second edition of his *Dissertation on the Seals and Trumpets* (1st ed. 1813), he threw off *obiter dicta* which correspond closely to the Irving-Drummond position and may have helped to shape it. In the first edition he identified, in a generalized manner, the probable 'second causes' of 'the approaching desolations' as

> those dreadful principles of political, moral, and religious insubordination and disorganisation, which burst forth at the French revolution, and have ever since been working, sometimes openly and at others more covertly, in the body politic. These principles are the natural and necessary fruit of unsanctified knowledge among all classes of society. . . . From this source proceed all those crude schemes of regeneration, whereby our modern political fanatics promise to correct the moral disorders of the world, and to bring in the millennium of philosophy, but which, if their execution be seriously attempted, as it possibly may be at the last great catastrophe, shall be found to have introduced the most awful disorder, and shall deluge the world with blood.[12]

In an elaborate later footnote he related this general situation to postwar British politics. In 1813 he had been content to call the attention of princes and their advisers to prophecy; in 1817 the state lottery prompted him to exclaim, with that typical prophetic propensity to link minute symptoms with massive diseases: 'But will God admit the plea of state necessity for disobedience to his eternal laws? Or is any failure of revenue an evil to be compared with that of drawing down upon our country the divine displeasure?' Great men, he went on, must do better than patronize Bible societies: 'They must fearlessly bring the principles of the Bible into the senate. . . .' This, not changes in the representation, would be true reform; in any case the Commons was already 'probably the purest representative assembly on earth'. He concluded with a flourish: 'This indeed is the fatal disease of the age, that men, instead of turning to God who has smitten them, are occupied with the dangerous and desperate schemes of state-quackery, learned in the school of that revolution which has already deluged Europe with blood.'[13] This however, was not the excitable Drummond but the professional Cuninghame; the analysis is a footnote, not a call to action.

In his *Letters and Essays . . . on . . . Israel* (1822) Cuninghame further prepared the ground for his excited successors by an undeviating literalism which established that the Messiah would reign on earth at Jerusalem over the restored Jews, that their return to Palestine would be a stage in the apocalyptic end, and that 'the final and glorious influx of the Gentiles into the church' would be a consequence of their restoration. The Albury prophets occupied the same ground, especially the opinion that allegorical interpreters were 'under the influence of a spirit of unbelief' comparable to the denial of the resurrection of the body, and that the conversion of Israel was 'the cause of God'.[14] This phrase implicitly down-grades conventional missionary activity, though Cuninghame in fact made no invidious comparison between types of missionary activity. However, in 1814 and 1815 he worked with Lewis Way to rescue the London Jewish Society from financial and denominational troubles, and undoubtedly thought very highly of this particular mission.

It is likely that Cuninghame and possibly Way were, like Frere and McNeile, insulated from sectarianism by this concern for the Jewish future. Cuninghame certainly went on as he had begun; that his hopes were fixed upon Palestine, and only in a secondary manner upon Great Britain, was shown by his *Letter . . . on . . . Jewish Colonisation* of 1849. He urged the formation of a society to promote 'the agricultural settlement of believing Israelites in Palestine'. He showed with elaborate calculations that the mass restoration was due to take place, concluding that it would be as well to do now what God will do in any case, lest he accompany it with Britain's destruction. The government should sponsor the scheme as an appropriate act of penance for the 'deep criminality' of the renewal of diplomatic relations with Rome.

Most that Drummond and Irving asserted is in Cuninghame, as it is in Faber, Frere, McNeile and Way. The differences are in tone, application, temperament. The latter were professional specialists within the establishment, correlating their beliefs with their situation by prudently interpreting the prophecies to point away from Great Britain where, they recognized, God's battle had been lost, to the Palestine of the future, where it had not yet been fought.

The case of Edward Bickersteth is distinctly ambiguous. Of all the commentators upon prophecy, Bickersteth was probably the most eminent in the 'religious world' so condemned by Irving. For fourteen years he was a secretary of the Church Missionary Society; as rector of Walton, Hertfordshire, from 1830 he was concerned with the Christian Family Library of religious classics, the anti-Tractarian series, Testimony of the Reformers, and the favourite evangelical hymnal, *Christian Psalmody*. In the 1840s he helped found both the Parker Society and the Evangelical Alliance. He did not tire of doing good, but, at least in the early 1830s, he must have wondered about the significance of good deeds. Early in his career this very respectable missionary organizer and preacher adopted (in the words of his son-in-law and biographer) 'the view that was then popular among serious Christians; and looked forward to the gradual conversion of the world, by the spread of missions, and a larger blessing on the ordinary means of grace'.[15] Political events shook this certitude—especially Catholic Emancipation ('I fear that we have displeased God, and may expect tokens of his displeasure') and the Bristol riots ('The Lord is shaking these kingdoms').[16] Prompted by the same events that obsessed Irving and Drummond, he became a pessimistic pre-millennialist. But, embarrassingly, he was already an eminent progressive post-millennialist; his well-known *Remarks on the Prophecies* of 1825 had a further wide circulation in later editions of *A Scripture Help*. Thanks to his conversion about 1833 the fourth revised edition of this work, *A Practical Guide to the Prophecies* (1835), was curiously Janus-faced. A considerably post-millennialist text was far-reachingly qualified by a distinctly pre-millennialist set of footnotes, in which Cuninghame is cited with very great respect. Bickersteth's intimacy with this rigid literalist began in 1833, and led to a series of annual gatherings devoted to the study of prophecy.[17]

Bickersteth's later pessimism and pre-millennialism did not fall far short of the extremes of the Albury prophets. Nevertheless, the distance, though small, was crucial. In his Visitation Sermon of 1831, he managed to strike a neat and businesslike balance between optimism and pessimism. The condition of England was indeed marred by the work of Satan. Sabbath breaking, popery, socinianism, 'neology', the encouragement of idolatry in India and slavery in the West Indies, irreligion, drunkenness, attempts at disestablishment, lack of zeal in the clergy were 'national sins' that amounted to a 'torrent of evil'. But Satan's works were stimulated by all that was good in English life: worthy ministers, sound preaching, church building, educational and missionary organizations. Where Bickersteth distinguished between the evil and the good, Drummond went further and demonstrated that his good was essentially evil. So, for Bickersteth, the belief that 'The times are Bible times' was a source of hope as well as danger. It was a stimulus towards more energetic preaching and the ending of controversy. 'THE JUDGMENT THAT IS APPROACHING' should be a spur to pastoral action. 'My beloved brethren' he concluded (he was addressing his fellow clergy) 'the period is fast coming on that will put an end to this world, and all its honours and distinctions; its frown or its smile, its contempt or its favour will soon pass away.' Much of this was close to the Irving-Drummond analysis, yet the overall tone was very different. There was just enough gloom and doom to stimulate action—not the action of a self-appointed leaven, but of the institutional Church. Bickersteth's underlying concern was the promotion of zeal rather than exactness in exegesis, a zeal for, not against, the Lord's traditional house.[18]

He retained both the sober zeal of the post-millennialist progressive and the probing alarmism of the pre-millennialist anticipator of crisis. He placed himself as precisely in the middle as it is possible for a man to get. His disenchantment, real enough, fell short of despair; he constantly tried to stimulate effort, but he did not rest his entire hope upon the usual channels of grace. He knew the practical value of pre-millennial exhortation; he also knew the perils of over-emphasis. He certainly relied ultimately upon the millennium as divine intervention, but meantime he hedged his bets by putting some of his money upon useful and continuing, albeit imperfect, institutions.

He gave his *Practical Guide to the Prophecies* a revealing subtitle: 'with reference to their interpretation and fulfilment, and to personal edification'. On interpretation and fulfilment it was cautious and non-committal; on edification, it was strenuous and emphatic. Bickersteth set down that the pre-millennial advent of Christ and the first resurrection of the saints were not sufficiently warranted by the evidence to be held dogmatically, but went on to note that those engaged upon benevolent works will 'obtain a most powerful reviver in the assured hope of our Lord's speedy return'. If the prophecies are obscure until fulfilled, this too is for edification: 'Light enough is afforded to guide and cheer . . . and darkness enough is left to check the pride of human speculation, and to try the spirit. . . .' With proper caution, he distinguished between what is necessary to salvation and what is helpful to the soul; prophecy falls into the second class. But this caution was cancelled by the assertion that prophecy 'is the generation truth, that is, the one which is peculiarly important in this generation, and opposes the whole stream and current of men's opinions by the simple testimony of God's word, and therefore it is the truth everywhere spoken against.'[19] Drummond and Irving rested a good deal of their case upon an identical assertion.

So too with the matter of the Jews. Their conversion is certain and their restoration highly probable. On the Jews as converters of the Gentiles, Bickersteth stayed carefully in the middle of the road; there are enough pagans for present work to proceed and for the Jews to have a hand in the *final* conversion of the Gentiles. Again, on missionary activity Bickersteth held to the mid-point. Where the societies thought it a work of mercy, and the Irving-Drummond group a work of judgement, Bickersteth settled for both, with an inclination towards judgement. Missionaries were, in the main, to separate the good from the evil before the millennium; they were not to bring the millennium about. As befitted a responsible clergyman, Bickersteth eschewed excess. He knew how far accepted scholarship would take him and where the appropriate cautions should be remembered. But he was overwhelmingly concerned with the promotion of zeal, as were Irving and Drummond, and this concern took him, in spite of himself, into extremes which negatived his cautions.

Because Bickersteth hesitates uneasily between extremes, he resists classification as either a pre- or a post-millennialist. Certainly, for practical purposes, he retained sufficient of his earlier optimism to encourage his readers in their pious works. Nevertheless, he refrained carefully from ascribing an ultimate value to such works. He did not assert that the second coming would precede the millennium, nor that Christ would come in the flesh; he simply described such a prospect as 'the blessed hope of every believer'. So he was able to characterize the activities of the religious societies as 'blessed exertions' (a description at which Irving and Drummond would have balked) but noted that they were only 'preparing the way for the Church's full glory—an expression they might have accepted. 'However useful Religious Societies have been or may be . . . yet we are not to expect through them more than a preparatory work. The Scriptures lead us not to anticipate a peaceful progress to a blessed reign of spiritual and universal blessedness. The image representing the four universal kingdoms is to be *broken to pieces*. . . .' The practical conclusion emerged clearly enough. There will be a second coming, but the prophecies make clear neither the form it will take nor precisely how it will be connected with the conversion of the world. The short term task is readily apparent, the work of conversion. If, indeed, this should be interrupted by a speedy second coming, it will be the better 'to be found among those labouring to make the day of grace known before it be too late, 2 Cor. vi. 1, 2, and hastening the coming of the day of God, 2 Peter iii. 12'. Bickersteth is best described as neither a pre- nor post-millennialist, but as an advocate who was ready to give scope to either form as long as it was appropriately shaped to excite devotion and energy.[20]

His ideas and those of the *Dialogues* ran closely parallel. He wished 'to view the subject more in the practical application than in minute anticipated declaration of future events'.[21] Irving and Drummond were as little interested in minute prediction and as fully concerned with practical application. But they relied completely upon an imminent end; Bickersteth contented himself with the safer belief that an imminent end was both likely and desirable. This difference, and differences in situation and temperament, allowed him to find a modest but real validity in the works which would occupy the interim. What were for the Albury prophets mere works of darkness were for him works of light—a faint enough light, but still a real one.

As his central teaching is close to that of Irving and Drummond, he and they also share many secondary positions. He held out, as they did, the prospect of especially heavy punishment for unfaithful rulers, magistrates and ministers. He expected internal disorder to be the prelude to the second coming. He contended that political quietism was the correct behaviour for believers, a modest relation to their divine right politics. He, too, saw about him the collapse of traditional social order. Like Irving, he reflected upon the incompleteness of the dead saints in their separate state. Again like Irving, he stressed the effectiveness of millennialism in shaping character and prompting action, similarly describing death as an object of terror rather than of hope. He insisted on a literal interpretation (noting his own past allegorical errors); the coming in the clouds, for example, meant just that. He offered the millennial kingdom as a compensation to sufferers in the present life. So extensive a correspondence between the zealots of Albury and Regent Square and the sober ecclesiastical statesman places them in a truer context than the extravagances that accompanied their decline.

Another notable evangelical, Henry Gauntlett, close friend to Rowland Hill and vicar of John Newton's parish of Olney, affords a further example of this correspondence, though few can have known about it until after his death. In 1817 he participated in a series of lectures at Ely Chapel addressed to the Jews on their future state. From these lectures grew his *Exposition of the . . . Revelation* (1821), a book which is said to have earned him £700. Gauntlett conceded that the hypothesis of a personal reign of Christ at Jerusalem was 'highly plausible' and 'exceedingly affecting to the mind', and that it had made some progress. Nevertheless, he firmly rejected it as unscriptural. These opinions were tucked away in an appendix to the second edition in which Basilicus (i.e. Lewis Way) was put right on the matter. Way replied in an ill-tempered pamphlet in 1822, and the two also engaged in controversy in the *Jewish Expositor*.

Though he anticipated some disasters, Gauntlett was optimistic and progressive. 'The dawn of this blessed era is already approaching. . . . Let us rejoice in the gradual progress which the gospel is making in our own age, and welcome those various societies and individuals engaged in promoting its universal flow. Hail! ye Bible Societies! Hail! ye Tract Societies! You will probably exist to witness the millennial glory of Christ.'[22] Even a determined post-millennialist could get excited, if rather humourlessly, when his mind ran upon missions and tracts. But this optimism did not last; a more overt and compensatory millennialism took its place.

His reaction to Catholic Emancipation was strikingly similar to that of Irving and Drummond, though it was expressed only in family letters which were subsequently included in the Memoir introducing his collected sermons. The new legislation 'would, he believed, accelerate the expected struggle between the christian and antichristian powers, previous to the establishment of the Redeemer's Kingdom, during the millennial age'. He saw the people of Great Britain as close to 'moral insanity' and ready to break loose from 'their social and religious obligations'. Scripture encourages 'the pleasing hope, that better days are not far distant', but only after 'great calamities and afflictions, and the triumph of evil in a very high degree'. Great Britain was 'no longer a Protestant country. What then must be the consequence? Shall we suffer with popery?' Gauntlett feared very much that she would. He compared the ministry and the Commons' majority to Caiaphas; they were acting only on expediency and had left God and religion out of the question. 'We live, my dear H. in a most interesting, extraordinary, and awful age of the world. I hope you, dear E., and the whole of our numerous and scattered family, may make our calling and election sure for the eternal state to which we are now hastening; into which, in a *short* time, I *must* and you *may* enter.'

The Reform Bill struggle turned his fears into near-certainty. He saw the 'prevalence of the democratic spirit' as the cause of 'revolutions, which will introduce the dreadful calamities to take place previous to a better and more holy order of things'. 'Probably' the Church of England would be afflicted and tried, even overturned, 'but if it be cast down it will rise again, purified by the furnace of affliction.' Early in 1832 the cholera came to Olney, producing 'an appalling sensation in the minds of the inhabitants'. Gauntlett shared their horror. 'May God . . . stop its progress in our beloved, but apostatizing country.' He went on: 'The latter epithet is a strong one, but I believe it is correct; although there are doubtless a large number of godly and devoted people among us. If our country is spared, it will be spared for their sakes.'[23]

The ingredients of the Albury response are all here: the apostate nation, inter-related social, political, religious and moral disorders, despair at the present situation, hope only over the bridge of calamity, judgement, wrath and purification, the saving role of a faithful remnant, and the millennium as the ultimate righter of wrongs. Gauntlett had not long to live when he wrote these pessimistic letters. Had he lived longer to bring out (like Bickersteth) a new edition, it would surely have been greatly revised. No more than Bickersteth can one imagine Gauntlett joining the excited groups at Albury and Regent Square; nevertheless, he too was a brother under the skin.

Bickersteth and Gauntlett, unlike Irving and Drummond, were professionals within the establishment, and as professionals disinclined to run to extremes, and especially to attempt to translate extreme opinion into extreme action. The same professionalism kept McNeile in line, Frere at a remove, and Faber wholly apart. These latter were professionals in a double sense; they were also specialist exegetes for whom the time-intervals and the symbol-values were an occupation rather than an instrument of regeneration. They were not distracted by strange happenings; they kept to their texts and their calculations, occasionally taking time off to condemn the exegetical errors of the self-styled students of prophecy. For them, prophecy was a gentlemanly occupation; they were not tempted to go into the market place with their message. Further, these professionals, after noting the imperfections of their country, looked beyond to grander and more remote visions: the future of the Jews, upheavals on the Continent and in the Near East, the revival of Catholicism. McNeile, Way, Wolff, Frere, Cuninghame, Faber and Bickersteth, all had their eyes upon these more distant horizons. A commentator had to connect Antichrist, Armageddon, the Messiah, the Jews and the millennium to Great Britain not merely as an abstract entity or as a disposable instrument, but as the critical locus of turmoil, disorder and active infidelity, and then to be obsessed with this connexion, before he ceased to be a prophetic specialist and became himself a prophet. It is in this obsessiveness, perhaps strangely but perhaps not, that Keble and Newman were closer in spirit to Irving and Drummond than were the professional specialists. They too were in revolt against the situation of their lives; they too were pre-occupied with prevalent iniquity and embattled virtue.

In its early years the Tractarian movement had a prophetic fervour and an apocalyptic flavour. Newman's reaction to Catholic Emancipation, his campaign against Peel, his horror of republicanism and his later speculation about the possible connexion between Antichrist and the Anti-Corn Law League, Keble's discovery of national apostacy in the ecclesiastical reform, all show the characteristic prophetic grounding of immense conclusions upon trivial evidence. Neither Keble nor Newman were specialists in prophecy; neither was tempted into excesses in print or in action. But in their sermons, designed for a pastoral situation, they had affinities with the other writers here discussed, affinities which are quite as significant as the very real differences.

The straightforward Keble is a clearer case than the more convoluted Newman. Some of his sermons for the season of Advent show that in a pastoral context he was as concerned as Irving or Bickersteth to use the anticipation of the last days to excite devotion and preparedness. This is more evident in his ambiguities than in his plain statements. Remarks like 'He will very soon be here, that is quite certain, and he has given us all notice', and 'the youngest will find he has but a short time', could in context refer either to the death of the individual or to the end of the world; one suspects that Keble was quite content with the ambiguity.[24]

As a preacher Keble invited his hearers both to believe that the end of the world will be soon and to act as if it will be soon. The second invitation interested him most, but the first is dropped into the exhortation from time to time as a bald assertion—'we are sure it will be; we are sure it will be'—to reinforce his pastoral appeal. This 'soonness' was backed up by a thorough-going literalism: the graves will in fact open, there will be a meeting of parted friends, physical defects and diseases will be cured, and earth will actually burn, and a select few saints will rule with Christ. There is not a little relish in his picture of the judgement: 'That which is all horror to the one will be most sweet and pleasant to the other.'[25]

All this was to encourage right conduct. Keble, far from speculating whether the last day was close or distant, argued that this information had been deliberately withheld by God so that men could never be sure that it will not be tomorrow. He explored this position quite elaborately in 'Watching for the unknown Day'.[26] If men know that something is going to happen like a schoolboy with a lesson to learn they seek to know exactly when it will happen. But, of deliberate purpose, men are never told when they will die or when the world will end. The information is 'kept back, that people might not, in their irreligious foolishness, fancy that it was far off'. Were men told when the day would come, were it early or late, they would not be in a correct state of mind: 'if we knew the exact time to be near, we should hardly be in a condition to choose; if we knew it to be what we call afar off, we should hardly, I fear, be minded to choose right.' Accordingly, men should always live as if the time were close. At this point, Keble, to diminish the force of the 'if' in his argument, set out considerations which the hearer was permitted to assume to be arguments for a fairly proximate ending.

Certainly no one knows when the end will come but 'certain events are foretold' which will be the sign of its coming: 'there are tokens of the old age of the world . . . great afflictions, false Christs, and false prophets, wars and rumours of wars, famines and troubles, the truth persecuted, iniquity abounding, the love of the greater part waxing cold.' Even the youngest of his hearers, Keble proceeded, 'must have seen and heard of too much of this sort of sign . . . a great deal of the news . . . is such as ought to put us in mind continually that the coming of the Lord draweth nigh.' Every war, plague, disturbance, bad season and 'gross wickedness' is a 'token of the coming of our Lord'. In the word 'token' lies that ambiguity typical of the preacher anxious neither to say more than he ought nor to surrender any sanction over conduct he could retain.

The sermon closed with a description of the conduct proper to Christians. On the one hand it is to perform duties in church, family and society, as clergy who rule and laity who obey, as children, parents, servants and masters, as contented poor and generous rich, as pure youth and penitent old. On the other, it is to be 'continually looking up . . . and running to the door, and watching every sound'. 'Friends,' the sermon concluded, 'neighbours, Christian brethren, I beseech you think on these things; for depend on it, the best of us has a great deal to do, and the youngest will find he has but a short time.' And with this calculated ambiguity the existentialist case for a belief in an imminent end may rest.

Newman also held that to believe in an imminent end was psychologically beneficial. But this opinion was part of a larger and more searching examination of the nature of human life in which he laid great stress upon the entire wickedness and moral nullity of the world, the merits even of superstitious and credulous opinions on the second coming, and the wickedness and/or folly of those who allow millennial imaginings to take them out of the confines of orthodoxy. The evidence for these statements lies scattered through the *Parochial and Plain Sermons*. Put together, it suggests that though Newman could not be considered a colleague either of the prophetic professionals nor of the self-styled prophets, he shared a significant territory with both, and further, that this shared territory was intimately related to the world-fear and world-hatred that underlay his hard-won urbanity. 'Life,' as he put it in one of these sermons, 'is well enough in its way; but it does not satisfy.'[27] One who found life so could not but be drawn to the ancient images of its cessation.

In 'The Religion of the Day'[28] he developed an argument very similar to the attack in the *Dialogues* upon 'unsanctified benevolence'. The devil is always at work to create a counter-religion sufficiently resembling Christianity to be a successful deception. In the dark ages the counter-religion stressed the fear to the exclusion of the love of God. Currently, 'the world's religion' was the opposite perversion. 'It has taken the brighter side of the Gospel,—its tidings of comfort, its precepts of love; all darker, deeper views of man's condition and prospects being comparatively forgotten.' Conscience and authority were replaced by 'the so-called moral sense' and 'the rule of expediency'. Guilt and 'prospective punishment' were rejected, and with them 'those fearful images of Divine wrath with which the Scriptures abound'. Benevolence was thought the prime virtue; austerity held to be absurd; bad conduct avoided only because it was vulgar. The cultivated mind busies itself seeking fresh information, novelties even in religion, and change for its own sake. This partial Christianity was a merely human thing, even though in taking a 'general colouring from Christianity' it was improved by what it borrowed. However, it 'includes no true fear of God, no fervent zeal for his honour, no deep hatred of sin, no horror at the sight of sinners, no indignation and compassion at the blasphemies of heretics, no zealous adherence to doctrinal truth'. Newman passed to a discussion of the consequences of this parody-Christianity, for both believers and unbelievers. For the latter it simply confirmed their assumption that religion did not matter except as a soothing appurtenance to a civilized life. For believers the result was equally disastrous.

One consequence of its influence was that 'Many religious men, rightly or not, have long been expecting a millennium of purity and peace for the Church.' Newman declined to say whether men are right or wrong to expect a millennium. But for those who do expect it, 'it has become a temptation to take up and recognise the world's religion. . . . They have more or less identified their vision of Christ's kingdom with the elegance and refinement of mere human civilisation; and have hailed every evidence of improved decency, every wholesome civil regulation, every beneficent and enlightened act of state policy, as signs of their coming Lord.' The indictment continued in terms closely parallel to those used by Irving and Drummond. Such millennialists have co-operated with open infidels; they have defended reforms in spite of the injustice so caused and the hallowed traditions so violated; they have thought 'that bad men are to be the immediate instruments of the approaching advent of Christ'. In brief, though Newman refrained from a verdict upon the general question of millennial expectations, he was as sure as the Albury prophets that the optimistic, progressive post-millennialism of his day was a grievous error. Their shared certainty was derived from a shared conviction that the world and the word existed in outright opposition to each other. Relations between the two were in the sphere of judgement, condemnation and wrath, not of co-operation, harmony and progress.

The sermon 'Watching'[29] had for its text 'Take ye heed, watch and pray; for ye know not when the time is'—a plain enough indication that Newman was not concerned with the timing of the second coming. He was wholly interested in the psychological benefits of watching expectantly for it. He developed the theme that 'watching' is the activity which chiefly distinguishes the true Christian from the false; it is a sure protection against 'a worldly religiousness'. 'True Christians, whoever they are, watch, and inconsistent Christians do not.' At this point, however, Newman took great care to deny that sharp distinction between the Christs of the two comings, between obscure humility and displayed power, which was always implicit and often explicit in adventist writings. 'This then is to watch . . . to desire His second coming, from our affectionate and grateful remembrance of His first.' Holy Communion too, is a constantly repeated new and identical coming. Newman will have nothing to do with adventist yearnings which spring from a distaste for the Church and its sacramental life, and from a disinclination to accept the incarnation as a complete revelation. Nevertheless the second coming will certainly be catastrophic, though in no way a further revelation. When it comes, 'what will this world have then done for us? wretched, deceiving world! which will then be burned up, unable not only to profit us, but to save itself.' Newman quite certainly believed that God had come into the world he had first made, but this belief did nothing to endear the world to him. Irving took the 'new earth' aspect of the apocalypse more seriously, possibly because he saw more far-reaching implications in the creation and the incarnation, implications which required a coming in power and glory.

Just because adventist expectations placed the world in such a sharp contrast to God, Newman had considerable sympathy with them when they took the form of humble credulity and superstition. He condemned two millennialist extremes: both progressive optimism and the wild imaginings of the Fifth Monarchy kind. But as long as he remained within the orthodoxy of the Church the most deluded watcher was not beyond approval. The sermon 'Waiting for Christ' exemplified this adventist application of his well-known argument for the conservative function of superstition.[30] Here he set out to answer the objection that since Christians have always been expecting the coming and have as regularly been disappointed, the whole thing is 'a mere weakness'. The answer lay in the assertion that superstition is preferable to 'high-minded security', that 'better a thousand times think Him coming when He is not, than once think Him not coming when He is.' The difference of attitude was that 'between Scripture and the world'. This expectation, he went on, had not been more regularly disappointed than the confidence of sceptics that Christianity was about to pass away. Indeed, in a sense, Christianity was always passing away. 'It is so uncongenial to the human mind, it is so spiritual, and man is so earthly, it is apparently so defenceless, and has so many strong enemies, so many false friends, that every age, as it comes, may be called "the last time".' It is, in fact, drawing to an end, it 'is likely to end any day'; it is 'a wholesome thing to live as if *that* will come in our day, which may come any day'.

At this stage in the argument Newman took up the Augustinian identification of the present age of the Church with the millennium. Before Christ came there were 'successive revelations' which led towards the full gospel. 'But when once the Christ had come, as the Son over His own house, and with His perfect Gospel, nothing remained but to gather in His saints. No higher Priest could come,—

no truer doctrine. The Light and Life of men had appeared, and had suffered, and had risen again; and nothing more was left to do. Earth had had its most solemn event, and seen its most august sight; and therefore it was the last time.' The final end has already happened. The contrast with the true apocalyptic exaltation of the second coming as the event which should lend dignity to the first is clear; herein lay the essential difference between Newman and the millennialists. It was, once again, the difference between Augustine and Joachim.

It cannot matter, then, if men were 'mistaken in what they took to be the signs of Christ's coming . . . they were not mistaken in looking out, and that for Christ'. Newman would 'rather be he, who from love of Christ and want of science, thinks some strange sight in the sky, comet or meteor, to be the sign of His coming, than the man, who, from mere knowledge and from lack of love, laughs at the mistake.' It was typical of him that he failed to consider the case of the man who had both love and science, and who pronounced the belief a mistake without laughing. Through such credulity, Newman continued, uneducated men, impressed by strange sights, earthquakes, famine and disease, and educated men, meditating on wars and revolutions, have contrived to keep 'their hearts awake for Christ'. One day the signs will be the right ones; it is not superstitious to look for them now. 'It is better to be wrong in our watching than not to watch at all.'

However, Newman excluded some men from the ranks of the acceptably credulous. 'Enthusiasts, sectaries, wild presumptious men, *they* have said that He was *actually* come, or they have pointed out the exact year and day in which He would come. Not so His humble followers.' This *caveat* begs a number of questions. First, it was altogether misleading to lump together, for example, the followers of Joanna and such eminently pious predictors as Faber and Bicheno. Second, the lack of humility displayed by many prophetic controversialists was simply a characteristic of theological argument in general. Third, the whole history of millennialism shows that as long as such expectations are considered legitimate some men will feel encouraged to predict the times at which the expectations will be realized. Newman's human sympathies were too narrow for him to be able to recognize all the men who were his fellows. Just as there is a continuum between Master Mede and the Fifth Monarchy men, so there is between Newman and the Albury prophets, for all his distaste for 'men who profess to work miracles, or who denounce the Church as apostate, or who maintain that none are saved but those who agree with themselves'. Such men, it may be, could be forgiven for passing over Newman's rather disingenuous argument that 'I come quickly' means 'I come suddenly' and not 'I come soon', and for taking more seriously his constant stress that it was right to watch for the signs of the second coming. They could go on to take heart from his abrupt distinction between the world and true religion, and from his disgust with the former. They could be greatly encouraged by his defence of attitudes which the world pronounced superstitious, especially the habit of seeing 'Divine meaning' in 'the accidents (as they are called) of life'. They could consider themselves untouched by the qualification that 'It is certain that this regard to outward occurrences does become superstition, when it is found in men of irreligious lives, or of slender knowledge of Scripture.' For it is clear that men of impeccable piety and considerable learning thought it proper to press enquiry further than Newman would allow to be permissible.

No one, not even Newman, could avoid an implicit embarrassment when dealing with the end of the world, nor a certain disingenuousness when applying it to a pastoral situation. If the biblical texts are taken seriously (and few at that time did not equate 'seriously' with 'literally') then they will invite the sort of speculative excitement which an orthodox apologist will deplore. Newman had not contrived to escape from the 'as if' situation in which Irving was caught; perhaps he was caught more deeply. Irving really believed that the last things would happen soon, and had a parallel argument that showed, even if this was not so, that it was good to live as if it was so. Newman did not believe that the last things were nearly upon him; nevertheless he argued for the benefits of believing and living as if they were. As an Augustinian, he could recover consistency by adding that the last events had, in principle, occurred, that the Church and the millennium were one. Could this be seriously said of the established Church in early nineteenth-century England? Newman told his hearers to find the last events in their lives within it. This was not an answer which would for long satisfy him; by 1845 he would be pointing to a life within another Church. Others, equally dissatisfied, had other exits: who is to judge between them?

All the millennialists, from the Southcottians to the scholarly professionals, were looking for a place in which God's will was wholly done, in which righteousness reigned. They found it in many places: in Albury chapel, in the Zion on the Mississippi, in the future Jewish kingdom in Palestine. Newman and Keble were not millennialists except in the Augustinian sense, but even the Augustinian has to go beyond equating the Church and the millennium, and ask himself where is the Church, where is the saving remnant? The Oxford movement and the movement to Rome are Augustinian equivalents to the millennialist quest for Zion. Fittingly, world-weariness and the apocalyptic shadow hang over both.

VII: John Ward—the Messiah as Agitator

All theorizing based upon the biblical images of world history and its ending is either implicitly or explicitly political. Not every expositor was a political controversialist but, mere hobbyists on one side, exposition usually required an expression of political and social opinions. The time and manner of the world's ending can hardly be separated from consideration of its moral character; the new world of blessedness is a comment on the world as it is. The biblical writers always had political reality in mind—the character of their own people and of its oppressors, the future of both, and the reversal of an actual situation of supremacy and humiliation. The great prophetic symbols, the statue and the beasts in Daniel, the wars and rumours of wars in the Gospels, the Babylon of Revelation, the time intervals and the periods of history, were already political statements, and were merely altered in focus when applied to the history of Europe. Antichrist, Armageddon and the returned Christ are never less than political, however much more they may be.

The stream of prophetic commentary from the 1780s to the 1830s was really if not solely a way of conducting a moralistic political discussion. The commentators, from professionals like Faber and Bicheno to those for whom the vocabulary was both available and meaningful, like Priestley and Newman, used the prophetic tradition as a way of evaluating their society and its political life. Irving and Drummond went further. They believed that they were embarked upon a programme of change which would begin with the Church and end with society and government. They invited Great Britain to remake herself according to a model of purity and righteousness. They would, surely, have been content to wait a long time for the end of all things if it had proved possible to talk the country into righteousness.

This politics was entirely one of aspiration; no important politician heeded Cuninghame's advice to take the prophetic gospel into the senate as a reforming programme. Evangelical politicians certainly chipped away at the grosser abuses of British life, secured public money for the building of churches and tried to tighten up Sunday observance. But only one politician of even minor note, the hapless Spencer Perceval, summoned the ministry and Parliament to total repentance and reformation. And he could be relied upon to empty the House. When the cholera came to Great Britain, the Government was persuaded to meet it with prayer rather than physic, reverting to the wartime habit of appointing a day of fast and repentance to implore divine favour. Though this was an evangelical rather than a prophetic achievement, it is noteworthy that Irving waited upon Melbourne to urge its adoption, and that Perceval moved the motion in the Commons. It is not likely that Earl Grey and his Whig colleagues took the matter very seriously—nevertheless, it says something for the prevalence of the habit of seeing the divine hand in these visitations that such a fast could be proclaimed. Radicals outside the House were enraged at what they considered an insult to the permanently fasting poor; John Ward, the main subject of this chapter, took a long step towards his imprisonment for blasphemy by ostentatiously feasting on a leg of mutton. He was incoherently denounced by Perceval when his friends petitioned the House for his release.[1]

Perceval himself was not quite happy with the fast; he questioned the motives which underlay its appointment. On its eve he delivered an apocalyptic speech in the Commons.[2] He had been especially angered by the omission of the name of God from the English Reform Bill, and reasoned that its inclusion in the Scottish Bill proved the English omission to be deliberate. It arose, he went on, from the fact that ministers obeyed the people rather than God, for which sin they and the country would be punished. Further, ministers had not proclaimed the fast out of proper motives: 'it has not been because they see in the cholera a scourge which is hanging over the land, or [in] the disturbances of the country signs of God's approaching judgments, that they have reluctantly determined to appoint a fast.' Their act was a mockery of religion for which God would punish them.

For most of his speech he was surrounded by members trying to quieten him—sons of prime ministers, even evangelical prime ministers, were embarrassing when enthusiastic—and much of what he had to say was inaudible to the reporters in what they called 'indescribable confusion'. Still, his drift was clear enough. 'I pray ye to turn to his love before it is too late; for be ye assured that the storm is coming, and that he is nigh, who is at once your God, your Saviour, and your Judge.' Clearly Perceval was behaving hysterically, and the Commons found the spectacle little to its taste; but his views were identical with those of the esteemed Gauntlett in private letters, the urbane Drummond in *Social Duties*, and the eloquent Newman in his pulpit.

Scarcely less intemperate opinions had been expressed in the House of Commons only a little earlier on the subject of Catholic Emancipation. Bransby Cooper echoed the prophetic nationalism of his namesake Edward Cooper in asserting that the 'vital principle was, that the government should be wholly, essentially, and exclusively Protestant. If that principle was once broken in upon, the constitution was at an end.' Catholic claims could not be granted without weakening 'the settlement of the House of Brunswick to the throne', reducing Great Britain from her eminence among nations, endangering the Church ('the glory of the Reformation'), and 'contemning that Providence, which had so long and so signally preserved our constitution'. Sir R. Vyvyan saw in emancipation the result of a conspiracy which had been hatched at Rome, furthered by the Holy Alliance and implemented by the Jesuits, to 'restore the Roman Catholic religion, not to its former purity, but to its pristine supremacy'. Sir R. H. Inglis, fresh from his triumph over Peel at Oxford, alleged that 'The moment that one Roman Catholic enters this House, and thus destroys the essential purity and Protestantism of our legislature, that moment is the commencement of a system, which will soon terminate in realising all those evils' which Peel had, in his earlier mind, predicted would result from concession. For Mr Hart Davis this was 'an awful crisis', while Mr Sadler of Newark saw Peel's conversion as 'apostacy' and the opposition to emancipation as 'this sacred, this deserted cause'.[3]

This language is not explicitly prophetic. It is evidence only of vehement anti-popery, desperate alarm at the removal of ancient landmarks and a providential view of history and politics. These are just the emphases that run through counter-revolutionary prophetic expositions since the French Revolution. Given the wide diffusion of prophetic opinions, it is likely that some politicians were at least aware of the prophetic dimension of the arguments they brought forward. The Albury prophets and the extremer evangelicals gave a particular shape to a more generalized response to political change. No doubt they hoped to gain currency and support from this general situation, and this would help explain their tone of complete self-confidence. But the confidence was misplaced; Perceval alone uttered apocalyptic from the floor of the Commons. The prophets and commentators remained political controversialists of the extreme right, well outside the limits of effective political debate.

But the language of prophecy and the image of the millennium was by no means restricted to the more alarmist forms of reaction.

It had equally valid uses among those seeking radical change by political revolution, by economic reorganization and by mass emigration. Succeeding chapters will deal with the millennialism of social change and social revolution, through the examples of John Ward, Robert Owen, James Smith, and the Mormon missionaries.

John Ward was an Irish immigrant, a shipwright and a shoemaker, a veteran of the Battle of Copenhagen, and a political agitator. In his own estimation he was also the Messiah, the Messiah of the first coming, not of the conventional second. He served a prison sentence for his blasphemous claim, but a careful reading of his pamphlets suggests that it meant something both a good deal less and a good deal more than might at first appear.

Though his writings are replete with ambiguities compounded by obscurity and incoherence, there is a good case to be made for the interpretation that his messiahship was essentially a way of claiming to be a new-made man rather than a newly revealed God. His background is intensely sectarian and biblicist; though his central message is post-Christian he did not fully discard the habits of his past. He could not avoid writing of God and of Jesus in conventional terms, though his essential teaching made nonsense of this terminology. Traditional habits die hard: Ward himself thought the historical Jesus to be a fiction, but a leading disciple, Charles Bradley, could write a hymn about him in 1831 which fell into traditional second coming language:

> Jerusalem, proclaim abroad
> The blissful tidings! say, The Lord
> A second time comes down!
> He who for thy Redemption fought,
> Whose strong Right Hand Salvation brought,
> Assumes the Royal Crown.[4]

Again, an ambiguity surrounds his attitude to his Southcottian heritage. Sometimes Joanna is the divine woman and Ward her spiritual son. But at others (and more centrally) he absorbs her role into himself. That the centrality of self and so of humanity was his vital principle is suggested by words taken down in 1836 by the same disciple during an illness not long before his death. He claimed to be 'the *Divine Woman* WISDOM *Herself*!' and went on: 'whatever I go through, I assure you the Lord *is here*—not THE DEITY, but the Man God, and you will know NO *other God* through all Eternity!'[5]

In the obscurer quarters of British towns a numerous population of eccentric zealots were ready for religious novelty and prepared to form new religious communities. Ward's career may be traced with a little assurance, thanks to the volume of his writings and his brief notoriety. In his case, one can achieve an insight into the operations of prophecy and millennialism at a normally sub-historical level. No observer made it his business to record the history of the Southcottian following over these years; Ward's fragmentary account enables one to know a little. He, together with James Smith, is certainly the most significant of Joanna's spiritual children, and easily her most endearing. He was, in spite of his verbiage, a good deal more sensible than many of his celebrated contemporaries. He was not, for all the apparent foolishness of his claim, as gullible as Edward Irving, as fantastic as James Smith, or as cranky as his respectable prophetic adversary Spencer Perceval. He was a radical reformer whose vocabulary of agitation was messianic and millennial. For many millennialists the surge of popular democratic demand signified the coming of Antichrist. For the plebian Ward, clumsy though energetic in utterance, coarse-grained and vulgar, this same surge was the sign of a new era of beneficent anarchy, and he was the first fruits of the time to come. So he called himself Zion ('the place where the Lord dwelleth'), and announced his messiahship. But his millennium is that of a self-liberated humanity.

Joanna Southcott, in ways and for reasons that remain mysterious, had created both a following and an expectation. One may guess at some of the reasons for her success. She had her personal charisma, cool but compelling enough to attract intelligent, educated and respectable men. But more than charisma is needed to explain the appeal of an obscure Devonshire countrywoman, barely literate and yet embedding her message (whatever it might have been) in a mass of preposterous publications. Evidently the illuminist currents of the seventeenth century still ran deep in hidden places, especially the expectation of a new age springing from a new revelation, symbolized by the woman who would be its mediator and, in whatever manner, give birth to the Messiah. The turmoils and terrors of the 1790s, which turned scholars and gentlemen to the hope of the Messiah returning in the clouds with glory, turned (so it must be) the minds of obscurer men towards a fresh revelation entrusted to a particular person and resulting in a specific birth. In a Bible-reading country, Revelation's 'woman clothed in the sun' was a familiar image. Joanna's success suggests that some were ready to believe that the metaphor had taken flesh.

Neither her failure in 1814 to bring the new Messiah, Shiloh, to birth, nor her own death, ended her influence. Could the history of Southcottianism be written, its real vigour might well be found in the 1820s and the 1830s. There were, it is sure, plenty of claimants for her mantle. George Turner went about efficiently turning the following into an institution. He and others, Mary Boon, Joseph Allman, Alexander Lindsay and John Wroe, fought for its control. By the later 1820s the main contestants appear to have been Wroe, Ward and, establishing his hold over a section of Wroe's Scottish followers and taking the battle to Wroe's stronghold of Ashton-under-Lyne, James Smith. Smith, however, had plenty of other irons in the fire; Wroe and Ward were the main contestants. Though Ward certainly claimed the right of leadership, he was not much interested at first in the business of running a sect. He and Wroe, on a minute scale, re-enacted the sixteenth- and seventeenth-century sectarian tension between the legalist and the libertarian. Wroe turned his followers into circumcised, bearded, minutely regulated new Israelites, even requiring them to learn Hebrew. Ward proclaimed the anarchic freedom of the new man, free from law and religion, from State and Church. When, by the mid-1830s, his following had evolved its own practices, it was a very loosely structured sect. There was no set worship; the faithful met in 'schools' in which Ward's writings were discussed, quite without special days of observance or fixed forms of procedure.[6]

Ward would have had no eminence beyond that of a Southcottian would-be successor had it not been for the Reform Bill. No editor would have seen fit to give him a place in the *Dictionary of National Biography*. But for a time his libertarianism coincided with the milder radicalism of the universal suffrage movement. The link was anti-clericalism, for Ward, speaking as the founder of the true religion, was second to none in denunciation of the officials of the false one. His vehemence coincided with the polemical needs of reformers outraged by bishops voting against reform, by clerical magistrates, by a national fast. Thus Ward, briefly, had a mass audience at the Rotunda in London and in provincial centres. Pamphlets and speeches poured from him; his trial for blasphemy became a *cause célèbre*; Henry Hunt presented to the Commons a petition pleading a miscarriage of justice, and Joseph Hume supported his appeal. After serving his sentence he sat quietly writing to his followers and publishing these lengthy letters as pamphlets. He died in 1837.

Before his death he had enlisted a scattered following of at least some hundreds. In 1832 a formal statement of belief was published to which were subscribed the names of representatives of congregations in London, Nottingham, Birmingham, Chesterfield, Ashover, Sheffield, Ilkeston, Huddersfield, Barnsley, Pontefract, Blythe,

Bristol and Ashton-under-Lyne. The movement's greatest strength lay in Nottinghamshire, Derbyshire and Yorkshire. G. R. Balleine[7] claims that Ward made hundreds of converts among 'solid . . . business-men' who financed his chapels. Certainly some money was found, for Ward began his mission in no position to pay for the flood of pamphlets which he sent out for nearly ten years. When he and his colleague C. W. Twort were charged with blasphemy in April 1832 they entered into recognizances of £100 each, with two sureties of £50 each. The previous month, at the first hearing, one Sam Dawson, described as a barber as well as an agitator, had been one of their bail.[8] Yet Ward directed his mission to the down-trodden; his prosecution was begun by the Attorney-General because his 'publications were calculated to have the most mischievous effect upon the lower orders of society in particular'. Witnesses testified that great numbers 'of the lower class' assembled to hear him at Derby.[9] It is not likely that solid businessmen crowded to hear him at the Rotunda in 1832. While it is clear that there was money about, and likely that men of some substance took the lead in settled congregations, it is probable that his following was of a lower status. A good deal of the money may have come from the Birmingham firm of Bradley and Holinsworth, tobacco, snuff and cigar manufacturers. Two Bradleys, father and son, figure prominently in Ward's published letters; C. B. Holinsworth remained faithful to the end of a long life. In the 1870s he re-issued three small volumes of Ward's writings and in 1881, to celebrate the centenary of his birth, a brief *Memoir of John Ward*. In 1899-1901 the massive twelve volume *Zion's Works* appeared, with extensive editorial comment by Holinsworth.

In 1881 Holinsworth referred to the sect simply as 'the Believers' and described their decline. 'Of the many hundred Believers that embraced this Faith during its Founder's life but few now exist; and, since his departure, these make no public appearance, living in the contemplation of, and being solely guided by the Written Works bequeathed for their instruction, and kept for future ages.'[10] It is the historian's bad luck that the nineteenth century was not an age of persecution; there is nothing to fill the gap left by the absence of the testimony of inquisitors and informers. The movement became a withdrawn sect and dwindled away. Twort lived on till 1878, dying in Walworth at the age of 93; perhaps he and Holinsworth presided over the shrinking remnant.

There are only fragmentary hints of this kind to suggest the social characteristics of the sect Ward created; a few hundred people in the northern and midlands towns and in London, recruited from small businessmen and workmen. For Ward it was the nucleus of a new humanity; to them and to all who would listen or read he addressed a body of ideas which, for all their confusion, have a recognizable shape. He drew on four main sources for his gospel; heterogenous as they will appear to be, he was able to weld them into a coherent programme. His starting point was the Southcottian expectation of a Messiah; to it he added seventeenth- and eighteenth-century illuminism and mysticism, eighteenth- and nineteenth-century rationalism and atheism, and nineteenth-century political radicalism.

Whether Joanna Southcott had read prophetic expositions or not is quite uncertain. She had undoubtedly read and re-read the Bible, and had absorbed ideas such as those of Jane Lead[11] which exalted the role of women in the new age—both in bringing it into being and in shaping its distinctive character. Her multitudinous writings, the persistence and fidelity of her followers and her cool self-assurance in announcing that she would give birth to the Messiah at a particular time, gave the millennial hope a personal immediacy which even the most assured of specialists could not lend it. The expectation, once excited, was not to be immediately destroyed. A line of visionaries tried to fill the gap which her death had left, each (no doubt) with a sufficient explanation for her apparent failure. Among the claimants was another Devonshire woman, Mary Boon, under whom Ward served his apprenticeship in millennialism.

About 1813 or 1814, over forty years of age, with a long experience of poverty and war behind him, and with a religious restlessness which had taken him in and out of half a dozen sects, he read one of Joanna's publications, *The Fifth Book of Wonders*, and was convinced that its message came from God. His troubles did not disappear at once—only in 1827 or 1828 did he achieve full assurance and peace—but *The Fifth Book* marked the turning point. He joined Mary Boon's group in Devon, becoming 'reader of the word to the people' and amanuensis to this illiterate prophetess. As she instructed him to become a eunuch for the sake of the Kingdom of Heaven, he left his wife and children—but not permanently yet, for his luckless wife was able to have him committed to the workhouse in 1828.

There are only a few points of clarity in succeeding years. From his new chronology, it may be taken that his belief in himself as redeemer first took shape in 1825: he and his followers numbered the years from that event. *The Fifth Book* had convinced him that God was love; it filled him with a love for the human race, made him seek to enlighten his fellow men and assured him that the time of redemption was near. Probably the experience of 1825 was the conviction that he was the selected agent of this redemption. The next three years Holinsworth interpreted as the complete transformation of his nature, culminating with the entry of the word of God into him with power late in 1827 and the commencement of his mission in 1828.[12] This began with a letter *To the Believers in the Divine Mission of Joanna*, dated 26 November 1828.

So a tormented life found resolution, and Ward's final decade of furious agitation and continual writing began. The fragment of autobiography from which these details are taken[13] shows a man who had known constant anguish. His childhood and youth, in Ireland and after 1790 in England, were filled with a fear of hell, reinforced by regular Bible reading. A life which he considered to be one of extreme dissipation, especially as a shipwright upon a man-of-war, deepened his conviction that he was damned. He looked at his dead shipmates after the Battle of Copenhagen and wondered why he, the wickedest man on board, should have been spared. On his discharge in 1803 he married a wife who was 'fond of going to hear preaching'. In Wales he joined the Methodists, but remained as full of sin as ever. He returned to London, his sin still with him. Here he heard a Baptist preacher shout 'Victory! Victory! Victory!' and this reminded him of a dream he had had three years before. An angel had taken him by ship to a place where lay chained to the ground a man sixty feet long. The angel gave him a trumpet and told him to sound victory, but he could not. Then the angel sounded victory so loud that he awoke. Until he heard the preacher this dream simply confirmed his conviction that he would never have victory over his sins. But the preacher's cry made him think that perhaps the dream was to tell him that he would not win until he knew what sin was. So he joined the preacher's chapel, and was dipped, and hoped that he would be a *little* changed, for the Baptists had told him that it was a divine ordinance—'but, alas! I found myself just the same being.' He went from chapel to chapel, without peace, from Calvinist to Sandemanians; he began preaching in country villages.

At this point he happened upon *The Fifth Book* and began his upward climb. However, his troubles continued. The Methodists made him a local preacher but then dismissed him for Southcottian heresy. He lost his friends and his shoe-making business suffered because he would talk to one and all of the prophetess. Nor would the Southcottians have him, for he had not known Joanna and he differed from them on many points. He had to work like 'an entire slave' to feed his large family, but his wife treated his views with scorn and contempt. Then came the time with Mary Boon; his desertion of his wife; his acceptance of his mission.

At first Ward's bid to lead the followers of Joanna was based upon a claim that he was in some sense the promised Shiloh. He simply held that she had been right in her belief that the Messiah, the new man, had come; he added that he was the new man. He did not say that any miraculous circumstances surrounded his birth; he meant simply that the spirit of God, which is the spirit of liberty, had entered into him. Other Messiahs have made more circumstantial claims, but none less supernatural. He made it his mission to share this spirit, this messiahship, with others. For all the fantastic biblical exegesis with which he dressed up his calling, he was in essence a prophet of human freedom, emerging with some force and cogency from the shadow world of the sectaries. It is difficult to imagine a later nineteenth-century agitator serving such an apprenticeship, but in the prophetic mood of the early 1830s it did not disqualify him. On the contrary, for a time it helped him.

In 1828 he claimed a miraculous transfer of authority from Joanna. In the letter *To the Believers* she is said to have visited him in the workhouse to which he had been committed on the complaint of his wife. Incorporated in the letter are her instructions to her followers to accept Ward as their leader. Under, as he believed, direct divine guidance he was able to escape from the workhouse and 'was led by an invisible hand to the house of Mr. Gompertz, Granby Gardens, Marsh Gate, Lambeth'. The account goes on: 'as I stood there, a Voice said to me—which I knew to be the Lord's,—"You must warn the people." I said, O my Lord, what shall I say? I was answered, "Tell them that SHILOH the SPIRIT OF TRUTH, that was to guide the people into all truth, IS COME!"'[14] This letter, the first of very many, has the characteristic signature 'THE UNITED ZION, THE LORD IS HERE!'

If there had been no more to it, Ward would be just another deluded sectary distinguished from others merely by the volume of his writings. But he felt other influences in the later 1820s, notably that of Richard Carlile. When he gave an account of the role of the woman in 1834, it is quite without references to Joanna. (Indeed Holinsworth felt it necessary to insert a note in the first letter explaining that the talk of Joanna and of the Mother was simply a way of appealing to the limited understandings of the London Southcottians.) In this later epistle[15] the whole argument was firmly grounded upon the glory of the love between man and woman; the entire dreadful history of so-called Christianity was described as a result of the 'unholy connection of men with men'. The goddesses of the Greeks and the Romans were anticipations of the 'Deification *of the Woman*'. Further, 'it is clear from the Scriptures, and from all prophetic writings, that in the end there was a Marriage union to take place between God [defined elsewhere as the eternal man] and His creature, Woman,—I mean the Spiritual woman or She-man, a being made for the express purpose of *introducing* the truth into *the world by a birth* of it.' This union could not occur till 'One . . . of our species is found, who possessed in his mere natural constitution a greater power of the natural love . . . than any other, and in whose heart was the *secret* and sincere desire to know Divine love and wisdom.' The masculine 'his' is significant here. The divine woman had become a way of talking about human goodness and freedom. He, because he was receptive to truth and filled with love, was chosen as the first fruits of those who should be free. If Joanna had made the mistake of re-mythologizing the mystical humanism of Jane Lead, Ward had done his best to demythologize her legacy.

Joanna's writings were not his only access to the mystical tradition. He referred to rabinnical writings and Jewish traditions, to an unspecified 'Quietist' tract, to Messiah stories in Chinese, Greek and Syrian legends and in the Vega, to Jane Lead and Emanuel Swedenborg. He was aware that he wrote within a tradition; he believed that he was the fulfilment of it. 'There have been many . . . visited by the Spirit, who went through an experience (both of evil and good, as they are called *in the world*), *as types* of the wonderful and marvellous work of the Regeneration and Transmutation of the human essence, showing how the human essence should pass into the divine, and become a "partaker of the Divine nature," thereby becoming God-man.'[16] Jane Lead, especially, he hailed as a precursor, quite properly in view of her stress upon the doctrine of the woman which Ward had first absorbed from Joanna. Probably he knew her through the 1830 Nottingham re-publication of her *Divine Revelations and Prophecies*. This work contains a set of heroic couplets looking forward to the birth of a new Benjamin in England, a prediction Ward applied to himself. Certainly he was keenly aware of the seventeenth century. In Derby gaol he consoled himself with the thought that George Fox and Ludowick Muggleton had been imprisoned here before him. He may, even, have talked with still-extant Muggletonians. In 1828 Carlile, to whom Ward was close by this time, had publicized in the *Lion*[17] the existence of tiny groups of Muggletonians in Nottingham and London, and was delighted with their lack of superstition and their simple humanism. Both towns were Southcottian centres, and it would be strange if such a sect-sampler as Ward had not sought them out. Ward found plenty to feed his messianism, especially in those branches of the mystical tradition in which individual illumination had developed into a straightforward humanism.

His message was, quite simply, a call to be free: perhaps to be free especially in that activity, sexual behaviour, in which men were then least free. There were other and easier ways to the same conclusion, but Ward's way, in the context of sectarianism and prophecy, was a valid one. And it was not, in the event, so very distant from the ways of James Smith and the St Simonians.

But liberation of the affections (so it may be suggested for Ward's writings yield nothing explicit on this point) demand a total liberation of all relationships. Whatever Ward may have taught his sect about sexual behaviour, he certainly taught all who would listen that the freedom which he enjoyed and was commissioned to impart was total freedom. Here the influence of Carlile probably counted for a good deal, and perhaps that of Carlile's co-worker, the ex-clergyman Robert Taylor. In particular, the bits and pieces of comparative religion which appear in Ward's writings may owe their origin to Taylor. For Taylor, such parallels helped destroy Christianity; for Ward they were corroborative evidence for his own correctness.

The impact of Carlile's version of eighteenth-century rationalism contributed to Ward's spiritual crisis of 1827.[18] During this decade Carlile published two strenuously anti-Christian journals, the *Republican* and the *Lion*, and founded a group of 'Zetetic' societies devoted to the study of science as the key to nature, a study which would free men from inherited superstition. Politically Carlile's influence was radical and democratic; religiously it was atheist and anti-clerical. In the *Lion*[19] Carlile jestingly referred to himself as Antichrist to the deluded Christians and Christ to the liberated Christians; he preached sermons; he published tracts with titles like *The Gospel according to Richard Carlile* and *Carlile's Sermon on the Mount*. The aping of Christian terminology was tactical, but Ward went through a similar process of personal indentification in deadly seriousness. Though the point is speculative, it seems reasonable to find here another element in Ward's messianic claim. From Carlile, too, he probably derived his rejection of most of the supernatural elements in religion, and his linking together of clerical and secular establishments into a total system of oppression. From deists like Rowland Detrosier writing in Carlile's journals, Ward may have taken his notions of the infinite spirit and the eternal reason. Through Carlile and his associates, the enlightenment of the philosophes flowed to meet native English millennialism. The theoretically distinct approaches of the progressive and the millennialist, the one stressing human effort, the other divine intervention, did not in Ward's propaganda preserve their separate identities. God had intervened in Ward; men would progress by following Ward.

It is easy to imagine Ward's despair when he met Carlile's arguments against the historicity of the Bible and the existence of Jesus. His violent and excitable nature, his persistent quest for religious assurance and his engrained biblicism can only have responded with anguish to an argument which held that the stories of Jesus had been invented by a corrupt clergy to underpin their system of fraud. Yet there were close links between the philosopher and the prophet, especially in antipathy to clerical establishments. Already Ward had seen the falsity of the churches in their rejection of Joanna; now under Carlile's guidance he came to see this piece of iniquity as part of a greater pattern. In meeting Carlile's ideas Ward suffered from something like cultural shock, but he was resilient enough to produce a synthesis, a sort of private adjustment cult.

There is ingenuity in this synthesis. He accepted the non-historicity of the Bible, but he went on to assert that while not a true description, it was a true prediction, especially of the coming of the Messiah. It was true of the future, not of the past. The book was of divine origin; only the interpretation that made it the record of a redemption already achieved was a clerical fraud. The Gospels did not tell of a Messiah who had come eighteen centuries ago, but of one who was at that moment going about his work. While the clergy had perpetuated a fraud and caused human misery by their talk of sin, Ward (who had tried out a number of their remedies) would tell the truth about religion and free men from sin. It was, in its way, an effective response to Carlile. It retained the fervour of prophecy; it added the cutting edge of radical criticism; it preserved plenty of opportunities for the habit of biblical exegesis, an essential employment for any prophet of the times. Ward spent page after page and hour after hour applying the total biblical corpus to his own person.

No part of scripture was immune from his personalization. Satan, abolished as a source of evil, became a symbol of unconverted man—that is, Ward himself before he was redeemed. Christ, by the same process, became the symbol of redeemed man—Ward after he was enlightened. Satan and Christ, B.C. and A.D., stood for Ward sinful and Ward sinless. This rather quaint christology was simply an elaborate way, and a millennial way, of explaining a conversion out of Christianity into a body of belief held to be more rational—the sort of conversion which was to become commoner in the nineteenth century. No one needs to take Ward's messianic claim as seriously as did the scandalized men who denounced and prosecuted him. It is not even necessary to conclude that Ward himself took it as seriously as he appears to say he did. From time to time humanism and pantheism stand out like rocks in the endless sea of allegory: an identification of the trinity with faith, hope and charity; a comparison of God and himself with the sun and the earth.

However daunting Carlile's influence may have been at first—and one is probably justified in regarding the crisis of 1825 to 1828 and its resolution as a product of the simultaneous impact of mystical humanist and rational humanist ideas—before long Ward established an amicable independence from Carlile. In his 'Epistle on Carlile' of 1832[20] Ward agreed that Carlile was right to say that for centuries the shell of religion had been preferred to the kernel, but wrong to think that he had cracked the shell and revealed the kernel. Ward, at this point, was still a deist (and he probably never ceased to be one in some sense); he questioned Carlile's honesty in talking of a deity as if he believed in one. The epistle attacked Carlile's allegorism; it did not defend biblical literalism, but rather Ward's rival allegorism.

Carlile, for his part, thought enough of Ward to try to convert him and his disciples. In 1833 and 1834 he advised Ward to give up all mystery, especially the use of the name 'Zion', and in 1835 there was a correspondence between Carlile and Ward's disciple, the younger Bradley. Possibly their last meeting was in Leeds in 1836, during a lecture tour on which Carlile was interpreting the scriptures in the light of science. Ward, in a wholly friendly tone, proposed to go to Carlile's lecture and challenge him there.[21]

With this complex but strangely coherent background, Ward enjoyed a brief prominence in the early 1830s, as a political agitator and as the founder of a sect. Political excitement is the fourth formative influence, and a vital one. It provided the mould into which all his energy and ardour was poured. He became a twice-weekly speaker at the Rotunda in 1831, and in the same year he hammered the clergy in the weekly parts of *The Judgment Seat of Christ*. He embraced the campaign against church rates, the denunciation of the national fast, and the resistance to the evangelical campaign to step up Sunday observance. He took his campaign out of London to the provinces, and at Derby, already tense from church rate riots, he was arrested, tried for blasphemy, and imprisoned for eighteen months. The libertarian and humanistic side of Ward's credo is obscured by the sheer volume of indigestible biblicizing. But it comes out unmistakably from time to time. In a lecture delivered at the Rotunda in 1831 he told 'True Reformers' to leave behind 'all the Doctrines and Commandments of men. . . . *Observe neither Sabbaths, Feast Days, Fast Days, Good Fridays, nor any other days*, but be free, for God is Love and changeth not. All the ordinances that God requires of us (the Reformers) is to love him that first loved us; to delight in his Wisdom, Goodness, Mercy, Truth, and Justice, who has decreed to destroy our adversary, and to save Man.'[22]

Redemption, he went on, cannot have come nearly two thousand years ago, for still, '*the working part of mankind have no comfort and cannot enjoy the fruits of their industry*. . . . But Redemption, if understood, what it is, and what it shall be when complete in every sense, both spiritually and temporally, is clearly set forth in the Scriptures and foretold for our comfort. For it saith: "Ye shall take them Captives, whose Captives ye were, and you shall rule over your oppressors."' Towards the end of this address he identified his own mission with this divinizing of humanity, which is as much a humanizing of divinity: 'Well, Believers, if this is your faith, surely you are all Christ's Humanity; you are his Human Nature in whom he dwells, and who shall, or who can, with justice, say to the first born, thou blasphemest, because I say, I am the son of God, since all are to be made Sons of God.'[23]

The radical Rotunda audience no doubt encouraged this sort of utterance, but it is far from isolated. A year or two later he made his anarchism abundantly clear. 'Why, I say, that you do not sin in anything that you do, no, not in anything, neither in thought, word, or deed, and that God never was, is not, nor never can be displeased with you, and the sooner you leave off being religious, according to the Old Man, or Devil's notions, the sooner you will know God, and be happy, for God is love.'[24] For Ward, being the Messiah was a role less grandiose and mystical than it was commonly held to be. Whether Ward knew it or not, he was advancing an antinomian solution to the problem of evil and the torment of conscience; not an antinomianism of the elect, but a universalist doctrine which would dissolve guilt and fear by establishing the unreality of sin and punishment.

In *The Standard of Zion* he had declared that at the root of all men's troubles lay wrong views of God and of God's will for men. Such wrong views supported a clerical establishment, a major and sustaining part of the total system of oppression under which ordinary people suffered. Babylon is not to be identified exclusively with the Roman Catholic Church. Rather 'this Mystery Babylon is the whole of outward Christianity altogether . . . from the Pope down to the Ranting Methodist.'[25] Further, the greatest oppressions are not material but spiritual. He spoke, in the quaintly entitled *Mince Pie for True Reformers* (1833), first of the load of taxes that oppress men, and then of 'the secret burden, that the mind has to carry for fear of not being cared [for] at last'.[26] The fear of death and punishment must have weighed heavily on men's minds in the evangelical conversion-ridden atmosphere of the period; Owen made much of it in one of his 1817 addresses. Ward had suffered its weight sorely himself, and from this fear he offered release. He also offered a release from other oppressors, from lawyers and doctors as well as from priests (in his terminology from the fox and the leech as well as from the wolf). Illness will disappear in the new order. It was at this time that Irving and his fellows accepted the validity of miraculous healings. Soon, too, the Mormons were to heal the sick miraculously. Nearly all depictions of the millennium, even Keble's, held out a prospect of long years of good health.

In two lengthy passages Ward expounded his universalist antinomianism quite explicitly and not unskilfully. In the first part of the *Important Discovery*[27] he explained the title 'Son of God' which he applied to himself. It meant that God had freed him from his fear, so that 'I no more pray, and cry, and fret, and grieve, as I did when I was only a servant, for then I felt liable for every fault to lose my place, and on that account was in continual fear and anxiety.' But more, 'I am only called to be the first of the race of sons, but God will now have many sons, for the time is come for his sons to be manifested, all hitherto in religion have been slaves under bondage.' He went on to describe the character of those made free and happy by their adoption as sons. They did not fear, they did not sin, they had no guilt, they did not pray for forgiveness or to be made clean, and in all this they were quite unlike those the world reckons to be religious and pious. Fear and guilt crippled the lives of his 'poor brothers' and so his mission was directed to those who knew no peace, who wished they had never lived, who could not stop convicting themselves of sin, who lived cheerless lives because they were afraid to meet 'the Great Judge'.

The way to happiness is to leap over 'that filthy black ditch' called priestcraft. Then 'you will immediately be free from sin and slavery, *I know it, for I was a slave . . . and you know this is the time they do emancipate the slaves.*' Up to this point the argument resembled Luther's crisis theology with its swing from the bondage of the law producing despair to the freedom of the gospel producing hope. But the resemblance quickly disappeared. Ward set out three attributes of God: that he is pure love, that he is unchangeable, that he has fore-knowledge. If he is loving and knew in advance every wrong thing that a man would do, then because he is unchanging he cannot by a man's wrong-doing be moved from love to anger. If, on the other hand, he was angry from the first, his unchangingness precludes the possibility that he could be deflected from his anger by good deeds. But, as the Bible makes clear, he is in fact loving as well as unchanging, and so it is not possible that he could be angry. His nature is love and it cannot change. Ward certainly described his mission, in traditional terms, as calling on men to repent their sins, but sins he defined merely as wrong thoughts about the nature of God. Sin, conventionally so called, becomes an impossibility. 'There is nothing that you do is sin—it is your thinking so that makes it evil to you.' The devil, he concluded, *'is an evil thought, thinking contrary to the eternal and supreme reason . . . when the eternal reason dwells in a man he is ever happy, he has quietness and assurance for ever'.*

A little earlier Ward had published a formal statement of belief, the *Creed of the True Believers* (1832). In some passages Christianity was diluted into a kind of humanistic pantheism. Many traditional doctrines were rejected: heaven as a distinct place, hell and eternal punishment, the trinity, the virgin birth and the very existence of the biblical Jesus, the crucifixion and the atonement, and the resurrection of the body. Positively, Ward and his followers believed in 'one Infinite Spirit, who is the Life and Existence of all things, and is without beginning or end, and who is infinite in Wisdom, Goodness, Mercy, Truth, Love and Power'. Of this God there had been no previous knowledge or true worship; on the contrary all 'Christian Teachers' had built an oppressive system upon erroneous ideas. These teachers were now known to be mistaken; if they persisted in their error they were fraudulent and sinful.

It was believed, further, that true knowledge came to Ward in 1825, so that the year of writing was not really 1832 but 7. This was the fulfilment of the prophecies, the beginning of redemption and the true resurrection. In spite of this, to Ward 'we pay no reverence whatever; only as a brother beloved of God as all men are, and we esteem him highly in love for his work's sake, believing him to be the minister of Christ (the True Light) to us.' The scriptures, this credo continued, are wholly predictive and in no way historical; they indicate what is now happening. The created world has no beginning or end; Genesis does not factually describe the creation of the world but mystically tells of 'the new Creation of Man'. After death no one goes to a place either of torment or happiness, but the spirits of the departed eternally live with God on earth; thus the comforts only of personal immortality are saved from the wreck of traditional Christianity. In spite of this, the millennium is emphatically this-worldly. 'WE BELIEVE that men will advance here on earth from this time forth, (Now that the Son of God is come,) from Glory to Glory, till by the Power and Spirit of God they are cleansed from all unrighteousness, and become perfect, holy, and happy beings, free from all corruption of mind, and filled with Light, Life, Truth, Love, and all Goodness.'

These are the doctrines which, aggressively propagated in a city already tense with strife over church rates, brought Ward to imprisonment for blasphemy. His trial (and that of his fellow preacher, C. W. Twort, reported to have given up a situation with the East India Company so that he could go preaching) was in itself an interesting example of the interpenetration of the sacred and the secular, and of the tendency of the secular to come out on top. James Dean, a clergyman, had an argument with Twort, and had later so infuriated him by pulling down one of his posters that Twort had attacked Dean with an umbrella, injuring him in one of his fingers. So Twort was charged with assault, and he and Ward together charged with a blasphemous libel, in that they had published 'certain tracts and pamphlets, tending to bring the proclamation for a general fast, and the Christian religion into contempt'. The radical orators and journalists responded to the fast by calling for a general feast. In Derby Ward and Twort had made a point of dining well, and had delivered speeches condemning the fast and abusing the clergy. They had, in fact, been making speeches and distributing pamphlets in and around Derby for about a month. The umbrella duel with Dean (who had used his own umbrella to pull down posters) gave the authorities their chance.

The prosecution emphasized the social aspect of the crime. 'These publications', it was contended, 'were calculated to have the most mischievous effect upon the lower orders of society in particular.' So it was the duty 'of every person who had the good of Society at heart' to put a stop to them. The defendants 'attacked the religion of their country, with a view, no doubt, to sap the morality of the age, and to make their doctrines a stepping stone to overturn the Government'. The judge, who spoke with great feeling, averring that he himself had benefited greatly from the consolations of religion, echoed and expanded this argument. The defendants intended 'to induce the the public to treat our excellent religion with contempt, and to so unsettle the minds of the lower classes as to deprive them of the best consolation in hours of affliction, and in short to sever those bonds of society which religion so happily supported.' Before sentencing each defendant to eighteen months' imprisonment he took the argument a step further: 'to endeavour to induce man to believe that there were no rewards and punishments hereafter, and that he was not an accountable being, would produce the most serious effect upon society, and ultimately overturn our excellent institutions.' For

Ward religion was a means of social revolution; for the judge it was a means of social control; for each, equally, the thing that counted was the social effect.[28]

The case was briefly discussed in the Commons. Henry Hunt presented a petition signed by two hundred people, praying that Ward and Twort be set free, that they were victims of a miscarriage of justice and that there should be no punishment for religious opinions. Joseph Hume expressed his disgust at this infringement of civil liberty. Thomas Denman, Attorney-General, evaded the issue by replying that they had been punished not for their opinions but for assault and disturbance. This, he must have known, was a good deal less than the truth. Then the half-crazed Perceval intervened. He accused Hunt of being the willing instrument of blasphemers, 'explained' his remark at the request of the Speaker, and was in the middle of an incoherent prophetic tirade when the House was counted out on the motion of Hunt.[29] But really Perceval and Ward were not so very far apart. Ward, with very different intentions, would have agreed with Perceval's denunciation of Church and ministry on the eve of the same day of fast: 'the Church of the land shall be laid low, for she hath corrupted her way before God.'[30]

All this would be no more than a quaint episode in a pathetic career if Ward's life did not further illustrate the inter-connexions of religious belief and political activity. His career suggests possibilities about the nature of millennialism and the nature of political radicalism. The idea of a millennium had often been put to radical purposes, in association with a broad popular movement with more limited aims. Ward's millennialism corresponds to that found associated with late medieval artisan and peasant uprisings; in both the millennialist identified himself with a movement with aims much less extreme than his own. The same was true of Owen, Smith and the St Simonians in their relationship to the trade union and co-operative movements. In the nineteenth century as in the later middle ages the take-over bid was doomed to failure. Ward, after his imprisonment, Owen and Smith, after the collapse of the Consolidated Union, were mere sectarians, as were the sixteenth-century religious radicals after the fall of Munster.

The range of the millennial impulse during the period would have been strangely limited if it had not included the dreams of the poor and the oppressed, if it had not taken root in the environment of political and social radicalism. Millennialism, except as a convenient metaphor for optimists, is a movement away from the *status quo*, either by revolution or by withdrawal. With Ward in politics, as with Owen in social and economic organization, it became revolutionary, fulfilling, in a post-Christian manner, the radicalism of Jurieu, Priestley and Bicheno, by identification with the most revolutionary forces in Great Britain. Irving and Drummond re-arranged the same elements into a counter-revolutionary pattern, claiming affinity with the right wing extremism of the same period. All of them, in the near future, took refuge in quietist withdrawal; a future already embraced at one extreme by the Southcottian congregations and at another by the expositors who dreamed of the restoration of Israel. In their activist phases, the various forms of the millennial impulse spanned the total socio-political spectrum; in their quietist final shape they merged into a single point of sectarian withdrawal.

Radical politics was a proper home for millennialism. The question remains—and Ward's significance depends upon its answer—was millenialism a suitable vehicle for political radicalism, at this time? Had millennialism a valid role in the context of the general working-class movement? Working-class radicals frequently used a Christian vocabulary to express their criticisms and their goals. This does not imply that political radicalism was in any credal sense a Christian movement; it is merely to say that the contemporary climate of opinion, its vocabulary and its concepts, were such that those who sought to create opinion and influence action often saw the advantage of doing so within Christian conventions. The personal beliefs of the particular radicals are irrelevant. The significant fact is that the Christian religion could still contribute to a vocabulary of revolution. This enabled Ward to play a millennial role in the radical movement. He was not talking to people who would have found too much strangeness in his language.

Many joined the political reform movement without altering their inherited religious beliefs. In 1828 Carlile described a Mr Wroe of Manchester, an old-fashioned believer in Christ as a political saviour; he regarded Jesus as, in his lifetime, a radical reformer both of bad government and bad priestcraft.[31] In the *Poor Man's Guardian* in 1831 one Samuel Sidebottom of Hyde called the bishops the 'head jugglers and deceivers in the church' who withheld from men the bounty God had provided for all. He asked: 'Are these the followers of the lamb that was slain, or the persecuting and crucifying Jews[?] Are these the followers of the meek and lovely Jesus, or of the autocrat of Russia?'[32] In the same journal an anonymous writer ('A British Slave') acknowledged that 'an immense class of conscientious Christians . . . are apprehensive that the efforts of the various Unions and Societies established throughout the Kingdom, are directed principally to the suppression or overthrow of that Divine religion.'

But, he went on, 'I would undeceive them as to the nature and objects of the Political Unions, which I am convinced are about to become a mighty instrument for the regeneration of these kingdoms. It is not for us to cavil at the means which God employs to effect his purposes.'[33]

Such people were probably a minute minority in the political unions. These unions, and their lecture rooms and newspapers, were rightly more celebrated for anti-religious propaganda than zeal for Christianity; Robert Taylor, an 'infidel' convert from the ministry of the established Church, is a characteristic figure. But conventional anti-Christianity was seldom as thoroughgoing as Carlile's. Where he treated the entire Bible as non-historical, the more usual agitator was content to demonstrate that the Christianity of the churches was a sham. There was a real Christianity beneath the sham to be disinterred and used against official Christianity. It is in the context of this secular Christianity, reduced to an ethical teaching, that the traditional religious vocabulary was employed against the traditional religious establishment. Thus a religious radicalism akin to Priestley's was extended well beyond the limits he would have imposed.

The contrast, as a writer in the *Poor Man's Guardian* drew it in 1833, was between superstition and religion: 'the grand aim of superstition is to reconcile the poor to the enormities of the rich, by inculcating the belief that all our evils are but so many dispensations of God's providence, or else the necessary results of our own innate corruption, for which we are indebted to the priest's theory of original sin.' By contrast, 'had we the religion of God and Jesus Christ among us, instead of that of priests and "statesmen", the *rich* could not maintain for a single hour their present unnatural dominion over the industry of the poor.'[34] Alexander Somerville, in his paper the *Political Soldier*[35] claimed to have learned from the Bible that kings and state religions were bad: 'I do not, with some, think that because the churches have become sinks of iniquity, that religion is bad also.'

An elaborate statement of this theme is to be found in Henry Hetherington's pamphlet *Cheap Salvation.* He laid down, as principles of true Christianity, that Jesus aimed to free men from the religious oppressors of his day, that the common people listened to him gladly while the plunderers put him to death, that to love God means to obey the moral and social injunctions upon which happiness is based, and that the parable of the good Samaritan is a proper guide for conduct. His attitude to traditional doctrines was not unlike Ward's: 'thinking men cannot embrace a religion falsely said to contain such absurd and mysterious doctrines as *Original Sin, the Trinity, the Miraculous Conception, the two Natures of Christ, Eternal Punish-*

ment, etc.' Primitive Christianity was intended to join men together in brotherhood through the power of reason and truth. To point up the contrast, the pamphlet concluded with calculations on the cost of the established Church. Doctrinally, Hetherington's Christian residue is almost exactly the same as Ward's *Creed of True Believers*.

That Hetherington was probably adopting a tactical device in order to wage the anti-clerical battle the more effectively is beside the point. More to the point is his failure to take up Carlile's position that talk about Jesus was nonsense because no such man had existed. Carlile had urged this argument with such energy that Hetherington could hardly have been unaware of it. But Christianity was too useful either to be entirely eliminated or to be left in the hands of the enemy.

Breakaway Christian groups have for centuries used a set of biblical statements for revolutionary purposes. These statements praise brotherhood, canonize the poor, condemn the rich and look forward to a reversal in which the rich shall suffer for their greed and cruelty. The Dives and Lazarus parable is at the heart of this argument. In the 1830s these texts were used by insurgent groups of all kinds, by trade unions in their ceremonies, by unstamped newspapers and by radical orators. Hetherington's *Cheap Salvation* was festooned with such biblical texts; if Christianity had been reduced to a radical ethical criticism, it was not to that *tout court*, but to a morality that was strident, revolutionary and even vengeful. A more important book that came out embellished with the same biblical texts was William Benbow's *Grand National Holiday and Congress of the Productive Classes* (1832), a pamphlet which underlay the vogue of the general strike idea through the 1830s and into the 1840s. It may be that the idea of the general strike derived much of its force from its apocalyptic tone and millennial promises. Benbow, a busy orator throughout the early thirties, commonly couched his denunciations in biblical and apocalyptic language.

In this he was not alone. Bronterre O'Brien and James Watson were not millennialists, but they could speak strangely on occasion. Watson wrote early in 1833 that it was 'consoling to reflect that the days of "The Church", as it is *falsely* called, are numbered, and that ere long, we shall have occasion to shout "*Babylon is fallen.*"'[36] A little over a year later O'Brien burst out: 'And will not God be avenged on such a nation as this? SURELY HE WILL! Since the beginning of the world HE has never sent warnings in vain . . . *one* million of men doing justly, loving mercy, and walking humbly according to the law of Jesus Christ, is better than *ten* of proud, covetous, cruel, oppressive wicked reprobates.'[37] For O'Brien to use the language of prophecy was unusual, but more than a matter of mere chance. Behind it lay the thick cloud of prophetic and millennial talk which had continued since the French Revolution; behind it, more generally, lay the impression the Bible had made on the British mind.

The clearest illustration of pressure of this religious context was provided by the development of that arch anti-Christian, Richard Carlile. Recent research[38] has shown that as early as the mid-1820s Carlile had been forced to recognize, with initial alarm, the capacity of small but vigorous humanist sects to draw off his Zetetic followers. By the later 1820s he and Taylor were deliberately aping the rituals and vocabulary of these sects. In this way Carlile paid his tribute to the vitality of religious forms. Though he retained to the full his belief that the Bible was wholly non-historical, his writings in the 1830s showed a keen awareness of the utility of the Christian vocabulary. He remained a believer in science as the great emancipator, but he no longer placed science and religion in opposition to each other. Instead he made an elaborate attempt to enlist traditional religion in the cause of 'scientific' propaganda. One of his last major pamphlets was entitled *Jesus Christ the only Radical Reformer* (1838)—a title which comments oddly upon his earlier scorn for 'Christian Reformers' —and his last newspaper was *The Christian Warrior*. How is this change of tone to be accounted for? In what way, if at all, is it significant?

For his left-wing biographers, Guy A. Aldred and G. D. H. Cole, these later activities were aberrations in the life of a radical hero, unfortunate but forgivable weaknesses. Cole suggested that ten years of imprisonment had impaired his mental as well as his physical health, and, without precisely saying so, implied that his later phase may be so explained.[39] He remarked that Carlile now thought 'that the correct method of reaching the minds of the people was to accept the language of Christianity and to use that language for an attack on superstitious belief'. It is indeed noteworthy that a leading anti-Christian should find the vocabulary of the Enlightenment so bankrupt and that of Christianity so helpful.

If, as seems likely, Carlile acquired his notion that Christianity was wholly allegorical from Robert Taylor, then, mercifully, he took it without the phantasmagoria of misplaced erudition with which Taylor obscured an essentially simple idea. Carlile retained to the last a capacity to put a straightforward argument in a straightforward manner. In an abstract of his lectures, published in 1837, he still asserted that no history is to be found in the Bible. On the contrary, the Bible is an elaborate allegory of the struggle between science and superstition. The fall of man is a fall into superstition; salvation is the victory of science; original sin is the animal ignorance man is born with. The function of Christianity, truly conceived, is to eradicate ignorance by education. The immaculate conception and the virgin birth, like the stories of the birth of Minerva and Bacchus, personify the birth of science in the human mind. Conventional Christianity originated in an error, that of mistaking allegory for history; the error became a conspiracy when Constantine and the priests foisted it upon the European mind. Thus all the churches are perversions; the Church of England, the Church of Rome, the Dissenters and prophets like Richard Brothers, Joanna Southcott and Irving, are all caught up in the same error. The established Church should be converted into a system of popular scientific education.

Actually, Carlile gave away a good deal less than his radical biographers felt obliged to apologize for. In the 1830s he said very much what he had been saying in the 1820s. The change was in manner and style. In a memorial to the king in 1837 he explained this change in terms which do not oblige one to account for it as a consequence of mental deterioration. In gaol, he said, he had studied the scriptures intensively. His first and mistaken response had been propaganda for atheism; more mature reflection, buttressed by the study of comparative religion, led him to see that Christianity and all religions were right if properly understood. Carlile had simply adjusted his propaganda to the prevailing ideology.

This ideology had a millennial dimension, to which Carlile also adjusted. In his lectures he gave a summary of the gospel story: 'Jesus is persecuted, driven about, has not where to lay his head, preaches and converts, is arrested and arraigned under the charges of sedition and blasphemy, insulted, condemned, put to death, has a resurrection and ascension, which is a true representation, in allegory, of the fluctuations and contingencies of mind among the generations of the human race, and very nearly exemplified in the life of the Lecturer.'[40] As his memorial to the king had gone unanswered, he greeted the young queen, Victoria, with another later in 1837, which showed 'That your Memorialist, though untutored at the University of Oxford or Cambridge, or at any of the colleges belonging to Dissenters, has really been a student of divinity or theology in some of the gaols of the country, and claims the distinction of being the English Champion of Divine Truth against all learned opponents.'[41]

Thus Carlile, for tactical reasons, adopted the stance of the millennialist, and the similarity of stance counts for as much as the dissimilarity of content. He argued, as in their different ways Newman,

Irving, Owen, Ward and Benbow had argued in the same decade, that an original deposit of truth had been overlaid by error and fraud, that the time had come to return to original purity, and that he had a role in bringing about this restoration. There is no talk of divine intervention, the wrath to come, or the reign of the saints. The millennial dream is pressed into the service of secular progress; the apocalypse is the anger of the people, not the wrath of God; the take-over has been taken over.

For all that, Carlile and Ward did not end up very far apart. Ward's view of himself as Messiah was essentially humanistic; he was closer to Carlile calling himself the Champion of Divine Truth than to Naylor greeted with hosannahs as he entered Bristol. Carlile was much more sophisticated than Ward, and yet his scientism shared with Ward's vaguer formulation the hope of complete human freedom. For both men the Bible was an allegory; for Ward it was predictive in a highly personal way, for Carlile it was a generalized allegory but one which included his own life. In agitation, the common result was an anti-clericalism which reduced all forms of organized Christianity to a single iniquity.

This analysis and comparison stresses the extent of the common ground occupied by two apparently (and actually) dissimilar men. It does not lead to the conclusion that Carlile was a millennialist or that Ward saw human liberation in terms of scientific education. However, it does show the more obvious dissimilarities are qualified and even balanced by significant continuities. These continuities remain obscure as long as one takes to the period an attitude of mind which is focused upon conventional dichotomies: religion and irreligion, obscurantism and enlightenment, faith and unbelief. The inter-relationships are a good deal more subtle than those of simple opposition; there is a great deal of commerce across the conventional frontiers. Christianity had a much greater relevance than could be measured by statistics of religious subscription, if they existed. Even the most hardened anti-Christian laboured under the necessity of using the language and imagery of his enemy. This language and imagery, in the 1830s, was still in some measure prophetic and millennial. Behind the millennialism lay the English Bible, still a major source of phrases, images and ideas. This, in the last analysis, is the factor which gave to working-class radicalism a Christian coloration, and gave Ward, 'named Zion by the call of God', his audience and his relevance.

VIII: The Empirically Proven Messiah

In August 1834 Robert Owen wrote the final editorial of the *Crisis*, the journal which he had founded more than two years earlier. This editorial coincided with the demise of the Grand National Consolidated Trades' Union, an organization which Owen had hailed as, 'of all the associations that have ever been formed, in any country, ancient or modern, the best calculated to effect, in the shortest time, the greatest amount of substantial and permanent good to the human race'.[1] Owen did not kill the Consolidated Union, any more than he had founded it; by the time the delegates of its member unions met to wind it up it had been killed in the cold hard world of politics and industrial warfare. This, however, was not a world Owen any longer inhabited (if ever he had). Early in August, when the union's defeat was plain enough to others—James Smith's editorial in the *Crisis* on 12 July began, 'One fatal blow succeeds another to accomplish the dissolution of the Grand Consolidated'—Owen anticipated that the delegates' meeting would prove a propitious occasion on which to reveal his full message to the world.[2] Evidently it fulfilled these expectations; the delegates turned the union into the British and Foreign Consolidated Association of Industry, Humanity and Knowledge, and made Owen 'Grand Master'.

These circumstances, as the world saw them indications of total failure, prompted from Owen an announcement that the millennium had arrived. From time to time during the year he had encouraged the belief that 1834 would prove to be the year of crisis; now, in a statement which must rank as extraordinary even among Owen's utterances, he narrowed the year down to a week. In this editorial he told the world what was, even as he wrote, taking place.

> The great crisis of human nature will be this week passed. The system under which man has hitherto lived dies a natural death, and another assumes its place. The accursed system of the old world of ignorance, of poverty, of oppression, of fear, of crime, and of misery, this week, this memorable week in the annals of man's history, dies for ever. The delegates of the British and Foreign Association of Industry and Knowledge, called especially from all

parts of the kingdom to their great council, held, during the last sixteen days in the metropolis of the most civilised nation of the earth, to consider in what manner the AWFUL CRISIS in which industry and knowledge were involved, should terminate, have, by their wisdom and firmness, now declared unanimously to all people, that the change from this Pandemonium of wickedness and lies shall not be by violence or by fraud, nor yet by any of the arts or weapons of the expiring old world; but that it shall be through a great moral revolution of the human mind, directed solely by truth, by charity, and by kindness.[3]

This was not the first time Owen had announced the turning of the corner, nor would it be the last. It is a typical example of Owen's prophetic technique: a portentous announcement, immediately qualified and explained in a manner which avoids the embarrassments of unfulfilled prophecy. The crisis is, even at this moment, passing—true; but its passage may be known by a decision on the part of a group of men which involves them in a continuing process of persuasion. Missionary advocates, similarly, were likely to announce both that the millennium had commenced and that their work would bring it about. Owen, a millennialist to the core and in his own way as much a Messiah as Ward, never quite lost the shrewdness that had taken him to the top of the commercial tree; he always hedged his bets and left scope for continuing activity.

From late 1833 onwards the *Crisis* had been owned by the publisher B. D. Cousins, edited by James Smith, and operated in a manner which brought Owen little satisfaction. So, in this same editorial, he announced that as the crisis was over the *Crisis* would close, and as the new moral world had begun, the *New Moral World* would commence publication. This, for the next few years, was his main instrument for the continuing work of reformation. Smith had been altogether too independent, critical and sharp-tongued—too little of a disciple—for Owen's taste. The new journal would not contain a sentence that contradicted his own opinions. This was a rational enough decision. To Owen his opinions were not just opinions, but the immutable principles governing human nature and society, experimentally discovered and demonstrated. Owen was an empirical Messiah.

Earlier in the year Smith had published some caustic reflections on self-appointed messiahs, and though he does not name Owen among them, one cannot avoid the suspicion that the great man was in his mind: 'we see individuals rearing the banners of salvation, and their followers idolising them as immaculate nonpareils, infallibles, whom it were well for the world to obey in all things; but alas, alas, the world is not wise enough.'[4] The list of examples which follows begins with John Ward, 'a very sensible, very good man, but . . . most immoveably obstinate in maintaining that he is the annointed of God, and the only man who was ever born again'. There was also Joseph Almond of London who had been over-impressed with the text 'and the *Almond*-tree shall flourish', Elias Carpenter who considered himself to be 'Elias, who was to come', 'old Silby' on the other side of London who expected to become King of England, as well as one John Dilks in Ohio, who had predicted the millennium for 1832, to begin in America.

Smith had had too much to do with millennialism either to over-value or to under-value these pretensions; messiahs were to be found all over the country, 'all foretelling the end of the old world; and if they are false in respect to their individual professions and expectations, they must surely be allowed to be so far true, that, taken collectively, they forebode a speedy dissolution to the old world.' Smith may or may not have silently included Owen in his list of self-appointed messiahs. If he had, he would have been perfectly correct, for Owen, as well as being a millennialist, held, in a way that requires more than usually careful definition, an opinion as to his own role and nature which can best be seen as a form of messiahship.

That Owen was not a Christian—except insofar as he would agree with the residue of all religions once the nonsense had been knocked out of them—is an initial obstacle to this assertion. Could a non-Christian be a millennialist? Clearly Owen was not a millennialist who accepted the biblical prophecies in a Christological sense and set about dating and describing the returned Christ's personal reign. But not all millennialists did this, even though most of them did. Two other aspects of millennialism help to locate Owen within the tradition. In the first place, and precisely among those most influenced by the rationalist, utilitarian temper of the later eighteenth century, among whom Owen is to be numbered, there had been a persistent habit of allegorizing the biblical images of Antichrist, Armageddon and the millennium into social and intellectual manifestations of decline, crisis and recovery. Second, the illuminist habit of transforming the Christ-figure (whether of the first or the second coming or of both) into the life of the particular visionary, of becoming oneself the Christ figure, not necessarily in a miraculous way but sometimes as simply a liberation-figure, has many examples, from Jane Lead to John Ward. This habit of mind thus intersects with allegorization, and here is almost the point at which Owen is to be found.

Almost, for his originality remains; he transferred the total process to an extra-Christian dimension. Others had come fairly close to this position. It was a Dissenter commonplace to subsume all ecclesiastical establishments under the image of Antichrist, and to argue historically that anti-Christianity had emerged as the original deposit of pure Christianity was overlaid and perverted by the falsities of oppressive establishments. Owen simply extended these two arguments further: from established churches to all churches of all religions, and from the original purity of Christianity to the original purity of human nature. It was a quite considerable step, but the ground on which he stood had been well prepared.

These transitions, from a situation within to one outside Christianity, mean that Owen's millennialism is recognizably Christian while being post-Christian: the content alters, but the form, the style, the vocabulary and the general shape of his utterances remain recognizably Christian-millennialist and even distinctly biblicist. Regularly, throughout his public life he was given to prophetic utterance, to biblical phraseology, to a millennial style and to messianic self-description. The message he delivered was normally cast in the language of political economy or of associationist psychology, but he typified the nature both of the message and the messsenger in the language of prophecy. It is certainly the case that this religious dimension became more apparent in his later years, when the 'Rational Religionists' had settled down to become a sect among sects. It is true, further, in this later period, that Owen used explicitly religious concepts much more regularly. But there was nothing in the later developments—apart from the habit of communicating with the departed—which had not been implicit and often explicit in his early writings. The sectarianism of the 1840s and the millennial announcements in the trade union excitement of 1834 are perfectly explicable in the terms of his first public utterances. Accordingly most of this chapter will be devoted to an examination of the statements he made in and around 1817, his first and greatest millennial moment, and of some of his reflections upon these distant events written down in his last years.

Owen was sharply distinguished from the great majority of millennialists by the role he assigned to himself. They were prophetic commentators, identifying the signs of the times and predicting the course of events. He was, in his own estimation, the most eminent of the signs of the times, and himself the occasion of the critical events. They looked forward to the return of the Messiah, either in an allegorical or a literal way; he saw himself as the redeemer, in a way which is both allegorical and literal. As he held no brief for the first coming, he had no reason to see himself as the Christ of the second coming—though he did occasionally apply this image to his message. In a general way he regarded himself and his ideas as providentially sent; in many specific ways he applied to himself the biblical characteristics of the Messiah; in a very emphatic way he represented his utterances of 1817 in London as the announcement of a universal gospel. Owen, then, did not write as a millennialist expositor; he acted as the person millennialism was about. He is much closer, that is to say, to John Ward than to Edward Irving.

Though Owen regarded his addresses and letters of August and September 1817 as the climactic revelation, all the themes are present, though muted, in his first publications—the four essays in *A New View of Society* (1813) and *An Address to the Inhabitants of New Lanark* (1816). The first of the four essays has the form of a sermon: it is built around the contrast between the misery that exists and the felicity that shall exist. He moved from his description of misery to his prediction of felicity by advancing a double argument: first that misery was approaching a crisis point, and second that the truth which will resolve the crisis into a happy outcome had been announced. This pattern was the stock-in-trade of the exhortatory preacher—the appeal was addressed to the heart of the sinner, to acknowledge his sinfulness and the possibility of an escape from it, and to move from death to life by a double recognition, of his helplessness as he is, and of his desperate need for the saving truth now offered. Specifically, Owen looked, in the company of a host of contemporary preachers, to the 'extraordinary events of the present times' for confirmation, and in particular to Napoleon's role in preparing the way for change 'by shaking to its foundation that mass of superstition and bigotry, which on the continent of Europe had been accumulating for ages, until it had so overpowered and depressed the human intellect, that to attempt improvement without its removal would have been most unavailing'.[5] This bore a close relationship to the role ascribed to Napoleon by such expositors as Bicheno, Faber and Frere.

Further, Owen (in this essay and in everything he wrote) shared with the preachers the certainty that the onset of the crisis and its resolution did not depend on human effort: 'the time is now arrived when the public mind of this country, and the general state of the world, call imperatively for the introduction of this all-pervading principle. . . . Nor can any human power now impede its rapid progress. . . . The commencement of the work will, in fact, ensure its accomplishment.' For the Christian preachers, God dominated the picture; for Owen, those principles which 'require only to be known in order to establish themselves. . . . They direct that the governing powers of all countries should establish rational plans for the education and general formation of the characters of their subjects.'[6] Men must follow and co-operate with these 'principles' which have the authority of an autonomous external agency. This brief introductory essay provided the framework which contained the lengthy and detailed exposition of the greater part of the *New View*. The keynotes of misery and felicity, enslavement and deliverance, the inevitability of change through sudden crisis, recurred throughout the succeeding essays. Owen's diagnosis and prognosis were of social ills and social goods, but his style and his cast of mind derived from millennialist exhortation. He was not, *au fond*, arguing a case; he was making a prophecy.

When he opened the Institution for the Formation of Character at New Lanark in 1816, Owen believed that he was doing far more than taking an important educational experiment a stage further; he was demonstrating that the future really worked, that the new age had begun. The purpose of the Institution was to '*give happiness to every human being through all succeeding generations*'. Hence his address upon its opening was more a millennial proclamation than a scientific argument. His was 'the only path to knowledge'; error had (like original sin) passed 'from one generation to another', so that 'none was in the right path—no, not one'; 'the minds of all men must be born again.' All men would be so impressed by the 'principles' and the 'system' that they would confess that they had previously been in error; they would greet the system of the Institution 'as the harbinger of that period when our swords shall be turned into ploughshares, and our spears into pruning hooks; when universal love and benevolence shall prevail; when there shall be but one language and one nation; and when fear of want or of any evil among men shall be known no more'.[7]

Though Owen was primarily interested in complete social reconstruction—hence his constant appeals to the great ones, ministers, emperors and presidents—he was also, like a good preacher, concerned with the regeneration of the individual. The recognition of the truth about the formation of character—that an individual is in no way responsible either for his original 'faculties and propensities' or for the circumstances in which he is placed—would lead all men to the new world, and (in the meantime) would lead individuals to a better relationship with their neighbours. His final exhortation to his New Lanark listeners was intended to help those who have been introduced to the truth to deal with the recurrence of 'injurious dispositions'. Owen, true revivalist, had a proper concern for the sins of the regenerate. The shadow of Calvinism lies heavily over the whole exposition. He summoned the individual to reject wholly his old life—'Yes! they will reject with horror even those notions which hitherto they have from infancy been taught to value beyond price.'

Behind conversion lay predestination: 'every infant has received all its faculties and qualities, bodily and mental, from a power and a cause, over which the infant had not the shadow of control.' But election and reprobation, as individual destinies, did not follow. There is no capricious God in Owen's theology; men in general, previously, have known 'every conceivable evil'; all humanity, from now on, will follow 'the true and only road which can lead to happiness'.[8] Hell and heaven have been socialized and he knew that the proper and time-hallowed term for a perfect society was the millennium.[9] Ignorance, the cause of all misery, was again a piece of socialized theology; the devil retained his terrifying aspect while being translated into a social force. Ignorance was 'the evil spirit which has dominion over the world . . . which has grossly deceived mankind'. It was 'the roaring lion going about seeking whom he may devour'.[10]

His doctrine of circumstances gave Owen an especially thorny problem in explaining his own immunity from inherited error. He had not much alternative but to 'deify' himself, or, at the least, to make himself the first new man of the new creation. In all his self-reflections (which are numerous) he oscillated between the role of redeemer and that of innovator. The former inevitably made him assume a messianic character. But even the latter required some pretty special explanation. Just as Christians have had to go to great lengths to detach Jesus from the chain of original sin, so Owen, simply as an innovator, had to work hard to show how he managed to be sufficiently immune from 'circumstances' to enable him to innovate. The logic of his own system required him to slide across from innovator to redeemer.

In the *Address* he made some significant approaches to self-messianization. His message, he stated, will arouse the scorn of the conventionally learned and wise, for their ignorance is especially great. Here Owen did not use biblical imagery, but his argument was close to that of the Magnificat, to the parable of the stone which the builders rejected, and to St Paul's well-known strictures upon the foolishness of the Greeks.[11] This description of the folly of the wise was meant to focus attention on the problem of Owen's immunity from normal human blindness. The answer, guardedly given in this *Address*, was a secular approximation to a special choosing, a sort of immaculate upbringing. 'Causes, over which I could have no control, removed in my early days the bandage which covered my mental sight.' Enabled, in this special manner, to see the truth, Owen went on, could he refrain from pointing out to all men the true path to happiness? 'No! The causes which fashioned me in the womb,—the circumstances by which I was surrounded from my birth, and over which I had no influence whatever, formed me with far other faculties, habits, and sentiments. These gave me a mind that could not rest satisfied without trying every possible expedient to relieve my fellowmen from their wretched situation, and formed it of such a texture that obstacles of the most formidable nature served but to increase my ardour, and to fix within me a settled determination, either to overcome them, or to die in the attempt.' Difficulties, initially appalling and apparently insurmountable, disappeared 'like the fleeting clouds of morning'. The path forward was now clear; no longer did he need to work silently and alone. 'The period is arrived when I may call numbers to my aid, and the call will not be in vain.'[12]

The language, still that of faculties, propensities and circumstances, is as unmystical as it could be. The problem of Owen's special role is simply met with bald assertion that, in his case, the faculties, propensities and circumstances were wholly different, and that the cause of the difference was wholly external to him. Providence is not excluded, but dressed in new clothes. The notion that he was specially selected, that he was the beginning of a new creation, grew upon Owen in later life, till it reached a climax in the infancy narrative set down in his autobiography. Owen, to repeat, was not essentially a millennialist, but rather the occasion of the millennium; this, as well as the special problems posed by his doctrine of circumstances, faced him with the need to give such an account. Here, for once, the example of Joanna Southcott is to the point. A society which contained a number of solid and reputable men ready to heed her claim to divine motherhood in 1814 would contain many more ready to go along with Owen's essentially mild and cool messiahship.

But the coolness—including the re-iterated assertion that the change must be carefully managed to prevent any abrupt dislocation, that his listeners must not try to move precipitately from the old to the new—should not obscure the highly personal excitement which underlay this studiously restrained *Address*. 'Old things shall pass away, and all shall become new'; 'in one generation' the rulers of the world will be able to make the change. The charge that he is insane was rehearsed and rejected; he will astonish theologians as well as politicians; he knew society as well as if it were set out on a map; he knew the thoughts of his listeners. With regular echoes from St Paul's discourse on charity he offered men his version of true religion and true Christianity.[13]

In the essays of *A New View* and in this *Address* Owen elaborated the principles which, with varying internal emphasis, he was to reiterate for the rest of his life. Here by argument and at New Lanark by demonstration, they had been shown to be true. The rest was proclamation. During a hectic few weeks, in London late in 1817, Owen proclaimed his gospel and called numbers to his aid. This was the millennial moment; not the time of the second stage in revelation history, but the time of the revelation itself. In old age, after nearly four decades of effort, Owen could adapt to his own life the words of the psalm he must have regularly heard as a child at Matins: 'it will in six months be just *forty years* that I may say "I have been grieved with this generation", while it has been passing through the wilderness of ignorance and gross superstitions.'[14] Specifically, in later life, Owen identified a precise instant as the moment of revelation: his delivery of the sentences announcing the error of all religions in his *Address* at the London Tavern on 21 August. This was the moment at which the new world began. Owen believed this to be so, at the time as well as in long retrospect.

Of course, Owen's manifest purpose in his 1817 campaign was to persuade the influential to adopt his scheme for poor relief. If this scheme was designed to be simply ameliorative, then there is an immense and inexplicable distance between the object sought and the means employed to urge it. But the scheme, because it was an application of the 'principles', was intended to be salvific not reformist, the beginning of a new, not merely of a better age. The gap, from this vantage point, narrows and disappears: no rhetoric can be too extreme for the millennium. At the London Tavern, on 21 August 1817, Owen inaugurated the millennium. The exact context of this millennial moment was the contrast between 'the Cottage system' of relief and 'the plan now advocated'.[15] The comparison shifted from a matter-of-fact discussion of food supplies to an eloquent discourse on problem of death—a transition which will appear less abrupt if Owen is regarded in the role of prophet and preacher, not of political economist or reformer. In the old order, death brought grief and despair; there was no communal comfort for 'All are individualised, cold, and forbidding.' But under 'the proposed system' it will be otherwise. 'The intelligent resigned sufferer waits the result with cheerful patience, and thus most effectually parries every assault of disease, when unaccompanied by his fell companion, death; and, when death attacks him, he submits to a conqueror who he knew from childhood was irresistible, and whom for a moment he never feared!' The bereaved will feel only natural grief, and no more, for 'around them on all sides . . . thousands on thousands, in strict, intimate and close union, are ready and willing to offer them aid and consolation.' Fittingly enough, the passage ends, 'O death, where is thy sting? O Grave, where is thy victory?'[16] Orthodox preachers offered a fearful generation one set of consolations; Owen a rather different set. But both were very concerned with death, and so, with religion as well.

Why, Owen went on, have 'the new arrangements' which would bring all these advantages not been introduced long ago? Because, simply, the ignorance perpetuated by all religions had not been destroyed; because no one had been prepared to sacrifice his life by bringing salvation through the destruction of these religions; because, in a word, Owen had not been brought to his millennial moment. The announcement of the falsity of religions, therefore, became the point of time at which the new world began. Here Owen, as an old man remembering, may provide his own commentary upon the occasion.[17] He described how he went to 'this meeting, ever-to-be remembered in the annals of history', determined 'at a particular place of my address, to denounce and reject all the religions of the world'. He believed 'the public mind' to be 'highly excited', that even the phlegmatic Lord Liverpool had been relieved of great anxiety by an interview with Owen, and indeed that the Government were so bewildered that 'they felt they were at my mercy.' He had copies of the address prepared for the reporters, but the copiers were instructed to leave the crucial passage blank for Owen himself to fill in before the meeting. He believed himself to be 'by far the most popular individual in the civilised world, and possessed the most influence with a majority of the leading members of the British cabinet and government.' He 'went to the meeting with the determination by one sentence to destroy that popularity, but by its destruction to lay the axe to the root of all false religions, and thus to prepare the population of the world for the reign of charity in accordance with the natural laws of humanity.' And as other phrases (both at the time and in retrospect) make clear, it was not simply popularity, but life, that he was prepared to lay down, and even expected to lay down, that all men might live.

At this point, so Owen continued his recital:

> I commenced my address, and continued amidst much applause and cheering from the friends of the cause which I advocated, until I approached that part in which I denounced all the religions of the world as now taught; when by my manner I prepared the audience for some extraordinary proceeding. And when in a firm voice I said—'A more important question has never been put to the sons of men—Who can answer it? Who dares answer it? but with his life in his hand—a ready and willing victim to truth, and to the emancipation of the world from its long bondage of error, crime, and

misery? Behold that victim! On this day! in this hour! even now! shall those bonds be burst asunder, never more to re-unite while the world lasts! What the consequences of this daring deed shall be to myself I am as indifferent about, as whether it shall rain or be fair to-morrow! Whatever may be the consequences, I will now perform my duty to you and to the world. And should it be the last act of my life, I shall be well content, and shall know that I have lived for an important purpose. Then, my friends! I tell you, that hitherto you have been prevented from knowing what happiness really is, solely in consequence of the errors—gross errors.—' The meeting here became excited to the highest pitch of expectation as to what was to follow; and a breathless silence prevailed, so that not the slightest sound could be heard. I made a slight pause, and, as my friends afterwards told me, added a great increase of strength of feeling and dignity to my manner, of which at the time I was wholly unconscious, and in that state of mind I finished the sentence . . . . and I then again paused for some seconds, to observe the effects of this unexpected and unheard of declaration and denouncement of all existing religions, in one of the most numerous public meetings of all classes ever held in the British metropolis under cover and at mid-day.

My own expectations were, that such a daring denouncement in opposition to the deepest prejudices of every creed, would call down upon me the vengeance of the bigot and superstitious, and that I should be torn to pieces in the meeting. But great was my astonishment at what followed. A pause ensued, of the most profound silence, but of noiseless agitation in the minds of all,—none apparently knowing what to do or how to express themselves. All seemed thunderstruck and confounded. My friends were taken by surprise, and were shocked at my temerity, and feared for the result. Those who came with the strongest determination to oppose me, had, as they afterwards stated to me, their minds changed as it were by some electric shock, and the utmost mental confusion seemed to pervade the meeting, none venturing to express their feelings; and had I not purposely paused and waited some demonstration from the audience, I might have continued my address in the astonished silence which I had produced. But when I did not proceed, and while I evidently waited for some expression of the feeling of the audience, after the long pause in silence, about half-a-dozen clergymen, who had attentively listened to all I had said, deemed it incumbent upon them on account of their profession to attempt to lead the meeting by a few low hisses. But these, to my great astonishment, were instantly rebutted by the most heart-felt applause from the whole of the meeting, with the exception stated, that I ever witnessed, before or since, as a public demonstration of feeling.

I then said to the friends near me—'the victory is gained. Truth openly stated is omnipotent.'[18]

Owen may or may not be a reliable reporter of the scene in the London Tavern, but this is a trustworthy account of his own motivation, expectation and general state of mind. It is not simply the product of forty years' hindsight, for it is perfectly in accord with the statements he made in 1817 about the occasion. The later account highlighted an expectation of martyrdom in the cause of truth. It went on to point up the vital significance of this day, 'the day on which bigotry, superstition, and all false religions, received their death blow'. 'The deed was done. Truth had escaped, as it were by a miracle.' There was, in this old man's recollection, more than a hint of divine guidance and protection: 'when I went to the meeting I felt uncertain whether I should return alive. . . . I never felt more strongly than at this period, that none of the power which carried me through these measures with the success which attended them was of my own creating. . . . On calmly recurring to these three addresses, it is now evident to me, through the experience which time has given, that the knowledge of the good and superior Spirit which directed and controlled all my public proceedings, was . . . far in advance of the age.'

This way of putting it was undoubtedly shaped to some extent by the convictions of Owen's last years—especially by his more habitual recourse to a deity as an explanation and by his belief in spiritualistic communication with the dead. But—spiritualism apart—the retrospect in no way contradicted Owen's view of his role as it may be deduced from the letters and addresses written in 1817. The most eloquent testimony comes from the *Letter* which appeared in the newspapers on 10 September, but the other documents of the period also point in the same direction.

The *Address* of 21 August itself was full of millennialist and apocalyptic language, quite apart from the lengthy passage quoted. He spoke of the wrong principles which in all religions have been 'fast entwined with all their fundamental notions'—a phrase which recalls the belief, commonplace among protestant exegetes, that an original 'pure' Christianity had been overlaid and perverted by the centuries of papal and political error which constituted the reign of Antichrist. He told his hearers that they 'must be attired in proper garments' before they could enjoy the new world—a direct reference to the wedding garment imagery which was commonly employed to describe the messianic feast.[19]

In the *Letter* published on 10 September, Owen asserted that the applause which greeted his announcement of freedom of opinion (which here and elsewhere he presents as a natural right, but which, within the terms of his own doctrine, would be more properly regarded as a consequence of the equality of errors) showed him 'that the world was delivered from mental slavery—that the shackles of ignorance, superstition, and hypocrisy, were burst asunder for ever'. Even in the brief period since he began his teaching, it had become clear that 'in the minds of all, the existing order of things has no secure spot on which to rest.'[20] The bulk of this lengthy letter was taken up with the details of community organization, a rather quaint exercise which, however, led to a full and sustained flight of millennial eloquence.

He explained, temperately enough to begin with, that his denunciation of existing religious and political systems was a required work of preliminary demolition; that it was necessary that he 'for a time offend all mankind'; and that men will in due time be given 'a new understanding, a new heart, and a new mind': 'Ere long there shall be but one action, one language, and one people.' As it is, the time had almost arrived 'when swords shall be turned into ploughshares, and spears into pruning hooks—when every man shall sit under his own vine and his own fig-tree, and none shall make him afraid.' Yet more marvellous, the time was close when men will love those who differ from them more than they now love those who agree with them.[21] Then followed three paragraphs of great significance:

> Yes, my friends, in the day and hour when I disclaimed all connexion with the errors and prejudices of the old system—a day to be remembered with joy and gladness henceforward throughout all future ages—the Dominion of FAITH ceased; its reign of terror, of disunion, of separation, and of irrationality was broken to pieces like a potter's vessel. The folly and madness of its votaries became instantly conspicuous to the world. When the benighted intellects of humanity were opened, and it was clearly perceived that *any* faith, however horrible and absurd, could be given to all of the sons of men, —it was in the same hour made known, that, therefore, Faith could be of no practical value whatever; but that its longer Dominion on earth must be productive of error and misery; and, if permitted to remain, that its continuance among the children of light would produce only evil continually.
>
> Now from henceforth CHARITY presides over the destinies of the world. Its reign, deep rooted in principles of DEMONSTRABLE TRUTH, is permanently founded; and against it hell and destruction should not prevail,
>
> Yes, on this day, the most glorious the world has seen, the RELIGION OF CHARITY, UNCONNECTED WITH FAITH, is established for ever. *Mental liberty for man is secured: and hereafter he will become a reasonable, and consequently a superior being.*[22]

This rejected age of faith is simply a post- and extra-Christian extension of the prophetically conventional reign of Antichrist. Owen nowhere used this latter term; it is hard to see how, writing from a vantage-point beyond Christianity, he could. For Christian millennialists Antichrist's reign was a period occurring at some stage between the first coming and the second. For Owen, talk of a first and a second coming could only be nonsense: Christianity was just another wrong religion. Still, his age of faith was quite close to the reign of

Antichrist as depicted by Dissenters like Priestley and Bicheno, for whom the term referred to that combination of religious error and Church-State oppression which had in the early centuries overcome Christianity and was still dominant in Great Britain as well as on the Continent. Owen's age of faith is radical Dissent's reign of Antichrist extended backwards and sideways to include all history and all religions. Such a concept was not an entire novelty: earlier English mystics had seen themselves as the inaugurators of the age of the spirit which should supersede the previous dispensations of the Father and the Son. Though Owen did not do anything with this venerable triad, there was a good deal of this kind of mystic about him. These mystics, still committed to the trinitarian framework, were not thoroughly post-Christian; Owen, concerned with a simpler transition from error to truth, and wholly untouched by ideas of progress, left all Christian apparatus except the simply millennial behind him. Antichrist became all error and so became all that had gone before, the age of faith. This whole past will dissolve before the onset of the religion of charity. Owen was not a commentator showing how all this would come to pass as a fulfilment of a change that had begun earlier; he was the Messiah bringing about the total change. But Christian vocabulary was less easy to discard than Christian theology. The concluding passages of the letter made this abundantly clear.

Here Owen defined this 'new religion' by means of a paraphrase on 2 Corinthians 13, inserting his rather awkward glosses upon St Paul's words from time to time: charity 'believeth all things (WHEN DEMONSTRATED BY FACTS,—BUT NOTHING THAT IS DISTINCTLY OPPOSED TO THE EVIDENCE OF OUR SENSES)'.[23] Abruptly, this exordium was concluded with the question, 'What are the signs of the last days of misery on earth?' This was answered by an adaptation of the central apocalyptic passage from the Gospel of St Luke (21:25-33): '"And there shall be signs in the sun, and in the moon, and in the stars; and upon earth, distress of nations, with perplexity . . ."' '"And then shall they see the son of man" (or TRUTH) "coming in a cloud with power and glory. And when these things begin to come to pass, then look up and lift up your heads, for your redemption" (FROM CRIME AND MISERY) "draweth nigh." "THIS GENERATION SHALL NOT PASS AWAY UNTIL ALL SHALL BE FULFILLED."' Abruptly again, the argument swung from the horrors of the last days to the joys of the new era, and again a central millennialist passage from the Bible was pressed into service: 'Then shall the wolf dwell with the lamb . . . . and a little child shall lead them. They shall not hurt nor destroy in all my holy mountain; for the earth shall be full of the knowledge of the Lord, as the waters cover the sea.'[24]

Owen then proceeded to use the past tense in speaking of the change:

> What overwhelming power has done this? Where is the arm that has crushed the mighty ones of the earth, and made them afraid? Who has said, Let there be light, and there was light, and all men saw it?
>
> This marvellous change, which all the armies of the earth could not effect through all the ages that have passed, has been accomplished, (without an evil thought or desire toward a being with life or sensation,) by the invincible and irresistible power of TRUTH alone; and for the deed done, *no human being can claim a particle of merit or consideration.* That hitherto Undefined, Incomprehensible Power, which directs the atom and controls the aggregate of nature, has in this aera of creation made the world to wonder at itself.

Carefully, Owen de-personalized his messiahship—and throughout his long life he was to insist that there was no special merit in him, that his disciples were followers of the truth, not followers of Owen. Nevertheless, this habit of self-deprecation needs to be set alongside the over-riding assertion that his teaching had destroyed error and established truth. Owen was not laying claim to any personal charisma (though he was to exert it later); he was simply a chosen vessel, a means of communication between that 'Undefined, Incomprehensible Power' and man; he was the available agent of the 'marvellous change'. The Messiah was not cast in the role of miracle-man, but of teacher; he was not constructing a sect, he was instructing mankind. But in the New Lanark address, and later in old age, Owen found it less easy to by-pass the problems raised by his individual significance.

He went on, in this letter of 10 September, to preserve impersonality by a brief world-view of history as a struggle between ignorance assisted by superstition, faith and hypocrisy, and nature aided by experience, knowledge and truth. This was a secularized version of the cosmic struggle between good and evil, light and darkness, God and Satan. 'Ignorance then called in Superstition and Hypocrisy to its aid; and together they invented all the faiths or creeds in the world; —a horrid crew, armed with every torture both for body and mind . . . . War was then openly declared against Ignorance, Superstition, Faith, Hypocrisy, and all their dire associates. The latter instantly sounded the alarm, collected their forces, and began to prepare for battle. . . . To their utter dismay, however, Charity . . . escaped their toils, and declared she would henceforward unite herself solely with Nature, Experience, Real Knowledge, and Demonstrable Truth. . . .' At this point the forces of ignorance were disheartened, were offered terms (by Charity) and accepted them—that is, to live on with their possessions intact in the territory conquered by Nature and her allies. 'And Charity, assisted by Demonstrable Truth and Sincerity, was to preside as the active agent over the whole dominions of the New State of Society.'

Here the apocalyptic-millennial style became explicit. Christians, in a long tradition, had seen the world as a battleground, had foreseen the victory of the Messiah, had lovingly depicted the social and political arrangements in the new world of the millennium. Owen modulated the *dramatis personae* into a secular cosmogony, demonology and angelology, a secular Messiah and a secular millennium. The modulation was of great importance, but it occurred within an inherited Christian myth, which it did not so much replace as re-structure.

When Owen came, in the 1850s, to write his autobiography, he reflected at length upon his career in general and upon the 1817 flashpoint in particular. There is no inconsistency between the early and the late statements; the chief difference is that in the later theological positions had become more explicit and more common. Thus in the introductory dialogues[25] he used phrases like 'the Great Creating Power of the Universe', 'the origin of evil', 'the good, wise and unchanging laws of God and Nature', 'after death through a life immortal' and 'the Millennium' itself, far more regularly and casually than in the earlier essays. There was also a heightened sense of crisis—entirely appropriate to the tense atmosphere of the mid-1850s—a situation referred to at one point as 'the awful suspense between such conflicting parties and principles'. A significant novelty was a fairly lengthy account of his youthful religious opinions, which will be taken into account later. The preface, further, contained a significant assertion of a 'double creation' doctrine, a secularized version of the ideas of baptism and original sin. Man is created twice: before birth by 'a mysterious and divine organisation of wonderful powers, yet more wondrously combined'; and by 'a secondary or new creation, super-added, to bring the first to its earthly maturity'. It is supremely important that 'this secondary creation should be in accordance with the first'; if it is not, 'man will be mis-formed, and will not attain the happiness for which he is evidently intended by the perfection of his first or divine creation.' The parallel with everyday Christian teaching is exact; man was created by God for perfection; this purpose is frustrated by original and actual sin; he may be restored by a new birth through baptism and the operation of grace. In Christian teaching the return to the original divine purpose is effected by a Messiah; in Owen's teaching he is that Messiah.

The following pages contain the history, step by step, of the progress of the mission to prepare the population of the world for this great and glorious change, which, when accomplished, will yet more demonstrate the knowledge, wisdom, and goodness of the Eternal Creating Power of the Universe. . . . In other words, and to simplify the subject, the mission of my life appears to be, to prepare the population of the world to understand the vast importance of the second creation of humanity. . . . In taking a calm retrospect of my life from the earliest remembered period of it to the present hour, there appears to me to have been a succession of extraordinary or out-of-the-usual-way events, forming connected links of a chain, to compel me to proceed onward to complete a mission, of which I have been an impelled agent, without merit or demerit of any kind on my part . . . . man may now be made a terrestrial angel of goodness and wisdom, and to inhabit a terrestrial paradise . . . . the earth will gradually be made a fit abode for superior men and women, under a New Dispensation, which will make the earth a paradise and its inhabitants angels.[26]

The straight narrative of the *Life* contains a good deal about the evolution of his religious opinions: Owen seemed to feel obliged first to show that his acquaintance with Christianity and with religion in general was deep and wide, and second to consider the problem of his own immunity from past error. In the dialogue cited previously he stressed his early religiosity, the Methodist overlay (applied by two evangelical ladies) to his Church of England parentage, his wide reading in religious tracts and books, and the seed of doubt planted by his reading of so many opposed controversial works. His general reading increased his store of conflicting notions; history and the accounts of discoverers 'exhibited to me in strong colours the endless variety of character'. The problem of variety, and of truth in variety, was resolved in ways which led directly to the doctrine of circumstances. The story of his religious evolution was carried further by the account of his time spent with the McGuffog family, during which he 'began seriously to study the foundation of all [religions] . . . Before my investigations were concluded, I was satisfied that one and all had emanated from the . . . same false imaginations of our early ancestors.'[27] He recounted at length the story of how, while yet a Christian, he wrote to Mr Pitt expressing the hope that the Government would enforce Sabbath observance, and how, to his gratification, the Government issued a proclamation to that effect within a few days. He did not seriously entertain the possibility that the letter caused the proclamation; but still he told the story with loving detail.

In Manchester, in the 1790s, Owen came into contact with the Unitarian Manchester College, where he had discussions upon 'religion, morals, and other similar subjects, as well as upon the late discoveries in chemistry and other sciences'.[28] It is possible, though no more, that here Owen became acquainted with the progressive millennialism of Priestley; it is, in fact, not likely that continued discussions of religion in the 1790s could have for long avoided prophetic commentary. For that matter, anyone seriously enquiring into religion in the later eighteenth century could hardly have remained unaware of prophetical publications. The two Methodist ladies may well have pressed tracts of this kind upon him.

This speculation becomes a little more substantial in the case of another acquaintance, James Haldane Stewart, who married Owen's wife's sister, Mary, and published a notable prophetic work in 1825, *A Practical View of the Redeemer's Advent.*[29] The relations between the families (including the household of another sister, Jane, who married another evangelical Anglican clergyman) were close, though the difference of opinions eventually brought the intimacy to an end. But, Owen added, 'Each knew the other's conscientious convictions', and he went on to recount how Mary, in a series of letters, constantly urged him to be converted. It is very likely that through the Stewarts, and especially through Mary's letters, Owen was brought into close touch with adventist doctrines. All these possible influences would have been felt well before the inauguration of his mission in 1817. The evidence is scrappy, but it leads (at least) to the conclusion that Owen had had, by that year, many opportunities to become acquainted with orthodox millennial thought. It is certain, from the text of his statements alone, that he set out his message and depicted his role in a manner which owed a good deal to the millennial tradition. It remains to identify the ways in which he is related to contemporary varieties of millennialism.

Millennialism is a way of looking at the world, not a set of conclusions; the conclusions which may be reached are extremely diverse, and though their family relationship is apparent, it is a relationship of style, concept, vocabulary and mood, dependent ultimately upon reference back to a common set of biblical texts and symbols. Millennialism is a mood of expectation, not a doctrine. Milliennialism is a cluster of attitudes united by a common core of images; the images may be explicitly explored, as is the case with professional biblical exegetes; they may be casually employed, either as figures of speech or as conveniently recognizable reference points, by writers and preachers adopting and adapting a means of communication. There is, then, a double range of variables, the first of the nature of the opinions and conclusions being urged within the millennial framework; the second of the way in which the symbols and texts are employed, extending from explicit exegesis to implicit reference.

Further, because millennialism has always tended to spill over into personal messianism, there is another range extending from personal messiahship to a total absence of such an identification.

In the fifty-year period which followed the French Revolution, the millennial style was employed as a vehicle for a wide range of arguments. For some it provided evidence of the truth of Christianity as they identified recent events which had been, arguably, predicted long ago by biblical writers. For others, it was a way of giving a cosmic significance to Great Britain's role in the international conflict, either that of the elect or that of the apostate nation. For evangelical preachers the picture of pending doom for the world leading to joy for some and grief for others was a normal way of calling individual sinners to repentance and a sinful nation to, for instance, stricter Sabbath observance. For a host of writers in missionary journals it was a way of enlisting effort in a process which should itself, under divine guidance, bring about a millennium which was in essence a perfected *status quo*. For the despairing 'students of prophecy' who gathered around Drummond and Irving, it was a way of condemning an apostate Church and nation which had, among other iniquities, conceded that Catholics could be citizens. For at least a handful of political radicals, among whom Richard Carlile may be ambiguously and John Ward palpably reckoned, it was a way of urging a libertarian programme. For a handful of trade union advocates in the mid-thirties, it was a vehicle for a producer-based socialism. For the Mormon colonizers, it was a recruiting argument to draw men across the Atlantic to the American frontier. For a few deluded souls, it was a way of staking out a claim to personal deification.

Owen does not fit neatly into any of these categories, but he is related to most of them. Obviously he was not at all interested in finding 'Christian evidences'. Nor was he anxious to settle whether Great Britain was on the side of Christ or Antichrist. Nevertheless, he shared with those who took that sort of question seriously a general excitement about the international situation. Again, he effortlessly assumed a view which was strenuously argued for by the 'elect nation' and pro-missionary commentators, that the millennium would begin in Great Britain and thence spread to the rest of the world. To continue down the categories, Owen could be at times (though he was not all the time) as anxious as any evangelical preacher to convert individuals by a finely balanced picture of opposed misery and felicity. Sometimes he was as progressivist as any Christian optimist finding evidence of divine activity in a variety of recent achievements, from improved navigation and efficient production to apostolic preaching and moral behaviour. But his progressivist appearance is superficial—he was more on the side of crisis than continuity. However, he did dwell upon the multiplying power of production and the spread of correct ideas in a way that had obvious similarities with the view that the millennium is a perfected *status quo*, its advent merely hastened by a recent acceleration of progressive tendencies: the spread of the gospel for some, the increase in production for Owen. It was not until the 1850s that his similarity to the Irvingites became evident: in his later writings (though it is to be detected in the earlier) there was the same urgent stress upon the imminent parting of the ways, the option open now but not open for long between disaster and deliverance. Further, there were the 'spiritual communications' of the later years—usually written off as the imaginings of an old man going soft in the head. Perhaps he was, but Owen saw in these intimations the same significance which Irving found the more spectacular voices speaking in his Church. They were a manifestation of the ruling power of the universe and 'the good and superior Spirits' responsible for the communications were 'actively engaged in their new spheres of existence to turn the threatening evil to good'.[30] His resemblance to the radical and unionist millennialists hardly needs emphasis; he and they provide closely comparable examples of the use of a millennial style for socially reformist ends—and the unionists, further, were considerably under his influence. Again, there are clear similarities between Owen's recruiting for communities and the Mormon colonizing campaign; both were calling men to come out of iniquity, to enter as much as could be had of the new world immediately, and there to await its early total arrival. He and they each used a glowing description of millennial bliss to attract recruits.

If Owen was related at most points to the millennial family of ideas, he was more closely related at some than at others. His unquenchable hopefulness (he no more believed that, at the crisis, men would take the wrong turning than the Irvingites believed they would take the right one) linked him in temper closely to the optimists. Like them, too, he allegorized millennial symbols into everyday if still striking phenomena of amelioration; and, still like them, he did not think of this movement to better and best as autonomous, but as the consequence of the initiative taken by some external agency. But he was quite unlike them on two major points. For them the movement towards their cosy millennium began from a situation which could be called good. For Owen, the departure point was distinctly more bad than good; crime, vice and misery were its leading characteristics. Set against this total darkness, very recent discoveries are not evidence of progress but heralds of sudden and total change.

Owen's favourite words were perhaps 'new' and 'crisis' and he took them both entirely seriously.

He had to do so, in an almost occupational way, for he was personally involved in the millennial process in a manner impossible for the normal millennialist progressive. They were speaking on behalf of an acknowledged Messiah who had come once and would (in whatever form) come again; he was speaking on behalf of himself, and his life was the first coming of the saving truth. So he was far more millennialist, though less Christian, than they. They spoke for the known dispensation rapidly progressing towards its millennial climax; he for a totally new dispensation only now revealed, his own—'his' in the sense of agency, not of personal responsibility. He, accordingly, thought of a sharp break; they of progress. Here Owen is closer to the 'students of prophecy', with the difference that he is confident of the irresistible onset of peaceful change, while they despairingly anticipate disaster as the purifying prelude to perfection. But for both, the old world was utterly to pass away.

However, the quest for a parallel cannot be limited to these respectable members of the millennial family. Owen was, for all his renunciation of personal merit, his own Messiah. The closest parallel is with the deluded ones of the period, with those Smith half (but only half) jocularly described in the *Crisis*. London, in the second decade of the nineteenth century, witnessed two messianic phenomena, Joanna Southcott and Robert Owen. Joanna was a pitiable victim of self-deception and the over-persuasion of disciples; Owen was a great man and a true prophet. But strangely, if one looks at their portraits, it is Joanna who looks composed and Owen whom one could readily believe to be possessed. Indeed, he was—possessed by his message and possessed by his mission. The message was the announcement of the good news; the messenger was, in a muted but recognizable manner, the Messiah. Owen well might look possessed, for the claim to have the good news is at least as portentous as the claim to be about to give birth to the Shiloh. Owen, too, in 1817, was great with child.

It does not appear from the works of either that Owen knew John Ward, and if he did he would surely have thought him an especially pitiable victim of adverse circumstances. Certainly Owen was much the greater man. But for all that they were not so unlike. Each emerged from a part of the obscure Celtic west; each had a strenuous religious upbringing; each passed through conventional religious beliefs; each believed that he stood for and indeed incarnated the ultimate revolution in human affairs. The differences between them are patent enough—from the simple fact that Owen could write clearly while Ward most of the time could not, to the larger distinction that Owen propagated a handful of important ideas while Ward could do no more than rather incoherently announce a gospel of ill-defined freedom. In millennialist terms, in spite of the basic shared conviction that each was in person announcing the new age, the difference is equally striking. Ward groped towards a depersonalization of the messianic claim, never fully able to throw off its sectarian and illuminist connotations. Owen was never concerned with these connotations; his young manhood liberated him entirely from the milieu in which Ward always moved. He was left with nothing but the vestigial problem of explaining his own nature and role. But, when he came to explain it, for all the deliberate and even arid precision of the language he chose, he was unable to avoid the messianic implications which in Ward are so explicit. If Ward was entrapped in his tradition, Owen did not fully escape from it.

Owen was closely related to contemporary millennial attitudes at three points—to the optimism of the progressives, to the crisis-expectation of the anti-progressives, and to the personal identification of the self-proclaimed Messiahs. He was, to revert to the three scales of classification suggested earlier, close to the progressive pole in terms of conclusions, to the implicit pole in terms of biblicism, and to the messianic pole in terms of self-identification. He reflected the whole millennialist tradition. When, in 1832, the young unemployed Scots minister, James Smith, after serving his apprenticeship with the Irvingites and the Southcottians, made his way to London, he fell in with Owen, quickly became the editor of the journal Owen had founded, and before long commenced to give regular Sunday morning lectures from the platform of the Charlotte Street Institution which Owen occupied on Sunday evenings. There was nothing curious about such a career nor about such an alliance. They were, after all, fellow millennialists.

IX: From the Southcottians to Socialism

In 1834 three millennial streams met and briefly flowed together: the native British illuminism of Joanna Southcott, the secular evangel of Robert Owen and the schematic world-view of the St Simonians. James Smith, the point at which they met, spent about twelve months in 1833 and 1834 as editor of the *Crisis*, and as co-worker with James Morrison, editor of the *Pioneer*, the official gazette of the Grand National Consolidated Trades' Union. Thus Smith was at the centre of the trade union upsurge of 1834; in preparation for this role he had served what must be the most curious apprenticeship in the history of trade union leadership.

He did not himself see his situation as curious but entirely appropriate. However, his explanation can only deepen the impression of oddity. He used the term infidelity to describe the popular movement with which he was associated, and he expected it to overthrow the old order. Such a position had been commonplace among prophetic commentators from Priestley to Irving; Smith, like Priestley, regarded it as a beneficial work. Again like Priestley, he rejoiced at the prospect; more, he deliberately enlisted on the side of the destroyers. He did not see himself as a Messiah, but his mission among the trade unions was otherwise comparable to that of his acquaintance Ward among the political unions.

He was, however, less whole-hearted about his commitment than Ward. He anxiously counted the collections taken up at his lectures and the fees for his articles in the *Pioneer*. This behaviour, though a shade too prudent to be convincingly messianic, is perfectly understandable. Smith had no resources and had to make a living; unlike Ward, he did not have well-to-do supporters. For a time he made a living in a manner which would have been impossible at any other time—as a prophetic preacher and journalist among the radicals and socialists. When the union movement collapsed in 1834, he kept on making a living, preaching and writing to other audiences, until he ended up as a perfectly ordinary working journalist with a religious flavour. This prudential approach was a kind of professionalism, and it protected him from the total commitment which sometimes destroyed the people he worked with, Irving, Owen, Ward and Morrison.

His experience before 1834 had brought him into contact with as wide a variety of prophetic teachings as the period could offer. He began his life in a theologically vigorous and unstable Scottish family; his father and a brother found a final home in the 'Irvingite' Catholic and Apostolic Church, the latter as a minister. In his teens he took a degree at Glasgow University and joined the ranks of the clerical unemployed, as a probationer licensed to preach but lacking a living. He earned his keep as a tutor, and tried his hand at painting and literature as well as theology. He was almost a caricature of the hungry young Scot, talented and poverty-stricken, heading for London.

The details of his education and upbringing are obscure. His nephew and biographer[1] says of Smith's circle that 'Prophecy was a fertile source of argument, and the "number of the Beast" divided with the "year of the millennium", the labours of skilful mathematical intelligences. In these labours, James Smith plunged with all the perfervid energy of his race, and his particular branch of it. An able mathematician, he, along with his close friend, afterwards Dr. James Napier, Letham, my mother's brother, filled MS. volumes with abstruse calculations on these questions, at that time looked upon as of vital religious importance.'[2] This 'coterie of Smiths and Napiers at Glasgow College' became, sometime in the 1820s, the nucleus of a small sect in which Smith was very influential until the early 1830s.

In the later 1820s he came under the influence first of Edward Irving and then of Joanna Southcott. In 1828 he heard Irving lecture in Edinburgh; this confirmed him in his recently formed opinion that the millennium was at hand and that it would be Christ's personal reign. The effect of the lecture was more extreme than Irving would have thought proper: 'There is nothing else, the death and resurrection of our Saviour, of course, are important parts of our creed, but they were merely preliminaries to the grand consummation of the whole in the kingdom.' He sent his father the pro-Camissard tract, *A Cry from the Desert*, which Drummond had recently had re-published, and urged him to consider the danger of rejecting 'the long-concealed truth which the Scriptures contain regarding the kingdom of the saints upon the earth'. He denounced orthodox divines in the manner of Irving denouncing the religious world. He rejected the unbelieving Church and looked for 'the speedy conversion of the Jews'. He took his father and many of his family into the

Irvingite camp, though he did not himself stay there very long.[3]

It appears that he achieved a little eminence among Irving's following, and looked to Irving to provide him with the career which was never far from his mind. 'I am like', he wrote to his brother late in 1828, 'to become an author soon in spite of myself . . . . Mr Irving has desired me to send up whatever I write upon the subject to London, and he and numerous friends of all ranks, whom I could name, are willing to superintend the printing, and spend and be spent in any way for the propagation of these opinions.' A little later he was anxious to go to London to inform Irving of his conviction that the second coming would take place very soon at Edinburgh. The family friend who sent this piece of news to Smith's father was convinced that James had become unhinged.[4] But worse than Irvingism was to follow. About this time Joanna Southcott claimed his attention; when he moved south it was not to Irving in London, but to John Wroe and his new Israelites at Ashton-under-Lyne.

In March 1829 the name of Joanna Southcott first appeared in his letters; by the middle of the year he had visited Ashton-under-Lyne to meet Wroe, and had seen 'enough of the Prophet to convince me that his work is from God'.[5] His orthodoxy continued to weaken; early in 1830 he described the New Testament as either seriously corrupted or full of blunders—the evangelists were not inspired and many apocryphal works were of equal or greater value. The Book of Hermes was 'next to the Revelation of St John, one of the finest books of the Christian age'.[6] But despite this suggestion of 'free spirit' Christianity, later in the same year he began a period under the legalistic regime of the prophet Wroe at Ashton, among the bearded new Israelites to whom he taught Hebrew.

Only a little previously Carlile and Taylor had taken an interest in the Israelites of Ashton. Their comments show that Smith, true to his more mundane ambitions, was attaching himself to a wealthy and respectable group. Carlile was struck by their new chapel, its band of twenty-one wind instruments and its pew fronts and sides of the best mahogany, and by the prosperity of some of the members, such as a Stockport corn chandler, and 'an extensive cotton manufacturer' who had sold up their property and given it to the poor before going to Jerusalem in the hope of meeting Joanna. For a time members of the community doing business at the Exchange had been dispensed from the obligation to wear beards. He commented: 'The consummation of earthly things was a favourite prophecy with Johanna Soutcote [*sic*], as it has been with almost every new and rising sect of Christians. When they get well and profitably established, they wish the world to go on as it is; they want no change;

but, when struggling with difficulty, they wish for, and they prophesy [*sic*], changes and revolutions.' Taylor, a little later, found the chapel being enlarged; the five hundred-strong community had grown 'opulent' through dealing only with each other. He described one Swyers (or Swiers) as patriarch; he had built a stone mansion and other mansions were under way, the whole intended to form the holy city, the new Jerusalem of Shiloh. The Ashton Israelites were, in an economic as well as a religious sense, a community, dealing with each other, looking after their own poor, and keeping their own shop for food and clothing. To Carlile this was an anticipation of co-operative shop-keeping at Red Lion Square in London. When in 1832, Smith met Owenism, both theoretical and practical, he had been prepared for it by the sectarian co-operative at Ashton.[7]

Little can be said about this period of his life, but that little is significant. He moved from Southcottianism to the vaguer 'doctrines of the woman's church'. It may be that he read Jane Lead; at least he acquired ideas of a new age of freedom to be inaugurated by a woman, or perhaps by the more receptive and spontaneous 'feminine' aspects of personality, and characterized by the dominance of feminine qualities. Here was the germ of an idea which was later to take a philosophical colouring from St Simonianism. Further, he formed his notion of the complementary nature of good and evil, God and the devil, Christ and Antichrist, which later led him to the paradoxical assertion of their identity. Finally, he engaged in a leadership struggle with Wroe. 'We have,' he wrote probably in the later part of 1830, 'chased away John Wroe, and I expect by and bye [*sic*] to have the sanctuary to preach in. . . . I would not take the best church in England or Scotland, though I had the offer; but I expect to be an instrument in the hand of God in battering them all to pieces.'[8] Through the incongruous comparison, the quest for a career is still evident; now that of a revolutionary sect-leader awaiting God's intervention.

The struggle with Wroe may well have been over the issue of freedom and law. In June 1831, Smith wrote that 'to me the happiest event of all . . . is the end of the law, which was a grievous yoke, by no means palatable to flesh and blood.'[9] This view would have accorded poorly with the minute regulations which Wroe was fond of enforcing. It resembles, rather, the libertarian gospel of Ward, whose acquaintance with Smith began during this period. In 1829 Ward had written an *Epistle to John Wroe's Followers*[10] in which he denounced 'John Wroe, who is setting up those laws which God shall abolish, because they cannot give life'. Holinsworth notes that this was addressed 'to his old associates'. Similarly, Holinsworth comments on Ward's *Answer to James Smith's Letter*[11] that 'The gentleman, after adherence to Zion for a while, started lecturing in his own self-wisdom.' The relationship was probably close; their ideas, especially the doctrine of the woman and the identity of good and evil, are similar. There is not enough in the evidence to encourage speculation, but conceivably the older Ward had some impact upon the impressionable Smith. Ward subsequently spoke of Smith as a disciple who had betrayed his leader. There are references to 'Shiloh' in Smith's letters; one of them, noting Shiloh's imprisonment, makes an identification with Ward very probable.[12] Finally, a letter printed in Smith's biography reads very much as if it were addressed to Ward. In it Smith accepts 'the grand spiritual work wrought within your being' but objects to 'your misappropriation of it to yourself'. This habit of '*Individualising* the Messiah in yourself' causes the whole of the teaching to be rejected: 'I feel great love is given me for all that you put forth, with the exception of this one delusion.'[13] Reconstruction is hazardous, but it is possible that Smith and Ward worked together to overthrow Wroe, only to fall out themselves over Ward's insistence that he was the Messiah.

In the event, Smith appears to have captured a fragment of the sect at Edinburgh, where there was a continuing squabble between the Wroe and Smith factions. But his future was not with this tiny band. In 1832 he left Ashton for London. He had, through all this sectarian activity, made a little money selling paintings, and he hoped to improve his position as an artist. His past connexion led him to hear Irving preach, not at the Regent Square church from which he had recently been driven, but in the hall he had hired from Robert Owen, which also housed the Equitable Labour Exchange. Observing its operations, and probably remembering the community shop-keeping at Ashton, Smith began to learn a new and social meaning for the word millennium.

He rented a chapel and supported himself by collections. Impressed by the number of atheists in London, he addressed himself directly to them in lectures published in parts under the title *Antichrist*. He taught that God was to be found in everything, in evil as in good; he reproached his brother (to whom he defended his teaching) for imagining that

> you speak very reverentially of God when you call him pure, clean, and holy, and would think it blasphemy to talk of God living in dung. If so, then I say you have yet to 'know the Lord'. The world does not yet know Him, and the only way by which it can come to the knowledge of Him is by 'blasphemy'. The age of blasphemy is coming, and that will put an end to all schism in

religion—for it will show men that God is all in all, and that words are mere wind. There will be a most furious resistance to the Church. Infidelity will triumph. I shall take no hand in it. I don't expect to be long amongst them. The infidels have a work of their own and I have another. I have never joined with infidelity, and never will; but you may depend upon it, it will turn the Church upside down.[14]

Thus he saw infidelity in a traditional manner as a force destined to overthrow old corruption; he identified himself with it for his own reasons and for a short time—quite possibly because he saw prospects of a living which were not to be found elsewhere. But whatever his motives and intentions, it was during this brief period (it was finished late in 1834) that he achieved all that lifted him, as the reform tumults had lifted Ward, from the ruck of petty messiahs and prophets. For, in this adventitious manner, he found himself briefly at the heart of a social movement of some size and vigour.

Through the *Crisis* and the *Pioneer*, he briefly had a mass audience, one which was excited to millennial expectations by the upsurge of the Consolidated Union. In his lectures, delivered at Owen's Institution and printed in the *Crisis*, and especially in the 'Letters on Associated Labour' in the *Pioneer* probably written in collaboration with Morrison, he moved towards (if not quite to) a secular millenialism of considerable interest. He explained his mission to his brother in March, 1834—at an early point in the short history of Consolidated Union, before it had had time to encounter a real enemy and so to begin its precipitate decline. 'I am very glad to see the popular side carry, although it will not make the Church a whit more pure. The Dissenters are, in my opinion, the worst of the whole clerical fraternity. However, it is a step in progress to the total overthrow of old Christianity, or rather Antichrist, the church of division and strife. *Men will never be made better by preaching*. It is only by improving their circumstances by an equal distribution of the produce of labour, and by setting all men to work at some useful occupation.' The letter continued in a newly Owenite manner: 'mechanical power' meant that plenty could be provided for all, so that 'moral crime' would disappear. Trading in necessities (food, clothing and shelter) must be abolished, and competition confined to the fine arts and literature, which would be a sufficient field when everyone was well educated. 'It is all vain to talk about the scriptural forms of government for the Church as long as there is such an unjust system of distribution of wealth practised. God works materially and spiritually, and his grace will never produce much consolation in a hungry belly. The Kingdom of heaven is within us, not within our heads and hearts only.'[15]

Antichrist and the millennium have each acquired a new dimension;

for such dissenters as Priestley both had been political and social as well as ecclesiastical; for Smith, under the guidance of Owen, both have become economic in addition. The new order to emerge from the pending conflict, the millennium to succeed Armageddon, has become a just society which is also a truly religious society; Antichrist has become an unjust society, irreligious in every aspect. In effect, Smith theologized Owen, for Owen's picture of the process had exactly this outline, but was much less explicit theologically.[16]

However, Owen's was not the sole, and perhaps not the main influence experienced by Smith at this period. St Simon's *Nouveau Christianisme* (1825) and the heady theorizing of Enfantin and the other disciples in their exposition of St Simonian doctrine were more precisely adjusted to his existing equipment. Had Smith been simply a millennialist of the Irvingite kind, Owen's influence could have taken him to the straightforward announcement that the just society was due and would be the millennium. But because he retained from his Southcottian period the 'doctrine of the woman' and the expectation of a new age in which femininity would prevail, the manufactured mysticism of the St Simonians struck a responsive chord quite beyond Owenism. It was, indeed, a more profitable influence. The analysis in the 'Letters on Associated Labour' is based upon an historical triad, which Smith could well have developed from St Simonian writings, but which is nowhere to be found in Owen's thought. It is a good deal more useful as a tool for understanding history than the simplistic before and after model which served Owen for history.

Even Owen, in the early 1830s briefly thought it worth his while to see what all the St Simonian talk was about. He asked the gentleman radical Julian Hibbert to translate for him. Hibbert sent him the opening pages of the general abstract first published in the *Revue Encyclopedique* in November 1830, together with his own reflections upon what nonsense it was.[17] There is no evidence that Owen took any further notice; he was ready enough to use religious ideas, but they had to be rather more straightforward. But for Smith this sort of theorizing was grist to a mill that was accustomed to feed upon paradoxes and elaborate patterns. In the early 1830s, he was in touch with reformist groups in Paris, as well as with the St Simonian lecturers, Fontana and Prati, who came to evangelize England. In 1834 he translated the master's last work, *New Christianity*. There is some reason for supposing that he knew more about St Simonianism than anyone in England at that time.

Through St Simonian ideas the ancient undercurrent of Joachimism became explicit once more, and fitted harmoniously with Smith's development of his native British millennial inheritance. The route they travelled to reach the nineteenth century was a long one, perhaps in detail untraceable; nevertheless, some interesting possibilities and parallels may be noted. It ended with St Simon's posthumous disciples, rather than with the master himself. For although one finds in *Nouveau Christianisme* a three-fold historical account of the Christian religion (Catholicism, Protestantism and New Christianity linked in a dialectical pattern of thesis, antithesis and a new thesis which is not a synthesis of the first two but simply a perfection of the organic qualities of Catholicism) the whole thing is rather evidently a clever construct. St Simon allowed himself some rather curious expressions, but his approach to religion was purely social: imperfect men expressed themselves in religions, so, at least to persuade them to change, new ideas had to be cast in a religious shape.

His disciples, it is well known, went a good deal further: they became enthusiasts. More specifically, they became Joachimite enthusiasts. Their master's rather jejune three-fold division of Christianity became once again the three ages of the Father, of the Son and of the Spirit, of law, grace and love, of Moses, Jesus and St Simon, a progressive series of incarnations spanning the evolution of religious consciousness. The triadic view of history was born again in a most improbable setting but with appropriate millennial excitements, for (as usual) the third age was about to begin. Enfantin is the most emphatic and the most bizarre of these latter-day Joachimites—to the extent of seeing in himself the third incarnation, so relegating St Simon to the role of a mere precursor. But for more clarity of statement one does better to turn to Eugene, the younger of the Rodrigues brothers, author of *Lettres sur la religion et la politique* and translator of Lessing's *Education of the Human Race*. Both works were published in a single volume with St Simon's *Nouveau Christianisme* in 1832. Thus, though Smith did not translate these writings of Rodrigues, he obviously knew of them.

Triads run riot in Rodrigues' *Lettres*. As there are three persons in God, so there are three functions in humanity, love, science, power, corresponding ecclesiastically to priests, theologians and deacons, and socially to artists, savants and *industriels*. Put in another way, the three basic activities of men are religion, dogma and cult, from which arise the fine arts, science and industry, the ideals of which are the beautiful, the true and the useful, and are personified by Moses, Jesus and St Simon. He describes this development as 'at once simultaneous and successive'—a formula which seems to mean that one dominates the others in successive eras. Certainly the process is cumulative: 'God is going to put the finishing touch to his work. We touch the definitive era, that of cult and industry.'[18]

This historical pattern is quite elaborately developed. The Judeo-Christian epoch has three phases (one of them future), but this is itself a culmination of a greater (and quasi-anthropological) three-fold pattern of fetishism, polytheism and monotheism. Fetishism here means no more than total religious individualism—each man has his own god; polytheism goes further so that each nation has its own god; the keynote of monotheism is of course unity, but in two ways. In the first place Moses revealed the unity of God, but in the second place circumcision at least symbolized, if it did not effect, the unity of man. Christianity is the second and improved stage of monotheism. Jesus founded a spiritual society of men on the principle of human brotherhood, but he realized that the time had not yet come for the religious organization of temporal society. So, in the Christian era, the papacy expressed the unity of man while the temporal rulers expressed its diversity. St Simonism is the third and definitive step in the development of Judeo-Christianity. Where, in the second step, God had been incarnated in an individual, now he will be incarnated in humanity as a whole. While the mission of Jesus had been to rehabilitate the spirit, that of St Simon was to rehabilitate matter. The Church and the kings have fought each other to the destruction of each. Thus the stage has been cleared for a new act in which the unity-principle will determine temporal as well as spiritual life—a distinction which will no longer mean anything. 'Yes, we march towards a grand, towards an immense unity; human society, from the point of view of man; the Kingdom of God on earth, from the divine point of view; that Kingdom which the faithful have called for every day by their prayers for eighteen hundred years.'[19] To complete the process the Jews, who held aloof from the spiritual reign of the Messiah, will accept him when his reign becomes temporal.

As the unity soon to be created would unify matter and spirit it is reasonable enough that Rodrigues should use either category to describe it. 'The State and the Church blend; for religion from now on includes all society in its breast.' For eighteen centuries an imperfect Christianity had 'repudiated the earth', that is, the material, leaving it to Caesar and respecting his power. This comment is obviously Joachimite, but it is also St Simonian, for Caesar is identified with the military and the idlers, who have battened on the producers, 'les vrais serviteurs de Dieu'. The future will rehabilitate the earth, the material; it will be the age of the liberated producers: 'The industrial capacity of man is the imperfect image of the creative power of god. . . .' The Franciscan ideal of limiting production for the sake of poverty is thus transformed into an ideal of maximizing production for the sake of abundance. But the paradox is not real; poverty and abundance are simply different ways of escaping from economic necessity.[20]

This is one side of the coin—and it presents the usual face of St Simonism. If it is turned over we see the antique lineaments of millennial prophecy. In a group of letters addressed to an unnamed Scottish Protestant of millennialist inclinations (who could have been, at least conjecturally, Smith), Rodrigues turned to a more conventional prophetic exposition. He stated that 'le regne de Dieu (*le Millenium*)' would come after Christ's word had enlightened humanity and after the power of Caesar had ended. He concluded: 'We recognise at last that the epoch has arrived, and that it is time to announce the Kingdom of God.' As Jesus fulfilled the ancient law of fear, so the St Simonians were fulfilling, '*with the aid of the holy spirit*', the law of love. The present epoch was 'completely similar to that of the establishment of Christianity'.[21]

At this point Rodrigues advanced a slightly different three-fold pattern, closer to St Simon's organic-critical dialectic. The religious antiquity of paganism and Judaism was destroyed by irreligious antiquity, Greek and Roman philosophy and Sadduceeism. Catholicism, the religious aspect of the succeeding era, was destroyed by Protestantism, its irreligious counterpart. All these have been 'preparatory and successive for humanity'. The perfect organic synthesis was emerging. The Catholic Church, which Rodrigues and the St Simonians generally admired greatly for its past, became a stage in the progressive socialization of the Judeo-Christian inheritance. St Simonianism is its total socialization.[22]

In these letters Rodrigues deployed a considerable range of theological reading: the Bible and Augustine especially, and of his contemporaries, Lessing, Kant, de Maistre, Ballanche and Lammenais. As a group the St Simonians saw themselves as providing the answer to the religious and intellectual ferment of their times. Their high praise for historical Catholicism met the demands of romantic medievalism; their authoritarianism coincided with that of the ultramontanes; their commendation of the savants met the enlightenment at least half way; their canonization of the *industriels* looked towards the economists; their elevation of the artists looked towards romanticism in literature and the arts. St Simonism was a very well designed synthesis—but was also too good to be true. It smelled altogether too strongly of the lamp; it was too obviously put together; it served to promote a brief enthusiasm but not to unite a coherent movement. St Simon himself proved to have more staying power than his febrile disciples. But the brief explosion of enthusiasm in Paris served to scatter these ideas widely in Europe. John Stuart Mill and Thomas Carlyle listened, but not uncritically, over the channel; and rather less critically, a handful of socialists. Smith, both a millennialist and a socialist, published his translation, *New Christianity*, in 1834. Not coincidentally, this was also the year of Owen's millennium, and of the great expectations poured into the entirely inadequate vessel of the Consolidated Union.

For all the great differences in situation and temperament, the St Simonian enthusiasts in their quest for myths with which to clothe human reason, and the British millennialists discovering a human future within their ancient myths, were strikingly similar. Ward and Smith (and, for that matter, Owen in his own way) began with God and religion and discovered man and society within them; Irving and Drummond did not know how far they were advancing along the same path. The St Simonians took man and society and discovered God and religion within them—with what 'sincerity' is another question, the answer to which depends upon the difference in quality between adherence to an inherited concept and to a consciously constructed one. And this is a difference which it would be rash to assert, on any except dogmatic grounds, is significant.

In 1828 Rodrigues, having relegated St Simon to the role of a precursor, wondered who would prove to be the Jesus of the new Christianity, and asked 'Who of us, who of us is going to become a God?'[23] The St Simonians, rather too self-consciously to be fully convincing, constructed a cult and used the word God as a metaphor. But it was a metaphor which they took very seriously. Ward and Smith, in their home-spun manner, had their answers to Rodrigues' question; for them the word God became more and more a metaphor, though not one exclusively. The point of convergence is a point of profound similarity, even of real identity. A Smith with a better mind would have been a major early Victorian religious and social thinker.

As it is, for a brief period and under influences ranging from the Southcottian to the St Simonian, he had some interesting things to say. No doubt Smith was drawn to St Simon and to his disciples by their religiosity; the doctrine of the woman and the expectation of a new dispensation corresponded exactly with his own ideas. But there was a good deal more to be drawn from them. In particular, three general ideas about human society merged with and considerably improved upon the theoretical naïveté of Owenism in the 1830s. First, there was the stress upon the organic nature of society, the notion that all social phenomena in a given situation are related to each other in a way that finds expression in prevailing religious ideas. Second, there was the view of history as a series of developments from one definable social pattern to another. Third, there was the canonization of human productivity, which the St Simonians and Smith both symbolized by the 'woman', and upon the need to control production in a socially beneficial manner. In a trade union and socialist context and in a millennialist atmosphere, Smith turned these notions into a fairly sophisticated explanation of the past and present and anticipation of the future.

The shape of the explanation is inevitably triadic. In *Nouveau Christianisme* St Simon had sketched out a threefold historical development—organic feudalism expressed by Catholicism, disintegrative individualism expressed by Protestantism, and a new organicism for the immediate future, an industrial corporatism expressed by the cultic apparatus of his newly invented religion. Rodrigues' triology of fetishism, polytheism and monotheism is another and more embracing account of human development towards organic unity, with the steps in the process identifiable by prevailing religious beliefs and practices. The same is the case with his more complex patterning of alternating religion and irreligion building up over three successive alternations to a fully integrated socio-religious unity. Through all these patterns, a notion of progress persists, towards a goal which is always the complete integration of belief and behaviour in a society which is also a religion.

It is clear from Smith's writings that he was greatly taken with St Simon's characterization of Catholicism, Protestantism and New Christianity. Though this pattern is progressive, it is also a return, for the third age with its extensive cultic apparatus and its implacably ordered social arrangements would far more closely resemble the first than the merely disintegrative second stage. From this source Smith probably derived the ideas of authoritarian hierarchy which characterize his lectures in 1834. He also found in St Simon's pattern a confirmation of the old opinion that the new age was to be inaugurated in Great Britain. For Great Britain was the Protestant nation; here negative disintegration had run fastest and furthest; here would the second age end and the third begin.

But in the 'Letters on Associated Labour'[24] there is none of this specifically religious theorizing. Here the threefold historical pattern and the stress upon the final value of productivity was related to a situation in which productive labourers were believed to be gaining control of their labour through the trades' union.

The result is an historical triad, culminating in a millennialist third age. There are three historical periods: that of enslaved or compulsory labour, which included serfdom as well as slavery proper; that of hireling or marketable labour, which represented a great advance for the labourer became socially free and could move from one master to another; and that of free or associated labour, in which the labourer will be freely associated with his fellows and not dependent at all upon a master. Each type of labour confers an overall character upon a society at a stage of its evolution. The second and contemporary period was characterized by capitalist ownership, the profit motive, over-production, long hours and low wages, Malthusian moral teaching and the institutionalized theft of the produce of labour. The 1830s were seen as the period of crisis during which, at least in England, the second age was dying and the third was being born.

There was no working out of the dialectic of change; it was simply asserted that the transition was caused by the factory system, machinery and education. History was moving towards a desired conclusion and this movement was beyond human control. Owen had announced the crisis of associated labour, 'but both *he* and *associated labour* itself, are the necessary consequences of events over which no powers on earth have any control.'[25] This secularized millennial confidence was also a mode of moral exhortation. The basic assertions were that the transition from good to evil was now possible, that to make it would be beneficial, that men may choose to make it if they decide to do what is right, and that if they do so decide they will be choosing to work with and not against history. The union, incorporating both the Consolidated Union and the complete social union of which it was the embryo, was the instrument of history.

Its essential principle will prevail in the end; the crisis will last until either 'the generous and Christian system of Associated Labour shall be generally adopted, or turbulent revolution overwhelm the civilised world.'[26] The word Christian in this context should be taken quite seriously; the union, both the actual and the ideal, was seen as a Church rather than as a collective bargainer, as the embodiment of universal goodwill, of the principles of morality and religion, of Christianity itself.[27] It was the nucleus of the ultimate social organization, and will be the great social and political regenerator.[28] All human well-being depended upon it; the individual as such was nothing, but as a union member he was part of the great body of producers and thereby a creator.[29] Smith and Morrison were, like the St Simonians, trying to create a new Church for a new Christianity, and like all churches it was both the promise and the foretaste of the millennial kingdom for which it prepared the way.

But the new Church and the new Christianity included the whole of human life, man's body as well as his soul, his economic functions as well as his beliefs. And so the union, as the foretaste of the millennium in which all man's faculties would be re-united into an organic whole, was actively introducing new productive arrangements which would, either persuasively or violently, supersede capitalist ownership and control. In this perspective, the small beginnings made in co-operative production and marketing become the beginning of the new age. The union, in its economic function, would persist into the new age, not as an economic controller but as society itself in its economic aspect. Politics would follow economics—as both St Simon and his disciples had insisted they must—and government would be functionally and hierarchically organized through the great union of producers. In other writings[30] Smith showed himself explicitly anti-libertarian, writing enthusiastically of single person rule and a strict hierarchy of subordinate levels of government. Morrison, in controversy with political radicals, also wrote slightingly of the universal suffrage ideas of the 'old republicans'.[31] They were though, like the St Simonians, contemplating the government of the new world, not of the old. In a situation of complete enlightenment (as Drummond had written of the absolute monarchy of the millennium) authority would be respected because it would be in the hands of the wise. There would be no need for the politics of the old world, which were the politics of exploitation. Government would become economic administration. Constant abundance would mean that good order, good habits and good health could be taken for granted; there would be no need for coercion. All this is Owenite, but it is also St Simonian; it is not an accident that the publication of these lectures, articles and letters coincided with Smith's translation of *New Christianity*.

The synthesis of the 'Letters' was no mean intellectual achievement. Much that was superfluous in the various sources was discarded: the fanciful and often frivolous rhetoric of the St Simonians, their cultic intensity and their more eccentric posturings; the finicky date-setting and image-interpreting of the long line of British exegetes; the unavoidable pretentiousness and bathos of the illuminists and would-be messiahs; the smug superiority, dogmatism and condescension of Owen and his closer disciples. But the impetus behind these currents of opinion persisted; if anything it ran more freely, simply and energetically than in any of the sources. There remained, free from dross and irrelevancies, a quest for a new age and a curiosity about its character. The 'Letters' represent an advance because this quest is all that is left, and because it is conducted in areas of experience which men could recognize as those they inhabited. The 'Letters' gave British workmen a better instrument for self-understanding than any other available to them at that time.

Its threefold pattern is both similar and dissimilar to that set out by Marx. Any comparison must begin by stressing Marx's immense intellectual superiority and the difference between a series of loosely connected newspaper articles and the deliberate work of a great system-maker. The possibility of comparison exists only in the basic shape of the idea, not in its articulated form.

There are three main points of similarity, the concepts of labour, of alienation, and of history. In the 'Letters' labour in one sense designates all those who work, but it also means the total result of their work and so the whole fabric of a society organized around the use of wealth. The idea of labour as the underlying social reality is close to Marx's forces of production, though it is quite unsupported by any explicit economic analysis. Further, the pervasive idea that men are unfree until they join together in work and remain associated to control the product of their work, is close to Marx's concept of alienation—the separation, in a capitalist system, of the worker from the materials he works upon, the product of his work, the work situation and society as a whole. For both, men are less than whole if they do not participate in the control of that major part of their lives which is an extension of their work. Finally, the movement of history is towards the liberation of labour, the end of alienation and the establishment of self-determination; this movement persists through three broad historical periods, the third of which is the culmination of the entire process, a self-administering society without politics.

The major difference—questions of scale on one side—is the absence in the 'Letters' of any developmental theory which identified the forces causing change and explained the mechanics of the transition from one phase to another. History is not creative; the original deposit of human fact is progressively re-arranged until it finds its ultimate form. Labour is an historical constant, persisting through all three phases; the proletariat is not brought into existence at a particular time. But in fact this is not too far from Marx, for though in his system slave, serf and proletarian are distinguished from each other by their relationship to the contemporary economic process, they have their own intimate relationship to each other persisting through the total historical development; they constitute a determinative historical constant.

The 'Letters' do not put forward, as a general theory of history, anything comparable to the Marxist argument that new modes of production arise within a social and economic order that can neither utilize nor control them. Instead, there is the routine Owenite statement that the increase of mechanical power in industry has thrown capitalism into dissarray and made a co-operative system both desirable and possible. Still, for all Marx's intention to supply explanations for history as a whole, his attention was in fact overwhelmingly directed to the collapse of capitalism and the embryonic existence of a new order. His account of the transition is not in essence other than that of Owen, St Simon and the 'Letters'.

There is, nevertheless, no hint of technological determinism in the 'Letters'. The essential motivating forces are moral and volitional: man evolves towards a better life because he wishes to achieve it. The better life itself, the millennial vision, because it exerts this influence upon men, is the nearest thing to an underlying force, and it is a great deal more like providence than technology. Marx is not too distant from this moralism. In the 'Letters' it is simply asserted that the ultimate good will come about because it is good. It is at least open to question how successfully Marx advanced from this simple moralistic starting point, in spite of all his strenuous efforts to demonstrate the objective inevitability of what he considered to be good. The argument of the 'Letters' is straightforwardly millennialist; the good needs no more power than its goodness. Goodness, now unrelated to God, provides the impetus towards the millennium. So, like all millennialists, Smith and Morrison did not organize a movement; they proclaimed the truth.

This comparison is not meant to suggest that the socialist theory set forth in these scattered and occasional writings was widely recognized or heeded at the time. Nothing certain can be said about the reception of this way of understanding the situation of labour. Certainly the *Pioneer*, in which the 'Letters' appeared, had one of the largest circulations of working-class journals; Smith put it at 30,000, but he may have been wanting to impress his brother.[32] Other important working-class journals, notably the *Poor Man's Guardian*, thought it necessary to attack the anti-political notions which Smith and Morrison propagated. Further, the conflict at Derby late in 1833, the scheme for co-operative production and a general strike which this conflict encouraged, the formation and rapid growth of the Consolidated Union, excited millennial hopes among many workers and apocalyptic fears among many of the more secure. On the masthead of each number of the *Pioneer*, the union's official journal, were the words 'The day of our redemption draweth nigh';

with some reason one may see in this rather more than the exuberant high spirits of its editor, James Morrison.

These general indications suggest that the secular millennialism of the 'Letters' may correspond to an upsurge of such aspirations among workmen, especially among the London, Midlands and southern artisans who joined the Consolidated. It may be that Smith's and Morrison's plan to unite the religious and the radicals[33] was at a working-class level not altogether fantastic. Within a few years the Mormons were to draw a great army of emigrants out of the humbler levels of the religiously minded; there was nothing absurd in the hope of drawing them to a local rather than to a distant utopia. Millennialism, in its ordinary theological forms, ran deeply among the religious; the Mormons were the most successful of those who attempted to complete it with a vision of a good society. They had, of course, this great advantage: America was unquestionably there. Ward, Carlile, Owen, Smith and Morrison could do no better than point to something they believed would quickly appear.

Neither the hope of forging a religious-radical alliance, nor the diffused millennialism of the 'Letters', the *Pioneer* and the Consolidated Union, were out of keeping with the nature of early nineteenth-century trade unionism. Trade societies and unions were not merely secular institutions. The lodge, the basic unit of membership, was a quasi-ecclesiastical society with distinctive ceremonial procedures. Of these procedures the most important was initiation—and certainly the best known, for in this period there were several prosecutions for administering unlawful oaths, including, of course, the case of the Tolpuddle martyrs. Further, so Morrison thought, union funerals were important demonstrations of solidarity; he published several graphic accounts in his journal. There was much more ceremony and ritual in these observances—and probably in ordinary lodge meetings—than would have been available in churches and chapels. Officers were clad in surplices and carried wands, the open Bible was carried in procession, the initiation ceremony was full of verbal and visual images: figures of death, swords, exhortations, oaths and vows. So firmly established were these usages that Owen, as intolerant of these as of other ecclesiastical habits, did not attempt to abolish initiation, but to replace it with more didactic and less irrational formulae. These ceremonies were designed to create and reinforce cohesion within the lodge by supernatural sanctions. The style is sectarian rather than secular; the formulae insist that the hope of a better life, here and hereafter, may be assured by fidelity to the lodge. Though there is no explicit millennialism, the ceremonies do include the swift movement from despair to hope which characterizes millennialism, and also the typical expectation that change will be effected by divine assistance. In some initiations, the new member is told upon acceptance that he has entered a new life. Morrison was not to know that these ceremonies were to decline into the theatricalism of friendly societies. Their vigour in the early 1830s would have encouraged the hope that the gap between religious and radical would be easily bridged, and bridged by millennialist teaching.

At a different level, the vision Smith and Morrison had of the Consolidated Union was a kind of secularized ecclesiology. Their ideal union is best understood against the model of the Christian Church. The union embodied goodwill, morality and religion; it was the means by which the individual acquired significance, the perfect society in embryo, the foretaste of the kingdom. They saw, behind the imperfect union in existence, the perfect ideal union—the regenerator of mankind, the ultimate social institution, the instrument of history. A rather turgid poem in the *Pioneer*[34] quite explicitly attributes to 'labour' the characteristics of the saviour:

> . . . under heav'n
> Labour rules each fateful hour;
> 'Tis the saviour HE hath given,
> Nature's evils to o'erpower.

The final stanza puts together echoes of the crucifixion and the millennium:

> It is finished! It is finished!
> Power supreme! Thy will is done.
> It is finished! It is finished!
> Quickly shall thy kingdom come.

Thus had men traditionally regarded the Church: the vessel of all human hopes, an institution to mediate salvation, to offer the truth to all, to recruit the elect, to transform the lives of individuals. Both as the promise of the kingdom and as a foretaste of its joys, the Church is the only wholly significant institution, for it was the agency which would either (according to the viewpoint taken) incorporate all men, or preside over the salvation of the elect and the destruction of the wicked. In these 'Letters' such an ecclesiology is transmuted into a wholly social context. The union-church becomes the agency through which the social millennium will come; the worker-saints will rule beneath the throne of a God who is now called history. The millennium, from being a supernatural regime under a messiah, becomes a just society under equitable laws, a social order organized for abundance. But even the most orthodox of Christians had depicted the millennium as a just and contented society. The greatest difference is whether God or history, acting through a church or a class, will guide men to it. Smith, quite as firmly as Drummond or Irving, believed that in the new age power would be in the hands of a dictator ruling through a hierarchy of wisdom. More orthodox men called the dictator the Messiah, and the wise administrators saints. When Smith went to hear Irving and stayed to listen to Owen, he did not make such a very great change.

This similarity between the apparently unlike is so marked because, in the end, all the millennialists were obsessed with the gap between virtue and power, and with the need to close it. All those who looked forward anxiously to the second coming felt they lived in a world where the good was powerless and evil was omnipotent. Justice required that the good should be omnipotent and evil wholly eliminated. Some found it possible to believe that progress towards this goal was in fact being made; in their optimistic moments Smith and Morrison were progressivists too. But millennialists more characteristically believe that the whole course of history ran the other way; evil was so powerful in the world that only God could defeat it by finally and fully manifesting his power to put Satan in chains. Morrison (more than Smith who moved off to other occupations) felt this way when the cause of the union foundered.

The transition from the millennialism of the exegetes to that of the socialists is effected if, in the foregoing analysis, labour and goodness are equated, and capital and power. The good with which Smith and Morrison were concerned was the human creative and productive capacity, the source of all that was useful, valuable and beautiful. The power they were concerned with was capital, the stored up wealth which labour created. The gap was the theft of this wealth by capitalists. The millennium they sought was the restoration of capital to labour; this uniting of goodness and power would defeat the capitalist—the secular Satan would be put in chains. They were not, however, writing for a persecuted remnant, but for a deprived humanity. They saw themselves as the spokesmen of a class that included nearly all men, not of a sect that excluded the great majority. Thus they did not see a social Armageddon as inevitable. While the union appeared to flourish they thought it possible that the enemies of labour would recognize their error and re-assume their humanity. Here the parallel with Christian orthodoxy fails—for few had held that Satan might be converted. But it does not fail when their writing was coloured by the possibility that the capitalists would prove obdurate sinners; in this case a social Armageddon became the likely way in which the crisis would be resolved. Morrison in particular, as the union fell to pieces under the hammer blows of rulers and employers, had recourse to the apocalypse in order to rescue a remnant of his hopes.

Since the 1790s well-to-do prophetical specialists had seen in democracy, radicalism and servile revolt the signs of the coming of the last days. Now the charge was turned back upon the accusers. Out of a strange mixture of Southcottian messianism, Owenite political economy and St Simonian philosophy had arisen an apocalyptic view of change in which the greed, the cruelty and the inhumanity of the possessors were identified as the wrongs to be righted, and the possessors themselves as the enemy in need of repentance and in danger of judgement. The apocalypse, socialized out of all supernaturalism, had returned to the actually oppressed, with whom it had taken its origin.

Millennialism, then, was a vehicle for emergent socialist thinking, not only in the simplistic and personalized manner of Owen and Ward, but also in the more comprehensive, thoughtful and generalized way of Smith and Morrison. From the opinions of the St Simonians, injected into a context already made up of class conscious labour-theory views and millennialist expectations, a lengthy step was taken towards working-class self-understanding as part of an historical process. There is nothing in Owen's writings which could have added this historical dimension; the St Simonian influence, mediated to a working-class audience almost entirely by Smith, was vital to this development. And Smith, in his turn, was able to act as a mediator because he had moved from an interest in prophecy to Irvingism and Southcottianism and thence to socialism. Had he not followed this progression, which he would have defended as perfectly straightforward, St Simonian ideas would have depended, for their working-class impact, upon the efforts of a pair of highly ineffective lecturers, Prati and Fontana. Because Smith had been an Irvingite and a Southcottian, St Simon and his disciples were to contribute to one of the most significant pieces of socialist theory produced in early industrial England. The course of history, inevitably, would have been much the same if they had not done so; but the purpose of this discussion is not to make any claim other than that millennialist ideas could be and were put effectively to work in this as in other milieus.

A Note on the Authorship of the 'Letters'

It has been assumed here that the 'Letters' are the joint work of James Smith and James Morrison. This assumption is based upon two pieces of evidence: first Smith's statement to his brother (Letter of 28 March 1834, W. A. Smith, p.98) that 'The article you allude to respecting Blackwood was concocted by Morrison and myself, but written by him'; and second, the appearance in the *Pioneer* for 22 March 1834 of Letter II taking issue with the article in *Blackwood's Magazine*. However, the *Pioneer* editorial for 8 March 1834 begins with a reference to 'Blackwood'. This means that the identification of 'Senex' (the pseudonym over which the letters appeared) cannot be over-confidently asserted. The analysis of 'labour' set out in the 'Letters' remains significant whatever the authorship, and it would remain highly probable that 'Senex' had been influenced by St Simonian ideas, though of course not so demonstrably as is the case with Smith.

X: The Mormons—Cosmic America

An official historian of the Mormons[1] thought that the condition of Great Britain in the 1830s was suitable for missionary activity. 'The new elements essential to the preservation of the work were found in the English people; for among them were given the evidences of the existence of the spiritual light and life which had characterised the work at its coming forth.' Indeed, upstate New York was not the only burned-over district; in Britain the fires of revival had regularly flared and faded since John Wesley first preached and the tide of millennialist and prophetic preaching had flowed strongly since the French Revolution. Though Mormon teaching added its own novel emphasis, there was nothing in it that had not been anticipated over the preceding half-century.

The Mormon mission has usually been treated as part of the history of emigration and colony-promotion and not as a religious phenomenon in its own right. But the first concern of the missionaries was to make converts, who were then urged to emigrate if they could afford to do so. The discussion which follows will be essentially directed to their preaching, and only incidentally to their effect upon emigration. There will, though, be some stress upon their theory of emigration, for it was a vital part of their eschatology.

The striking success of the Mormon preachers was closely related to four aspects of British life. First, religion flowed easily across the Atlantic. Since at least the 1820s there had been a continuing stream of American influences of a revivalistic, enthusiastic and millennialist character. Second, and precisely in the 1830s, the America of Andrew Jackson gained a reputation among British radicals as a model society, free, mobile, and without inherited rank and privilege. This reputation was an essential part of Mormon preaching; America itself was a part of their eschatology. Third, the vision of a Zion across the Atlantic, simply as a place where industrious and virtuous men could live well, has obvious affinities both to the communitarian aspect of Owenism and the colonizing propaganda of E. G. Wakefield. This appeal was not at all neglected by the

Mormon preachers, for, again, prosperity was a valid part of their doctrine. Fourth, and of quite basic importance, there was no part of Mormon preaching which had not become a commonplace of British prophetic theology.

In the mid-1820s the widespread advocacy of prayer for a special outpouring of the Holy Spirit had drawn heavily upon American revivalistic experience for examples; the pages of the *Evangelical Magazine* contained many accounts of American revivals, invariably accompanied by admonitions to follow this example. In 1822 a serialized article ('Thoughts on the encouragement to implore and to expect a more copious effusion of the influences of the Holy Spirit') asserted that such an effusion was prominent among the prophecies which refer to the millennium, described American revivals and conversions to the mission field as sure signs of the beginning of a millennium of effective preaching, and appended a lengthy list of examples from across the Atlantic.[2] In the following year the same writer exhorted his readers to special prayer, and continued: 'then it will be no presumption to indulge the hope, that an effusion of the Holy Spirit, bearing resemblance to that which has effected so glorious a revival in many of the churches of our trans-Atlantic brethren, may ere long descend, in all its vivifying and gladdening influence, upon the churches of Britain!'[3] Though this writer probably did not, in the event, welcome the Mormons, their arrival less than twenty years later was a direct consequence of the ferment which he so much admired.

But America was more than a scene of revivals; it was also a new socio-ecclesiastical fact, an example of Church-State separation of immediate relevance to British Dissent, and to the versions of prophetic history propagated, for example, by Joseph Priestley. By the mid-1830s this argument was being energetically advanced in England by the followers of Alexander Campbell, in terms which closely anticipated Mormon millennial preaching. William Jones, a London Baptist preacher and bookseller and a writer on church history and on the Apocalypse, published in 1835 and 1836 two volumes of the *Millennial Harbinger*, a periodical substantially made up of items reprinted from Campbell's American journal with the same title. Much of his argument drew upon the stock-in-trade of the commentators: that primitive Christian purity had been perverted by Constantine, that Antichrist's reign had then begun, that Luther had started its decline which was due shortly to be completed, that the Europe now ripe for destruction was the remnant of the fourth monarchy of Daniel, and that the coming kingdom would grow from a little stone to a vast mountain filling the whole sky.

Though commonplace enough in its main themes, the argument was developed in an unusually thorough libertarian manner. The kingdom is this world's opposite, so that any form of establishment and any activity taken over from worldly kingdoms is a sign of Antichrist. The clearest present sign of the coming kingdom is the total freedom of the Church from the State in America. 'Above all, we have seen the Church in America seated down under a gracious and efficient government, affording her and all men an unprecedented security of life and property.'[4] Clerical oppression, under the cover of state establishment, is a pre-eminent mark of the anti-Christian past. The changes from popery to protestantism, to Presbyterianism and Anglicanism, to Independency and Methodism, were changes of form not substance, for the clerical principle persisted. When men really begin to heed the gospel, then will the millennium begin; meanwhile, simply because bigotry and despotism prevailed in Europe and because in Britain efforts were being made to consolidate the Church-State alliance, America appeared more and more as a foretaste of the kingdom: 'America possesses a stronger hold than ever on the hopes and affections of those who desire an amelioration of the general condition of man.'[5]

This millennialism does not fit readily into either the progressive or the catastrophic category. On the one hand there was talk of amelioration and political progress; on the other, there was the assurance that the Roman-European kingdom 'is ready to be ingulphed in the yawning judgements of Almighty God'. In this duality lay the characteristic Americanness of the Campbellite and later of the Mormon position. For British millennial pessimists, doom and ultimate hope were both seen as the product of catastrophe; human political and social reform were merely signs of actual disorder and pending disaster. For British millennial optimists, doom disappeared entirely, and with it the heart of the prophetic world-picture. The two attitudes could be combined when America was given a cosmic role. Catastrophic doom could be limited to Europe; progressivist hope could be located in America, a continent which, as the Mormons were to make very clear, had been no part of the four doomed kingdoms symbolized by the statue in Daniel. The Mormon 'discovery' of a separate revelation and apostolic succession in America exempted that country from history and provided for the purity of its churches; in addition it was a way of solving the problem of continuity through the anti-Christian papal centuries.

The Mormons, through this historical fiction, could depict the American Church as apostolic and yet quite untarnished by the European anti-Christian past. Further, America itself was a new society, fit to be the location of a new Church. For both Campbellites, and Mormons the two innovations were linked; secular America was a major part of the divine plan. They could thus combine progressive and catastrophic views, because progress and disaster were geographically separated; God was working for man's improvement on one side of the Atlantic and for his destruction on the other. Accordingly, for the Mormons (though not for the Campbellites) crossing the ocean became an act of obedience to the command to come out of Babylon. But emigration was not merely an act of obedience—progressivism exacts its tribute. Emigration was also commended as a way to a better temporal life; for the Campbellites, in a similar manner, the American constitution was a better political order in its own right. Here American religion intersected with British political radicalism. Cobbett had been telling the British for decades that their goals were the facts of everyday life in America, and by the 1830s it had become a radical commonplace. The Mormon mission coincides with the early peak of the chartist movement; it was a radical phenomenon politically as well as ecclesiastically.

The Mormon missionaries identified their message with the anticlericalism of British radicalism, though, perhaps conscious of their vulnerability, they limited their attack to the established Church and did not extend it to crown and aristocracy. For all this prudential reserve, however, they made it clear that America was a land of total freedom—social, economic and political as well as ecclesiastical. But though this libertarian aspect was real enough, the core of their message lay in the exposition of prophecy, the fourth of the correspondences listed previously. They came as prophetic specialists to an audience well versed in prophecy.

Two Mormon preachers in London discovered that the ground had, if anything, been a little too well prepared. Their open-air sermons fell flat, not because they were Baptist,' with outrageous novelties, but because everything seemed too familiar.

> When we arose to preach unto the people repentance, and baptism for the remission of sins, the cry of 'Baptist, Baptist', would be rung in our ears. If we spoke of the Church and body of Christ being composed of Prophets, and Apostles, as well as other members, 'Irvingites, Irvingites,' would immediately dash into the mind. If in the midst of our remarks, we even for once suffered the saying to drop from our lips, 'The testimony of Jesus is the spirit of prophecy,' 'O, you belong to Johanna Southcote,' would be heard from several places at once. If we spoke of the second coming of Christ, the cry would be, 'Aitkenites.' If we made mention of the Priesthood, they would call us 'Catholics.' If we testified of the ministering of angels, the people would

> reply, 'The Irvingites have their angels, and even the Duke of Normandy is ready to swear that he has the administering of angels every night.'

So often were such responses heard that the preachers 'were about ready to conclude that London had been such a perfect depot of the systems of the nineteenth century, that it contained six hundred three score and six different gods, gospels, redeemers, plans of salvation, religions, churches, commandments, (essential and non-essential), orders of preaching, roads to heaven and hell.'[6] The reference to the Duke of Normandy is obscure. That to the Aitkenites indicates the followers of Robert Aitken, an adventist who published *The Second Coming* in 1839 and founded a sect. He is not to be confused with the celebrated Anglican preacher of the same name. The conversion of an Aitkenite group at Doncaster is reported in 1841, and in a Liverpool elder found his way from the Methodists to the Saints through an Aitkenite society.[7] Though London, probably because its inhabitants suffered from revivalistic overkill, did not become a strong Mormon centre, the account illustrates some of the interconnexions between native English and imported American millennialism.

Joseph Smith's instructions to the first missionaries made the most of these connexions by requiring them 'to adhere closely to the first principles of the Gospel, and remain silent concerning the gathering, the vision, and the Book of Doctrine and Covenants'.[8] If the tone of the early preaching may be gauged from the *Millennial Star* (founded in May 1840) these instructions were in the main obeyed. Thanks to this reserve, early Mormon preaching does not differ markedly from the normal pattern of British prophetic exhortation, except by its greater comprehensiveness. The Mormons were as strong on church order and the sacraments as the Tractarians, as insistent upon believer baptism as the Baptists, as receptive to tongues and healing as the Irvingites, as concerned about the future of the Jews as McNeile or Bickersteth, as quick to pounce upon signs of the coming judgement as Frere or Cuninghame, as vehemently anti-clerical as Ward, and as persuasive about material advantages as Owen. The Mormons, in fact, were complete millennialists, spanning the total English spectrum, but adding a novel American dimension.

A long essay on 'The Millennium', published in the first and fourth numbers of the *Millennial Star*,[9] may be taken as a reliable guide to early Mormon preaching. It held that 'the seventh, or last thousand years' would be 'a rest, a grand release from servitude and wo [*sic*]'; that these delights would be known upon earth; that the kingdoms of the world would become the kingdoms of God; and that on earth the saints would rule forever. The conclusion could almost have come from the *Dialogues on Prophecy*: 'In the Millennium, all the political, and all the religious organizations that may previously exist, will be swallowed up in one entire union—one universal empire—having no laws but God's laws, and saints to administer them; while the very priests of that happy period will be those who are raised from the dead.'

A series of divine interventions would bring in the millennium. First, God would restore the Jews 'to their national rights, to the favour of God, and to their own land', judging the nations according to the help or hindrance they gave to this gathering. The second coming would be 'intimately connected' with the restoration; it would be '*personal* and *visible*', and accompanied by 'the destruction of the wicked, and the establishment of his universal kingdom'. The dead saints would rise immortal and rule from the holy city, the re-built Jerusalem. Those spared alive at the second coming would not be immortal but would be 'possessed of the earth with all its riches and blessings'. The earth itself would be wholly fertile, 'sickness, premature death, and all their attendant train of pains and sorrows will scarce be known upon its face: thus peace, and joy, and truth, and love, and knowledge, and plenty, and glory, will cover the face of the earth as the waters do the sea.'

Robert Owen would hardly have needed to alter these last phrases at all, though he would have been impatient with the prelude about the Jews and the Messiah. However, these aspects had been the stock-in-trade of pessimistic British exegetes. As the essay continues, however, it moves from the pessimistic to the optimistic side of the British debate, from catastrophe to progress, especially in listing the indications which show that the end is near. Though 'Bible Chronology' does not yield precise dates, it is clear enough that 'we live somewhere in the latter end of the sixth millennium.' This useful vagueness enabled the Mormons to make secular provision for an elastic interim, and also to deride more exact predictors who had been contradicted by the passage of time. The essay listed five indications of coming change, which show something of the distinctive shape of Mormon millennialism.

'Modern inventions and discoveries', such as the mariner's compass, printing, steam navigation, railways and the finding of America, were necessary before news could spread and before the Jews could be gathered from every corner of the world. God inspired Columbus and all the inventors, though they did not know it, to do all those things necessary for the literal fulfilment of the prophecies. For similar reasons, civil and religious liberty had to be established before messengers could go out freely with the summons to the gathering—in this context the gathering of Jews. Liberty had grown since the reformation 'and especially since the bright constellation displayed its glory in the West'—an event identified in a footnote as the 'Establishment of the American Republic'.

Further, the gathering of Israel required the weakening of the Turkish Empire, a 'despotic principality which had for centuries held the land of Israel in bondage'. Greek independence, the victories of Mahomet Ali and the navies of the Christian powers had effected this change. More, the Protestant powers (so it was asserted) were 'contemplating the establishment of the Jews in Palestine', an assertion supported by the recent appointment of a British consul to Jerusalem. This last detail was wide of the mark, but the error was a common one at the time. The vice-consul appointed in 1838, 'embraced a very early opportunity of spending a few days under Mr. Bickersteth's roof, and conferring with him on the hopes of Israel, before he set out.'[10] The Mormons made the mistake in the best of company. They had plenty of company, too, in believing that there had been an abundance of signs over the last ten years showing the nations' distress and perplexity and men's hearts failing them for fear. But more, 'the Latter-Day Saints have other assurances'—the Book of Mormon itself showed that the time had indeed come for 'THE WORK TO COMMENCE AMONG ALL NATIONS, IN PREPARING THE WAY FOR THE RETURN OF ISRAEL.

The early numbers of the *Star* as a whole contain plenty about the gathering of the Jews but hardly anything, until early 1841, about that other gathering, of the Gentile saints to an American Zion. But from the beginning the journal made much of the American quality of the new revelation. The activities of the saints in America were frequently reported; it was made clear that a special revelation had been given to Joseph Smith, and that this was related to America's providential destiny. Under the innocent, even coy, heading 'Discovery of an Ancient Record in America', Smith's visions and the discovery of the Book of Mormon were described, and the two pre-Christian Israelite migrations to America were mentioned. A lengthy account was given of Christ's post-resurrection preaching in America and his commissioning of the American Church. Significantly enough, the 'rock' passage was altered to remove all Petrine and so any papal connotations: 'this is my doctrine; and who so buildeth upon *this*, buildeth upon my rock; and the gates of hell shall not prevail against *them.*' America is mankind's second chance with God; it is made so through a wholly recast sacred history.[11]

Three aspects of this use of prophecy are notable. First, at the core of the Mormon message lay a very familiar group of symbols and statements. Second, however, the arrangement of these familiar elements was quite novel. The popular image of America as a second start was sacralized by this re-arrangement; the second chance became a new dispensation, shored up theologically by early Jewish settlement, by the commissioning of a non-European Church, and by a special revelation which summoned the new world to rescue, for eternity as well as for time, the old. The third aspect is a consequence of the second. The American Church, superficially new but in this way represented as wholly original, presented total claims to the world. Possessed of such an ancestry, the saints did not think of themselves as another enthusiastic sect. The world was offered an elaborate new church order, fully grown jurisdictionally and sacramentally as well as spirit-filled. In America alone was to be found *the* Church, wholly untainted by the anti-Christian centuries of Europe. Hence emigration became a theological imperative. There were three elements, then, in the Mormon prophetic preaching; an entirely familiar general interpretation of biblical texts, a strikingly novel theology of America and a summons to a decisive personal action, to leave the European Babylon for the American Zion. The three elements combine into a striking variant of the millennial theme.

The gathering of the saints to the American west was, of course, the characteristic doctrine of the Mormons. Theologically it contained two elements. Essentially, to gather to Zion was to obey the command to quit Babylon for a place of safety from the wrath to come. In the interim, while the wrath was awaited, to gather would be to enjoy the pure worship and social delights which only a complete community of saints could offer. Further, and beyond theology, gathering became mere migration to a place where prices were lower and independence could be achieved. Still, this characteristically Mormon gathering did not preclude a vital interest in the gathering of the Jews to their ancient home. The Mormon teaching depicted two future and cosmic gatherings, which, at least initially, held equal status in the divine strategy. Each was part of the prophetic world picture upon which the new religion rested.

The conviction that the last days were close—indeed, that they had actually begun—made it urgently necessary to set about organizing the gathering of the Gentiles. An editorial of November 1841 illustrates the interconnexion. 'A general spirit of emigration', wrote the editor about the British saints, 'seems to prevail amongst them;

and the more they are oppressed, persecuted, and wronged for their religion, the stronger their desire and determination to be gathered with the saints, where, becoming a great nation, every man may sit under his own vine and fruit tree, and none molest or make them afraid.' He concluded by putting this feeling of urgency in a context much wider than that of mere local persecution. 'We have received several interesting communications from different places . . . . The purport of them is, that the sick are healed, the lame walk, the old men dream dreams, the young men see visions, the servants and handmaids of the Lord speak in tongues, and prophecy [*sic*]. While the Lord is showing wonders in heaven above, and signs in earth beneath—blood, fire, and vapour of smoke. All these things admonish us that the coming of the Lord is near. "Amen.—Even so.—Come Lord Jesus."'[12]

The hour was late; the last days were upon men; the gathering of the saints to the new Jerusalem, there to await the day and escape the wrath, became imperative. That it would also bring about a life-giving injection of British capital and labour was a further and by no means irrelevant consideration. One constantly wonders, reading the *Star*'s emigration propaganda, if one has not exchanged the world of Edward Irving for that of Edward Gibbon Wakefield, and if the two were really so far apart.

The first call to gather in America had appeared in the *Star* in February 1841, in the form of a long letter from a British elder who had emigrated earlier.[13] This was quickly followed by a letter from Joseph Smith and a 'Proclamation to the Saints scattered abroad' from the presidents of the Church.[14] From that time on the campaign was energetically prosecuted. Thousands crossed the seas, doubtless prompted by the usual opaque mass of mixed and fluctuating motives which attend any major colonization. From the three statements just mentioned one may deduce very little about motivation; but one may discover something of the framework of belief within which the Church conducted its enterprise. Perhaps this framework was not wholly unconnected with individual motivation.

In his letter to the British saints Elder Moon advanced a three-part argument. 'Now it appears' he went on after opening with the deliverance of Israel from Egypt, 'that we live in a time in which the Lord is going to gather his people, to that land that was promised to Joseph and his seed, which is a land choice above all lands.' He set out two basic reasons for the gatherings: 'first it is the design of the Lord to deliver his people from the troubles that are coming upon the earth'; second, it is desirable 'that they may build a sanctuary to the name of the Most High, that there they may behold the glorious going forth of the Holy One, and learn of his judgements and attend such ordinances and receive such blessings as they could not while scattered upon the face of the whole earth.' These advantages will more than compensate for the pain of parting with friends. But, if more persuasion was needed, Moon had a third inducement: 'the land . . . is extremely good, and there is every prospect of being happy, having the things of this world and every opportunity of receiving the things of another.' In fact, Moon felt obliged to warn emigrants against becoming so content that they might forget God. He ended his letter with a brief lesson on the value of American currency, the level of wages and food prices, and the nature of farming practices. 'What we want', he concluded, 'is some persons with property for to raise these places [corn mills and factories], and then men to work them, and then the clothing would be at a less rate, and we English would feel more at home.' So could any settler have written, from, say, New Zealand, at exactly the same time. Joseph Smith and the presidents were fully alive to the advantages of attracting settlers with private capital and to the disadvantages of penniless saints.

Smith's letter (in the following number of the *Star*) was addressed to the Elders in England, and contained only one paragraph, an extremely cautious and businesslike one, on the matter of emigration. Certainly Nauvoo 'has been appointed for the gathering of the Saints', but the process must be controlled in a spirit of prudence. Many of the English saints were poor and unused to farming; therefore 'let those men who are accustomed to make machinery, and those who can command a capital, though it be small, come here as soon as convenient, and put up machinery and make such other preparations as may be necessary, so that when the poor come on they may have employment to come to.' The saints were indeed to come out of Babylon, but not helter-skelter; they were to depart in an economically desirable order.

The Proclamation of the Presidents was a more elaborate document, a prudential clarion-call, if that is possible. It placed an interesting emphasis upon the advantages of political liberty. In Illinois, in contrast to the persecution suffered in Missouri, both state authorities and citizens at large had welcomed the Saints. The state government, by granting the three foundation charters (to the city, to its university and to its army) had guaranteed 'all those great blessings of civil liberty, which of right appertain to all free citizens of a great civilised republic'. In this way 'a foundation for the gathering of Zion' had been built. However, the summons—'let the Saints come *here*—THIS IS THE WORD OF THE LORD, *and in accordance with the great work of the last days'*—came late in the proclamation, and when it came it was preceded and followed by words of clear-headed and businesslike caution.

Those who 'appreciate the blessings of the gospel, and realise the importance of obeying the commandments of heaven, who have been blessed by heaven with the possession of this world's goods, should first prepare for the general gathering.' So, by establishing factories and farms, saints in whose persons are joined right principles and private capital 'will secure our permanent inheritance, and prepare the way for the gathering of the poor'. This carefully qualified message, firmly described as '*agreeable to the order of heaven, and the only principle on which the gathering can be effected*', was to be delivered to all the saints in Great Britain by the elders.

The proclamation defined the Zion to be set up in America in a way which made it more like a progressive Utopia than a waiting remnant. The city, the army and the university would give the saints all they needed for the good life: a place of their own which they could defend, where they could educate their children in, among other things, 'the arts, sciences, and learned professions'. Utopia came close to driving out the millennium; at Nauvoo would be effected all 'those things which are of such vast importance to this and every succeeding generation'. Whether these generations would live in a fortress Zion, an armed camp in a wicked world, or would succeed each other through the millennium itself, is not made clear. Indeed the distinction has disappeared. The difference between Zion in the wilderness under a tolerant American constitution and Zion the centre of the new dispensation would remain significant theoretically, but in practice paradise would have been regained whatever the label attached to it. In form the Mormons remained firmly pre-millennialist, but in substance the optimistic post-millennialism of the 'redeemer nation' took over.[15] The good life, spiritual and temporal, was to be built by men under the guidance of God.

For British pre-millennialists the transition from the old to the new, from evil to good, could only be through the suffering which the great catastrophe would inflict on all men; their own suffering would be made tolerable by the promise of justification on the farther side of the crisis. For the Mormon saints, the transition was a voyage across the Atlantic and up the Mississippi, a voyage which would leave the catastrophe behind, a mild experience of suffering more than relieved by the prospect of immediate earthly as well as eventual heavenly joys. Though they talked and wrote of the second coming and the wrath of the last days, they planned a millennium made by human hands, such a substantial instalment of blessedness that its fullness would hardly be missed. The gathered saints were indeed to wait, but in great comfort and with full human freedom and dignity. The British prophets always described, rather zestfully, the trials of a suffering remnant; the American saints, quite as enthusiastically, the triumphs of a prospering remnant. In their proclamation the presidents of the Church told the British saints to expect 'a scene of peace and prosperity'. Almost as an afterthought they added: 'In addition to all temporal blessings, there is no other way for the Saints to be saved in these last days.' They recalled their doctrine in time, but not before they had set down a good deal which stretched its strict limits. And they concluded with an invitation that doctrine alone could never have induced them to issue, an invitation to all good people, irrespective of religion, to come and settle.

The characteristic mixture of eschatology and community-building was revealed in detail by an editorial written to deny newspaper stories about the savage and inhospitable condition of Nauvoo.[16] Though the writer made much of the unique opportunity to experience the joys of pure worship, he made much more of the benefits of political liberty and prosperity. The moment the emigrants 'bid farewell to their native shores, they hoist the *Flag of Liberty*—the ensign of Zion—the stars and stripes of the American Union; and under its protection they completely and practically NULIFY [*sic*] THE BREAD TAX.' But there was as much stress upon power as upon liberty. The young and the middle-aged will serve in Zion's armies 'to strengthen her bulwarks—that the enemies of law and order, who have sought her destruction, may stand afar off and tremble, and her banners become terrible to the wicked.' This is the Church literally militant; the new dispensation is not only to be built, but also to be defended. Zion will resemble Munster as well as New Harmony. The remnant will not suffer in meekness; it will prosper in defiant strength.

Emigration enabled the Mormon propagandists to offer British members three attractive prospects: temporal well-being, independence in a militant Zion, sure survival through the catastrophe to come. This attractiveness would be increased rather than reduced by the tendency of the three prospects to blend. But emigration was never the sole appeal of the Church, nor even the main one. Quite without it, the Mormon preachers were able to offer, in the life of the new Church, a range of satisfactions finely tuned to many familiar elements in British religious life. It is striking how complete this range was. It included a firm insistence upon Church order, a strong emphasis upon ministry and sacraments, a sufficient scope for gifts of the spirit, and a clean break from existing denominations. In an examination of these aspects of Mormon life and teaching will be found the basic, but not the total, relationship of the Mormons to the British religious context and specifically to its millennial characteristics.

To become a saint meant passing through a four-step initiation: obedience to the gospel, repentance of sins, baptism by total immersion for the remission of sins, and the reception of the Holy Ghost by the laying on of hands for perfecting in the faith.[17] This is obviously close to the traditional pattern of profession of faith, penance, baptism, and confirmation; though the Mormons had no love for Puseyites, to an extent they spoke the same language. But only to an extent; the Mormon Church was much more universalist and worldly. An exposition of 'Four Kinds of Salvation'[18] contained doctrines to which Tractarians and orthodox Christians generally could not have given assent. The believer is saved from original sin by Christ, whose sacrifice applies to all men; thus little children, incapable of actual sin, are holy. Baptism saves the believer only from actual, pre-baptismal, sin. Further, he may enjoy temporal salvation, either in Jerusalem or in the American west, from the judgement to come. Finally, he may achieve eternal salvation by keeping the commandments of Jesus until death. Within the Church, he will be enabled to keep the commandments while enjoying a foretaste of the joys to come. Here the high Church parallel becomes valid again. The Church will provide the total context of the life of the believer and train him for the blessedness he already in part enjoys. The Church is a projection of eternity into time, of heaven into earth.

The possession of a true priesthood was one of the major Mormon arguments against other churches. The false priesthood of Rome and the derivative priesthoods of the Church of England and of Dissent were set against the true priesthood of the saints, which was reckoned to be a necessary consequence of the true revelation of the latter days. The Mormons did not move in a free-spirit manner beyond priesthoods and ordinances, but into a more rigorous application of both. 'In every age of the world where God has had a gospel church, there has always been connected with that gospel a priesthood, whose duties and privileges it was to hold intercourse with heaven, receive instructions from the lord, administer in the ordinances of the gospel, and govern the kingdom of God or church of Jesus Christ.'[19] Again, the tone and the pattern is traditional and conservative; the language is that of authority, hierarchy, order and sacraments.

In the so-called Irvingite Church a high view of the Church, a hierarchical ministry and a veneration for the 'gifts of the Spirit' co-existed. The same combination occurred on a much larger scale with the Mormons. The British saints also enthusiastically embraced speaking in tongues and healing the sick. Such gifts, accepted as authentic signs of the reception of the Holy Ghost and of the coming end of the world, were a prominent feature of their church life. But equally notable was the realistic caution with which its leaders treated these manifestations, their insistence upon distinguishing between good and evil spirits, and their determination that the gifts should not disrupt the decorum and discipline of an orderly Church.

In its very first number, the *Star* emphasized that the Church was an institution both disciplined and free. Its life was characterized by the sacraments as well as preaching, hierarchy as well as democracy, regularity as well as enthusiasm, ordinances as well as revelations. Rival churches could be criticized from either of two vantage points—either as too enthusiastic or as too unenthusiastic. Thus the Church of England was criticized precisely for its lack of spontaneous spiritual phenomena. 'Do they teach them to believe in, and pray for the gifts of the spirit, such as revelations, visions, prophesyings, miracles, tongues, interpretations, healings, ministering of angels, etc?'[20] The correct answer would not, in fact, be the 'no' anticipated by the rhetorical question. Over the past twenty years quite a few English clergymen had been seeking such gifts, though they would not have felt at ease with the shape in which they came to the Mormons. The British, in fact, or some of them, had a great appetite for the extraordinary in religion. Many of them satisfied it in the Mormon Church, to such an extent that the elders, like Irving in this as in so much else, tempered their initial and indeed obligatory approval with caution—with, in fact, rather more caution than Irving.

The belief that unusual manifestations were valid spiritual gifts was firmly held, but carefully balanced by exhortations to keep their appearance within decent bounds. Inexperienced saints, it was laid down, were all too likely to cry aloud and deliver judgements, and to feel that they should not restrain these promptings lest they grieve the spirit. But 'the spirits of the prophets must be subject to the prophets.' Paul's advice to the Church at Corinth was quoted at length; the saints were advised to 'strive earnestly for the best gifts—the gifts of charity, wisdom, and knowledge', to edify each other in their own language and to seek interpretation should they speak in an unknown language. Never were they to hold meetings simply for this purpose, nor to speak in tongues in front of people who came especially to hear them do so.[21] While the gifts were in essence good,

Satan could manipulate them to lead the saints to rebel against the authority of the priesthood.

A very full discussion of the subject, first published in America, showed, besides the typical combination of approval and caution, a keen desire to separate the experience of the Saints from that of other groups celebrated for unusual happenings.[22] As such phenomena were not necessarily of God but might come from Satan, the proper authorities within the Church must exercise discernment. Outside the Church, four rival groups were selected for especially severe treatment: the Camissards, the Southcottians, the followers of Jemimah Wilkinson and the Irvingites. Much of the case against them rested upon the argument that women have no place in church leadership: 'where do we read of a woman that was the founder of a church in the word of God?' The conventional strictures against women being heard in church were recited with considerable emphasis.

The Irvingites were singled out for the most elaborate condemnation, because they were 'a people that have counterfeited the truth perhaps the nearest of any of our modern sectarians.' Irving had great ability, but he was 'wild and enthusiastic in his views' and fell 'into the common error of considering all supernatural manifestations to be of God'; he let the prophetesses dominate by allowing them to speak in church, to rebuke him and other ministers, and to be (so it was claimed) responsible for the organization of the church. Further, the Irvingites did not observe the true principles of church order; it was remarked that a man was permitted to prophesy before baptism and the laying on of hands. Finally, the Irvingite predictions, like those of the Southcottians, had been proved false by the passage of time. If such a critique had been found in, say, the high Tory *British Critic*, little of it would have seemed out of place. It is with some surprise that one finds the followers of Joseph Smith equally sure that 'there was nothing indecorous in the proceedings of the Lord's prophets in any age.' The writer of this admonition admitted that the saints themselves had suffered from their share of false manifestations, but only because members had been recruited from all the sects and were not fully converted. Within the Church the authority of the priesthood was used to correct those running to excess; members who would not repent of such error were cut off.

The Mormon apologists, then, offered a surprisingly comprehensive image of the Church; it combined, for example, a vindication of authority with an acceptance of signs and wonders. But the former, very definitely, prevailed over the latter. Contemporaries (and later writers) who mistook them for a handful of cranks had no good reason for their mistake. In contemporary England only the Irvingite Church rivalled its positive affirmations and its scope. But, unlike that body, it was not the creation of a group of middle-class devotees, overdependent on a few fitfully charismatic individuals. The Latter-Day Saints did not see themselves as a sect and they did not behave like one; they saw themselves as the new and the true Church which reached back over Antichrist to the apostles and was, through special revelations, the continuation of the Church of Israel. Its posture towards the world was that of a Church proudly conscious of being *the* Church; it did not call to itself a righteous handful, but all humanity. Mormonism provided a much more energetic version of church-centred millennialism than the British were able to create for themselves.

This millennialism, spanning the whole range of British variants and annexing to the new dispensation the material and ideological attractions of the new world, was Mormonism's main feature. It was the Church of the new age, called into being (re-called in its own estimation) at the end of the old dispensation to guide humanity in its passage to the new, and then to preside over the new world—new, in senses of the word that range from the conventional to the eschatological. A few autobiographical fragments will illustrate the satisfying shape of this theological artifact.

One of the leading British elders, Joseph Fielding, told his story in the *Millennial Star* at some length.[23] His father was a devoted Methodist local preacher whose attachment to that church diminished as he grew older, even though 'he evidently increased in the spirit, and drew nearer to God as he drew nearer his end.' In 1832 Fielding left for Upper Canada 'as cheerfully as though I had been going home; the Lord was with me in all things.' There he and a small group of neighbours 'began to look more closely into the scriptures, from which we saw many things which had not been taught us; for instance, the first and second resurrection, the destruction of the wicked in the last days by the judgements of God, the coming of Christ to reign on the earth, in the millennium, and the apostacy of the Gentile churches.' A Methodist preacher who stayed at Fielding's house began to preach these ideas, but was forced to desist by the threat of expulsion. Fielding continued: 'our constant cry was that God would bestow upon us the Holy Ghost'—but they did not know where to exepect it to come from. Parley P. Pratt came from Kirkland to this little flock and satisfied their yearnings with baptism and the laying on of hands. Where before Fielding had 'mourned because I could not keep the Spirit of God . . . and this was the experience of the Methodists there in general', now members of the group began to speak in tongues, prophesy and heal the sick. 'What could I wish for more as evidence that it was the pure Gospel of God [?]' At the same time Irvingite missionaries from England began to convert other of Fielding's neighbours, but he had no difficulty in concluding that their spirit was evil. 'When the Saints began to speak in tongues, it filled the soul with joy and sweetness, but the other's [*sic*] (for they had what they called utterances) filled one with horror.'

When Pratt prophesied great troubles for Canada—'the steamboats would come loaded with rebels'—Fielding 'again began to think of getting out of the way' and readily accepted a command to preach in England. Before he came to England (where the short-lived hospitality of his brother at Preston gave the saints their first foothold)[24] he spent some time at Kirkland where he became fully convinced that 'The prophets and the seers are no longer to be covered up, the vision is no longer as the words of a book that is sealed, but the light of the glory of God has begun again to shine as in times of old, and it will shine brighter until the perfect day, until it shall cover the earth as the waters the great deep; and, as we are no monopolists, we invite all men to come and look for themselves, and share in the blessings.'

Another English convert, James Wood of Yorkshire, told a similar story.[25] He had learned early from the scriptures that two precepts are there set down: First, that its instructions should be minutely followed, for example on baptism by immersion and other matters of church order, and second, that he should look for the second coming. Only 'the followers of John Wroe . . . and the believers in the late Joanna Southcote, with some clergymen of the Church of England' preached this latter doctrine. He obeyed the first precept by joining a Baptist congregation, 'but to my surprise and sorrow I found they had no ear to hear of the second coming of Christ.' Then he heard of 'a people called "The Latter-Day Saints", or Jerusalem Saints,' read an open letter Pratt had addressed to the Queen 'touching the signs of the times and the political destiny of the world,' and became convinced of the truth of their teaching, without, it seems, having had any personal contact with any of them. Another convert, formerly a Wesleyan local preacher, G. Mitchelson, noted in his account of his conversion the importance of three changes of opinion: from an allegorical post-millennialism to a literal pre-millennialism, from credal statements to free interpretation of the scriptures, and from sprinkling infants to immersing adults.[26]

Clearly, from these personal accounts, motivations vary, but running through them is a constant millennialist search, an anxiety to find a church in which the teachings about the new age were clearly and prominently set forth. This they found in the doctrine of the Mormon preachers, as the informing principle of the new Church's ecclesiology. This ecclesiology, already half-familiar to British hearers, was in essence a new version of sacred history.

This version of sacred history had clear points of relationship with ideas already made familiar in Great Britain by such writers as Jurieu, Priestley, Bicheno, and later Beecher and Campbell. Further it was not wholly unlike the widely propagated views of Owen, Smith and Ward. Perhaps one should not be surprised to find, in the columns of the *Star*, Mormon preachers defended from Wesleyan disrupters by socialists, nor a Mormon comment that the socialists were better Christians than the so-called orthodox, nor even a report that in Glasgow the saints were accused of being socialists. But the chief resemblance is with Dissent. It arises in two ways: first, from the value placed upon civil and religious liberty within the divine strategy; second, and consequentially, from the broadening of the Antichrist concept to include all established religious groups. The Mormon version is distinctive in that it is not unambiguously libertarian (one cannot be sure that liberty is valued as more than a pre-condition for propaganda), and that it is much more explicity theological and ecclesiological than the older versions. Nevertheless, there is an unmistakable family likeness.

The whole family of views pronounces the papal period a time of entire darkness, in which the original purity of the gospel was perverted. But while Jurieu had seen a clean break at the time of the Reformation (not complete but still an effective beginning), the Mormons could see only a false start. Luther's initiative was not taken up; the protestant period was no more than sub-papal. The restoration of the true Church waited upon the special revelations of the early nineteenth century, when ancient true priests revisited earth as angels to re-establish continuity.[27] In spite of many other differences, Priestley was not so very far from this viewpoint in holding that the protestant establishments had so involved themselves in the interest and in the fate of the old iniquity that a new start was necessary. Priestley believed that the unitarian profession was both a new start and a return to primitive purity, though of course he did not surround this belief with special revelations and a new church history.

The chief claim of the Mormon preachers was that they had a new church based upon a new revelation, that this newness was true antiquity, and that continuity between the new and the old was effected in a way which escaped contamination from the anti-Christian interim. Every aspect had an American imprint: the double migration of pre-Christian Jews to America, their prophets' knowledge of the incarnation, the confirmation of this knowledge and the commissioning of a new Church by the risen Christ, the revelation of these truths to Joseph Smith in a way which was both a restoration and a new start, the spread of the Church of the Saints from America to the whole world and the American location both of the actively waiting Zion and the millennial kingdom. The familiar pattern of British prophetic teaching was given a new and engaging shape by this American orientation. This orientation, the theology of America as a cosmic fact, is the significant innovation of the Mormons.

The American location was fully providential. There was nothing adventitious about the way in which revelation sought out an American, Joseph Smith, for he was chosen to preside over a restoration of a true Church that had previously existed in America, not in Europe under the shadow of the Danielic statue. The stone that was to shatter the statue was an American stone; as a consequence America itself, social and political, is made sacred. The path of empire indeed took its course westward. 'The Kingdom of God, Or the Stone cut out of the Mountain without Hands'—this is the title of an essay in the *Star* concisely presenting in prophetic terms the concept of cosmic America.[28]

Here it is laid down that the 'great image' of Nebuchadnezzar's dream 'was a representation of the forms of government, and institutions, both civil and religious, from the days of Daniel, down to the present time, including the four great Monarchies [Babylon, Persia, Greece and Rome], and all the modern kingdoms, forms of government, and civil and religious institutions which have been perpetuated by, or handed down, or borrowed from the Roman empire. No[t] only the Catholics, but the Protestants of every sect and name constitute parts of this image, either directly or indirectly from popery.' All this tyranny and corruption, civil and ecclesiastical, is on the verge of destruction. The kingdom of God, 'represented by a stone cut out of a mountain without hands', will 'rise over the ruins of fallen empires, and control the world'. The description of the stone, so the argument proceeded, implies that it has no relation at all to the image; the kingdom it represents must be quite separate from the regimes included in the image. It must be a 'land separated, a country secluded, a nation by itself'. This kingdom set up by God must have 'a government, a civil, a political, and religious organisation under his immediate directions, at once a theocracy'. Where shall these characteristics be found? 'America is such a country, the Book of Mormon contains, and is connected with such oracles and institutions, and the Latter-Day Saints are such a people.' The writings in the Book of Mormon 'were all written after they [the Jaredites and the Nephites] had gone into the wilderness as a free people, or after they had arrived in America, and had become entirely distinct and separate from all the forms of government represented by the image.' This remains, after all, the world of Thomas Jefferson; he wrote of one migration and Joseph Smith of another, but they were both explaining how a people became free by sailing away from corruption. The impulse behind *A Summary View of the Rights of British America* is not hard to find; the theological disguise which has to be penetrated is not so very heavy.

America, however, is not the stone; it is the mountain out of which the stone was to be cut: 'the country where, or the mountain from which this kingdom should originate'. The so-called history of the world is only the history of half of it—'the western world reposed in security from all the commotions of the eastern hemisphere.' America was 'the land held in reserve from the dominion of the image, and destined to give rise to the kingdom . . . the holy mountain where God's purpose lay concealed, and from whence they were to originate in the latter day.' The modern history of America is of a piece with the ancient records. It was colonized by refugees who 'threw off the yoke of oppression . . . and laid the foundation of a free and independent government, and of free institutions. A Washington and others were raised up and inspired by the spirit of freedom (which is the spirit of God) to form the constitution, and to organise and defend a country and government as different from the tyrannical and oppressive governments of the old world as light differs from darkness, or as heaven is higher than the earth.'

This is a high destiny for America. True, she was the mountain, not the stone, but she contained, preserved and liberated the elements from which the kingdom was made. At this still elevated level her destiny was sacred and providential. All the events of her modern history were designed 'to prepare the way for His church and kingdom to be re-established as in days of old, and to come forth out of the wilderness as a bride adorned for her husband'. No sooner had free government been established, than 'lo! the heavens were opened and angels were commissioned to bear glad tidings of great joy to the people of that favoured land.' The imagery quite deliberately recalls that of the incarnation. So were brought into being the Saints of the Latter Days, 'a people every way governed by direct revelation from the King of heaven and earth, the Lord Jesus Christ.' This people, maintaining 'the freedom of their country and the cause of God', must increase their 'dominion and power by the dissemination of truth until the great image which has so long held men in bondage . . . shall disappear [*sic*]; and then shall the government of Jesus Christ, under the administration of his saints, extend its dominion so as to form a universal kingdom over the whole earth.' Manifest destiny, like immemorial rights, was contained in the language of prophecy; America was more than a cosmic fact, it had also a cosmic mission.

Perhaps a good deal of the Mormon preachers' striking success arose from the new shape they gave to a familiar prophetical message. Perhaps, too, they were successful because the re-arranged message led to a belief in the possibility of effective action within the scope of actual possibilities. While orthodox exegetes told men to live purely, and Irvingites told them to come together and wait, and Owen invited them to find harmony in a community, the Mormons made exactly the same biddings, and also pointed to the place where they could be obeyed immediately, the wilderness Zion. A man might be hard put to know how to be pure, or to wait indefinitely, or to find a community, but he could think he was beginning to do all these things if he paid down £5 and took ship for America.

Still, the greater number of the British saints stayed at home. They could, at least, feel sure that something was doing in a far and famous place that was part of their own salvation. They could add to the disembodied outline of the millennial dream the firm contours of America, the fresh start, the second chance, the new society. No British prophet produced a millennial vision as complete, as compelling or as concrete as Joseph Smith's fellow workers when, for the time between persecution in Missouri and his murder in Illinois, they and the American dream seemed to thrive together. No British millennialist enjoyed a success comparable to that of the Mormons. It was better to set the millennium for this year in America than for next year in Jerusalem.

XI: Some Possible Futures

The argument of this book is that in the later eighteenth and earlier nineteenth centuries the habit of looking at the world in a manner shaped by biblical prophecy was a normal and widespread activity, and that the thought-forms and conceptual vocabulary associated with this habit were employed well beyond the limited area occupied by specialist prophetical commentators. The intellectual respectability of a habit of mind which is to be discovered in Priestley, Irving, Newman and Owen, should be evident enough from a recital of their names. Nevertheless, the claim made here on behalf of prophetic and millennialist thought is not, so much, that it was an eminent way of thinking about man and society (though, as used by some, it was). The chief claim is that it was a commonly and widely used way of thinking, and that accounts of the intellectual history of the period should not ignore it.

Though research has not been taken further than the 1840s (and, in that decade, concentrated upon the Mormons), and though it is apparent that some people went on thinking in this manner from that time to the present day, it remains highly probable that the habit suffered an at least relative decline in the later nineteenth century. It is necessary to attempt an explanation of this decline and to relate the earlier phenomena to the apocalyptic style of the twentieth century, in many ways a very different style.

Few parts of the Bible were as vulnerable to modern critical scholarship as those dwelt upon by prophetical exegetes. There had always been a marked element of arbitrariness in their scholarly conventions, so that arguments of the kind used by Maitland were damaging enough before 'higher criticism' added its effect. When a critical system designed to clarify the literary form, authorship, dating and historical circumstances of biblical writings became widely accepted, it became difficult for serious scholars to practise the kind of exegesis which had seemed a reasonable intellectual activity to men like Faber and Cuninghame. As a consequence, the uses of biblical prophecy explored in this book remained valid only for those groups and individuals who were untouched by new habits of biblical scholarship. The output of books, tracts and sermons on these themes has been continuous to the present day—in terms of sheer volume it has probably increased—but this activity has ceased to be a normal part of the scholarly work of the major Christian denominations. Eschatology remains a branch of theology, but chiefly (for eminent theologians) either an exercise in historical scholarship or an explanation of 'realized' eschatology—realized, situationally, in the life of the individual and of the Church. This latter, though not too far from the probable inner motivations of prophetic preachers, is still a good distance from the professed concerns of earlier theologians.

The decline of biblical literalism and the related decline of providential world-views centred upon a constantly intervening personal deity, probably did as much as anything else to make prophetic thought a minor element in intellectual history generally, and also within the spectrum of Christian thought. Two other developments probably contributed to this end: first the transfer of the apocalyptic style to non-Christian ideologies, and second the erosive effect of the strenuous, if less than total, optimism of the later nineteenth century. The first will be taken up shortly. The effect of the second can be suggested by pointing to the optimistic post-millennialists of the early part of the century. Here, in the end, millennialism was extinguished by the idea of progress.

It is still the case, of course, that the partial decline of a specific kind of eschatology has not seen the end of attitudes which are profoundly, though less biblically, eschatological. Apocalypses are a twentieth-century commonplace; secular and sacred varieties have abounded, at least since the First World War. National Socialism's 'Reich of a thousand years' would be worth exploring as a deviant millennium. 'Socialism in one country' has at least some affinities with the Zion-Utopias which were to incapsulate and establish the coming kingdom. Nor have Western responses to the Kaiser, to Hitler and to Stalin lacked benefit of references to the Beast, Antichrist and Armageddon. Every turn in the Middle East conflict has sent fundamentalist tract writers back to their Bibles for an explanation and a forecast. The twentieth-century world has not yet lost contact with the images of calamity and survival which were so much more familiar earlier. Fundamentalist Christianity is anything but expiring, and its biblical arithmeticians are still busy. Less literalist Christians are still apt to be struck by the wickedness and destructiveness of the world; preachers still remind their congregations that God will bring evil to an end and wonder if the time will be soon. Among Roman Catholics, the Fatima cult showed the apocalyptic mood in full flower. The strange marriage, in protestantism, between some fundamentalist groups and the newly emergent 'Jesus Movement' shows the same stream running in other, and perhaps more surprising, places. The spread of pentecostal and charismatic beliefs and practices carries with it a yearning for what would have been called, in the 1820s, a 'more copious effusion' of the spirit and a comparable expectation of Christian renewal. So great has been the recent revival, in part through fundamentalism and pentecostalism, of anticipations of the end of the world, that it may be no longer proper, in the later 1970s, to treat such Christianity as of marginal significance.

Nevertheless, if all the evidence was added together, it would probably not be shown that specifically Christian apocalypses predominated in the later twentieth century. Earlier, if one wanted to identify and give a total characterization to a potentially disastrous contemporary phenomenon, one called it Antichrist. Today the phenomena have achieved their conceptual autonomy: the atomic bomb, the population explosion and the ecology crisis are apocalyptic enough on their own. One would not add much to their capacity to alarm if one labelled them Antichrist. In the early nineteenth century, if one called the Revolution, or popular democracy, or the Napoleonic Empire Antichrist, one added a great deal. Today's apocalypses appal in their own right—their mythological shoring up, if it exists, is as likely to come from science fiction as from Christianity.

Yet, as science fiction, the U.F.O. hypthesis and related beliefs show, many of the old symbols are transmuted rather than eliminated. Very frequently in novels, in the statements of U.F.O. writers and in religious beliefs which seem to stem in part from such sources, one finds a scenario essentially made up of three acts—original purity, intervening disorder, restored purity. Purity, both original and restored, comes from elsewhere—and whether it be from another planet, or another galaxy, or from heaven, and whether the restoration be effected by an incorrupt alien or by a returning Messiah, does not alter the basic concept in any essential manner. In a truly millennialist fashion, one not wholly alien to the early nineteenth century, the evil that happens down here is being set right by goodness sent from up there.

Again, the apocalyptic mood deriving from the population and its pressure on the environment, has an element of relationship with the earlier period. The alarmed conservatives of the Revolutionary period and after saw in the emergent masses the chief sign of Antichrist and the chief agency of destruction, because they were controlled by forces which were destroying established pieties and conventional order. The parallel should not be pressed too closely, but today there is a similar alarm at the pressure of masses upon resources, impelled by ideas and aspirations which are fundamentally subversive.

The resemblances between earlier Christian and later secular apocalypses recede, however, at a point that can be indicated by the word 'God'. The viewpoints explored in this book were highly providential, either directly with the theologians, or indirectly with, for example, Owen. The rest of the nineteenth century saw an abrupt and, for some, total attenuation and depersonalization of providence. As this took place in response to the apparent affirmations of geology, biology, science and social science, the forces of nature and history absorbed and objectified all, or most, that had been projected into the highly personal concept of 'God'. Perhaps it is at this time that the forces of disorder achieved their autonomy by shaking off their conceptual inheritance. Few contemporary apocalypses, except those still reproduced by Christian fundamentalists, retain the intimacy and comfort of a prospective providential rescue, except the markedly post-Christian versions of science fiction. No one else appears to believe that we can save ourselves from the bomb, or from people, except by our own arduous effort. Whether this is gain or loss is quite another question.

That it is loss for some is suggested by the current vogue of end-of-world oriented religiosity, both in its more traditional forms, and in the 'Jesus Movement' phenomena. Maybe, too, it is reflected in the persistent growth of pentecostal and charismatic religious practices and organizations, in which, as with the Irvingites, ecstatic phenomena, a belief in significant change, and an emphatically providential view of man, society and history, co-exist. If this speculation should be justified, the old symbols may yet prove to have a long life ahead of them.

In a quite different social context, that of adjustment cults, cargo cults, 'religions of the oppressed', these images may have already had a long and fruitful career. The outlines of this possibility are simple enough, though the details would, were they found to exist, be infinitely complex. If ever the long-awaited marriage between history and sociology should take place, the benefits for the study of prophecy and millennialism would be especially great. One would be able to advance some distance towards an answer to the question: How are the more closely studied movements of a prophetic and millennialist kind among third-world and tribal societies related to the currents of opinion and action described in this book? Bryan Wilson has recently published a major synthesis which goes a very great distance towards answering the question in terms of a classificatory system based upon types of response.[1] But this typological approach, eminently satisfying in itself, cannot help but leave the question unanswered from an historical point of view. The historical concern with continuities over time, with probable causal relationships, with the problem of relationships in specific spatial and temporal contexts, requires its own kind of answer.

This answer would emerge from a series of detailed studies aimed at seeing what connexions might be found between specific missionary initiatives and specific tribal and third-world millennialist manifestations. At the moment, this problem can only be approached in the most general manner. The fifty years covered by this book saw, as well as a significant level of prophetic and millennialist theorizing, the beginning of a missionary outreach which was to send messengers of salvation from Europe and America into almost every part of Africa, Asia, Oceania and Latin America. At least it seems reasonable to suppose, if only because the great majority of missionaries had a literalist attitude to the whole Bible, and because it is evident that many of them understood their activities in the light of eschatology, that the missionary message and the indigenous response could well have a close relationship. The supposition that there was a lack of relationship would, in the face of it, require more justification.

To suppose that a real relationship would be found to exist does not suggest that the indigenous response would be a mere mirror-image. On the contrary; the variant of millennialism which appealed to the great missionary societies of Great Britain and America was optimistic and progressivist, the variant least disposed to the 'rejection of prevailing cultural values, goals and norms'.[2] More typically, the indigenous response is a rejection of such norms and an attempt to mobilize a power to overthrow them. The 'mutations of sectarian response'[3] would have to be extended to include the creative innovations of the objects of missionary enterprise. However, a movement from an optimistic and progressivist to a pessimistic and apocalyptical use of prophecy could be made well within the bounds of the span of attitudes discussed in this book. It should not be presumed at the outset that the indigenous responses Wilson calls 'revolutionist' and 'introversionist' could not as readily have been derived from the missionary deposit as those he calls 'reformist' and 'utopian'.[4]

The attempt to see if such correspondences exist would require an immense labour, chiefly directed to identifying the specific versions of the gospel which particular missionaries imparted to particular communities, and relating these to the subsequent religious history of these communities and their neighbours. Whether, in fact, the actual terms of missionary preaching would be recoverable in such detail, it is not possible to say.

However, it is already possible to be sure that one perennially fruitful influence was transmitted, in accessible vernacular translations, by missionaries to those they regarded as converts—the Bible. Over the whole Christian history of Europe its visions of divine wrath and reconstruction had continued to shape a millennialist response to the world, often enough without apparent benefit of explicit instructions and commentary. There is no reason to believe that they did not continue to do so in non-European contexts, long after missionary influence had been withdrawn or rejected. If, in this more general way, and in ways related to the specific content of missionary preaching, the initial impact and subsequent utilization of Christian prophetic and millennialist thought proved to be sufficiently recoverable, then the most significant twentieth-century residue of an earlier time's prophetic excitement would, probably, have been discovered.

References

1: Biblical Prophecy and Millennialism

1. Purposes which are indicated by their sub-titles: Norman Cohn, *The Pursuit of the Millennium*, 1957, sub-titled *Revolutionary Messianism in Medieval and Reformation Europe and its Bearing on Modern Totalitarian Movements* in 1961; and Ernest Lee Tuveson, *Millennium and Utopia, a Study in the Background of the Idea of Progress*, 1949.
2. In S. L. Thrupp (ed.), *Millennial Dreams in Action*, 1962, pp. 37-39.
3. B. Wilson, in *Comparative Studies in Social History*, VI, pp. 93-114, October 1963.
4. E. P. Thompson, *The Making of the English Working Class*, 1963.

II: A Sketch of the Traditions

1. *Shapes of Philosophical History*, 1965, pp. 13-23.
2. Eric Voegelin, *The New Science of Politics*, 1952, pp. 110 ff.
3. Primarily M. E. Reeves, *The Influence of Prophecy in the Later Middle Ages, a Study in Joachimism*, 1969, and G. Leff, *Heresy in the Later Middle Ages: the Relation of Heterodoxy to Dissent c.1250-c.1450*, 1967. See also: M. W. Bloomfield and M. E. Reeves, 'The penetration of Joachism into northern Europe', *Speculum*, XXIX, pp. 772-93; M. W. Bloomfield, 'Joachim of Flora', *Traditio*, XIII, pp. 249-319; F. E. Manuel, *Shapes of Philosophical History*, 1965; K. Löwith, *Meaning in History*, 1955 ed.; M. E. Reeves, *Joachim of Fiore and the Prophetic Future*, 1976.
4. G. H. Williams, *The Radical Reformation*, 1962, pp. 857-8.
5. *A Dictionary of Writers on the Prophecies*, 1835, lists an immense number and variety of works in its 114 pages. Its only entry for Joachim is an early sixteenth-century edition of a work on Isaiah, which it pronounces dubious.
6. Two seventeenth-century mystics, whose writings were reprinted in the early nineteenth century, echo very strongly the more heterodox aspects of Joachism, the stress upon the superiority of the third Age of the Spirit. See John Saltmarsh, *Sparkles of Glory: or Some Beams of the Morning Star*, 1811 and 1847, and Jane Lead, *Divine Revelations and Prophecies*, 1820.
7. C. Hill, *Antichrist in Seventeenth-century England*, 1969.
8. E. L. Tuveson, *Millenium and Utopia*, 1949, p. 28. Though this polemical purpose certainly encouraged the idea of progress, millennialism is in essence anti-progressivist.
9. William Haller, *Foxe's Book of Martyrs and the Elect Nation*, 1963.
10. W. M. Lamont, *Godly Rule: Politics and Religion, 1603-60*, 1969, and criticizing Lamont's extreme view of Brightman's importance, Bernard Capp, in *Past and Present*, 52, pp. 106-17.
11. Thomas Fuller, *The Worthies of England*, ed. John Freeman, 1952, II, p. 183.
12. *Christian Observer*, XXV, pp. 496-7.

13. Richard Hurd, 'An Introduction to the Study of the Prophecies', 1772, *Works*, V. p. 256, 1969 reprint of the edition of 1811.
14. Thomas Newton, *Dissertations on the Prophecies*, 2nd ed., 1759 and 1760, I, pp. 1-2, 5.
15. *Works*, V. pp. 169, 172, 175. Priestley attacked Hurd's position with some vigour in his *History of the Corruptions of Christianity*, II, p. 483.
16. David Hartley, *Observations on Man*, 1966 reprint of 1749 edition, Part II, pp. 366-81.
17. F. E. Manuel, *Isaac Newton Historian*, 1963, pp. 7-8, 165, 256n. One of his protégés, Nicoas Fatio de Duillier, was discredited for his alleged connexion with them.
18. *Remarkable Extracts*, ed. E. May, 1790 and 1793, p. 22. The page of the copy consulted (Bodleian Library, Oxford) which contains these views is heavily marked in pencil, and annotated 'Socialism predicted, *after* 1785'.

III: Responses to Revolution

1. Joseph Priestley, *History of the Corruptions of Christianity*, 1782, II, p. 466.
2. ibid., I, pp. v-vi. Priestley's *Description of a New Chart of History*, 1777, pp. 21-22, contains a similar use of images from Daniel, 2:31-45.
3. Part one of *Two Sermons*, 1794.
4. *Letters to the Jews*, 1794, p. 48; and *Two Sermons*, p. 28.
5. *Two Sermons*, p. 41.
6. *Letters to the Jews*, p. 9.
7. *A Continuation of the Letters to the Philosophers and Politicians of France*, 1794, pp. iii-iv.
8. *Two Sermons*, p. 49.
9. *Letters to the Philosophers and Politicians of France*, 1794, p. 24.
10. *Continuation of the Letters*, p. 92.
11. *Two Sermons*, p. 30.
12. ibid., p. 31.
13. ibid., p. 36.
14. James Bicheno, *Signs of the Times*, 1793, p. 7.
15. ibid., p. iv.
16. ibid., p. 101.
17. *A Word in Season*, 1795, pp. 43-44, 47.
18. *The Fulfilment of Prophecy Further Illustrated*, 1817, pp. 10, 12, 18.
19. ibid., pp. 109, 112.
20. ibid., pp. 195-6.
21. *The Restoration of the Jews*, 1800, p. 95.
22. ibid., p. 65.
23. *The Man of Sin*, 1794, pp. 10, 14, 18, 26.
24. *Critical Disquisitions on the Eighteenth Chapter of Isaiah*, 1800 (American edition), pp. 21, 94, 98, 99-100.
25. *British Magazine*, IV, pp. 717-41.
26. ibid., V. pp. 131-41, 261-2, 406-12, 517-23, and VI, pp. 10-18.
27. *The Watchers and the Holy Ones*, 1806, pp. 24-27.
28. 'Memoir' by F. A. Faber, in G. S. Faber, *The Many Mansions in the House of the Father*, 1854.
29. *History the Interpreter of Prophecy*, 1799, III, p. 7.
30. *Two Sermons*, 1799, p. 25.
31. *Dissertation on the Prophecies*, 1806, I, pp. xix-xx.
32. ibid., I, pp. 317-8.
33. ibid., I, pp. 324-6.

34. Frere's *Combined View of the Prophecies*, 1815, answered by Faber in the *Fifth Apocalyptic Vial* in the same year.
35. *Dissertation on the Prophecies*, I, p. 342.
36. ibid., I, p. 103.
37. *Fifth Apocalyptic Vial*, 1815, p. 5.
38. *Dissertation*, II, p. 408.
39. *General and Connected View*, 1808, II, p. 319.
40. *Supplement to the Dissertation*, 1806, p. 181.
41. *General and Connected View*, I, pp. vii-ix; II, pp. 318-19.
42. *Dissertation*, I, p. xxiii.
43. *General and Connected View*, I, pp. vi-vii.
44. *Treatise on the . . . Dispensations*, 1823, p. 22.
45. *Sacred Calendar of Prophecy*, 1828, I, p. 74.
46. *Three Sermons on the Jubilee*, 1810, pp. 42, 54, 56-7, 63, 70, 88.
47. ibid., p. 180.
48. *The Crisis*, 1825, p. 259.
49. ibid., p. 221.
50. *The Apocalypse of St. John*, 1827, pp. xv-xvi.
51. ibid., p. 283.

IV: Arguments about Prophecy

1. *Dissertation*, II, p. 413.
2. *Practical View of the Redeemer's Advent*, 1825, p. xi.
3. ibid., p. 156.
4. *The Cause and Remedy for National Distress*, 1826, p. 22.
5. *Christian Observer*, XXIII, pp. 281-2, 347-51, 408-11.
6. ibid., XXV, pp. 422-35, 489-520.
7. *Brief Enquiry into the Prospects of the Church of Christ*, 1828, pp. 709.
8. ibid., pp. 152, 16, 18, 21.
9. ibid., pp. 150, 117-18, 149.
10. ibid., pp. 154-5.
11. ibid., pp. 278-9.
12. ibid., pp. 279-82.
13. *The Prophecies Concerning Antichrist*, 1830, p. 61 of 1853 edn.
14. *Second Enquiry into the Grounds*, 1829, p. 108.
15. *An Enquiry into the Grounds*, 1826, pp. 53-57.
16. *Modern Fanaticism Unveiled*, 1831, pp. 191, 200, 202, 209-10. The British Museum catalogue attributes the work to a Mrs Henderson.
17. ibid., p. 210.
18. ibid., pp. 101-2.
19. Paris, 1817, and noticed in the *Quarterly Review*, XXXIII, pp. 375 *et seq.*, 1826.
20. *The Latest Heresy*, 1832, pp. 16-17.
21. cited n.6 above.
22. *Sermons Preached in London at the Formation of the Missionary Society*, 1797, pp. xi, xix.
23. ibid., pp. 118, 119, 121, 122, 130.
24. ibid., pp. 176-9, 182, 201.
25. Eugene Stock, *History of the Church Missionary Society*, 1899, I, p. 71.
26. *Annual Sermons of the Society for Missions to Africa and the East*, p. 172.
27. William Canton, *A History of the British and Foreign Bible Society*, 1904, I, p. 12.
28. Alexander Shand of Aberdeen according to an MS note on the copy at the Bodleian Library.

29. *An Explanation of the Interesting Prophecy*, 1817, p. 40.
30. *Four Sermons*, 1806, p. 90.
31. *A Sermon preached in Aid of the London Society*, 1811; see pp. 40-43 for references to the meeting of the Sanhedrin in Paris in 1806.
32. *Address in Behalf of the London Society*, n.d., p. 2.
33. *Letter to the Rev C. Simeon*, 1828.
34. *Sermon Preached Before the [London Jewish] Society*, 1817.
35. *Reviewers Reviewed: or, Observations on Article II of the British Critic for January. 1819*, 1819, pp. 7, 12, 44.
36. *The Latter Rain*, 1821, pp. viii-ix, xxvi, xxix, xxxii, 62; *Christian Observer*, XX, pp. 505-10.
37. *Dissertation on the Seals and Trumpets*, p. vi of 1817 ed.
38. *Letters and Essays . . . on . . . Israel*, 1822, pp. 278-9, 286-92, 293.
39. ibid., pp. 184-90.
40. *Evangelical Magazine*, XXIX, pp. 52-5; and for similar discussions, XXX, pp. 7-9, 53-6, 98-102; I (N.S.), pp. 12-16; III (N.S.), pp. 184-5.
41. ibid., XXX, pp. 305-9, 436-8, 469-72.
42. ibid., III (N.S.), pp. 361-5, 239-41.
43. ibid., V (N.S.), p. 68.
44. ibid., VI (N.S.), pp. 142-5.
45. ibid., VI (N.S.), pp. 347-51, 387-91.
46. ibid., VI (N.S.), p. 481; VII (N.S.), pp. 190-2, 407-8.
47. ibid., VII (N.S.), p. 404.
48. ibid., VI (N.S.), pp. 569-72.
49. *Wesleyan-Methodist Magazine*, VII (3rd Series), pp. 31-35, 441-51, 515-17.
50. ibid., IX (3rd Series), p. 19.

V: Irving and Drummond

1. Introduction to *The Coming of the Messiah*, 1827, p. clxxii.
2. ibid., p. xlvii.
3. ibid., pp. liv-vi, lix-x.
4. ibid., p. l.
5. G. Carlyle (ed.), *The Prophetical Works of Edward Irving*, 1867, 1870, I, pp. 464, 459-90.
6. Introduction to *The Coming of the Messiah*, p. lii.
7. ibid., p. lxi.
8. ibid., pp. lxii-xv.
9. ibid., pp. lxv-xvi.
10. A. L. Drummond, *Edward Irving and his Circle*, 1937, pp. 56-57; M. Oliphant, *The Life of Edward Irving*, 1862, I, pp. 186-7.
11. Quoted in Oliphant, pp. 190-1.
12. *A Defence of the Students of Prophecy*, 1828, p. 115.
13. ibid., p. 50.
14. ibid., p. 116.
15. ibid., p. 51.
16. ibid., p. 124.
17. *Social Duties upon Christian Principles*, 1830, pp. 160-1.
18. ibid., pp. vii, viii, 3, 6-7.
19. ibid., pp. 89, 143, 171-2, 173-4.
20. ibid., pp. 155, 121, 131-2.
21. ibid., p. 154.
22. G. Carlyle (ed.), *Prophetical Works*, II, p. 498.

23. *Dialogues on Prophecy*, 1828 and 1829, III, p. 463; II, p. 240.
24. ibid., I, pp. 58-59.
25. ibid., II, pp. 242, 245.
26. ibid., II, pp. 244-5; I, pp. 348 ff.
27. ibid., II, pp. 250-2.
28. ibid., II, p. 253.
29. ibid., III, pp. 250, 253-4.
30. ibid., III, p. 256.
31. ibid., I, p. 366.
32. ibid., II, pp. 358, 360.
33. ibid., III, pp. 422 ff.
34. ibid., I, p. 363; II, pp. 355-6; III, pp. 436-7.
35. ibid., I, p. 369; II, pp. 291, 295.
36. ibid., II, p. 296.
37. ibid., II, pp. 291-2, 297.

VI: The Albury Group and its Context

1. *Dialogues on Prophecy*, I, p. 217.
2. T. R. Birks, *Memoir of the Rev. Edward Bickersteth*, 2nd ed., 1852, II, p. 43.
3. *British Critic*, II, pp. 1-27.
4. ibid., VIII, pp. 393-426.
5. *Evangelical Review*, VIII (New series), p. iii.
6. *The Times of the Gentiles*, 1828, pp. iv-v.
7. ibid., pp. 12, 16, 18-19, 25-26, 39.
8. *Popular Lectures on the Prophecies Relative to the Jewish Nation*, 1830, pp. 167, 177.
9. *Letters to a Friend*, 1834, pp. x, 177, 188-9.
10. ibid., pp. 138, 150.
11. J. H. Frere, *Eight Letters on the Prophecies*, 1831, pp. 54-59, 61-67, 77-80.
12. *Dissertation on the Seals and Trumpets*, 2nd edn, 1817, pp. 351-2.
13. ibid., pp. 356-7.
14. William Cuninghame, *Letters and Essays . . . on . . . Israel*, 1822, pp. 184-90.
15. T. R. Birks, I, p. 42.
16. ibid., I, p. 421; II, p. 17.
17. ibid., II, p. 45.
18. *A Sermon Preached in the Parish Church of Hatfield . . .*, 1831, pp. 9, 29, 32.
19. *A Practical Guide to the Prophecies*, 1835, pp. ix, 8, 32.
20. ibid., pp. 64, 65, 67, 120, 72.
21. ibid., p. 104.
22. *Exposition of the Revelation*, quoted in 'Memoir' in *Sermons: by the late Rev. Henry Gauntlett*, 1835, I, p. cxv.
23. ibid., I, pp. clxxiii, clxxx-clxxxi, cxcvii-cxcviii.
24. *Sermons for the Christian Year*, 1875-88, I, Sermons XI and XXII.
25. ibid., I, Sermons VIII, IX, XVII.
26. ibid., I, Sermon XXII.
27. *Parochial and Plain Sermons*, 1908-16, V, Sermon I.
28. ibid., I, Sermon XXIV.
29. ibid., IV, Sermon XXII.
30. ibid., VI, Sermon XVII.

VII: John Ward—the Messiah as Agitator

1. *The Dictionary of National Biography* (XX, sub. Ward, John) wrongly identifies the M.P. as Alexander Perceval.

2. *Hansard*, XI (3rd series), cols. 577-81.
3. ibid., XX (2nd series), cols. 331, 333, 522, 798, 572-3, 1166, 1168.
4. *Zion's Works. New Light on the Bible from the Coming of Shiloh, The Spirit of Truth*, IX, p. 247.
5. ibid., XII, pp. 296-7.
6. ibid., VIII, pp. 38-39.
7. *Past Finding Out*, 1956, p. 97.
8. *Derbyshire Courier*, 31 March, 21 April 1832.
9. *Derbyshire and Chesterfield Reporter*, 16 August 1832.
10. *Memoir of John Ward*, [1881], p. 7.
11. See Chapter II.
12. *Memoir of John Ward*, p. 3.
13. John Ward, *The Judgment Seat of Christ*, 1831, pp. 65-74. See *Zion's Works*, X.
14. *Zion's Works*, XI, p. 188.
15. 'On 2 Esdras VII, 28', ibid., VI, pp. 264 *et seq.*
16. 'Priestcraft Fairly Exposed', ibid., III, pp. 211-12.
17. *Lion*, II, pp. 321, 385-92.
18. Balleine, p. 95. Balleine does not document the statement.
19. *Lion*, I, p. 141.
20. *Zion's Works*, II, pp. 280 *et seq.*
21. ibid., V, pp. 37-38, 57-61, 64-65; VI, pp. 324-38; VII, pp. 175-7, 325.
22. *Standard of Zion*, 1831, p. 28; see *Zion's Works*, XII.
23. ibid., pp. 4-5, 63.
24. *Important Discovery*, n.d., part 2, p. 3; see *Zion's Works*, VIII.
25. *Standard of Zion*, pp. 4-5, 63-64.
26. *A Mince Pie for True Reformers*, 1833, p. 8.
27. *Important Discovery*, part 1, pp. 4-8.
28. Details of the trial are taken from the *Derby and Chesterfield Reporter*, 16 August 1832.
29. *Hansard*, XIV. (3rd Series), cols. 1410-11.
30. *Hansard*, XI. (3rd Series), col. 580.
31. *Lion*, I, p. 69.
32. *Poor Man's Guardian*, 19 November 1831.
33. ibid., 3 September 1831.
34. ibid., 31 August 1833.
35. *Political Soldier*, 7 December 1833.
36. *Working Man's Friend*, 12 January 1833.
37. *Poor Man's Guardian*, 22 March 1834.
38. I. McCalman, 'Popular radicalism and freethought in early nineteenth century England', A.N.U. thesis, Canberra, n.d.
39. *Richard Carlile*, 1943, pp. 30, 34-35.
40. Abstract of the Lectures, 1837, p. 11.
41. ibid., pp. 27-28.

VIII: The Empirically Proven Messiah

1. 'Letter to the Lord Chancellor', *Crisis*, 10 May 1834. See also 'The Legacy of Robert Owen', *Pioneer*, 29 March 1834.
2. *Crisis*, 2 August 1834.
3. ibid., 23 August 1834.
4. ibid., 14 June 1834.
5. G. D. H. Cole (ed.), *A New View of Society and Other Writings*, 1949, (Everyman edition), p. 18.

6. ibid., pp. 17, 19-20.
7. ibid., pp. 93-4, 95, 97.
8. ibid., pp. 109, 102, 103, 104.
9. See his careful introduction of this term in this *Address* (ibid., pp. 104, 106), where the phrasing suggests that Owen knew that he was inviting a new content into an old concept.
10. ibid., pp. 103, 105.
11. ibid., p. 107. But in later life Owen did apply to himself the image of the stone which 'the builders up of society' rejected. *Life of Robert Owen. Written by Himself. With Selections from his Writings and Correspondence*, I. 1857, p. 203.
12. Cole (ed.), pp. 108-9.
13. ibid., pp. 111, 114, 115, 116, 117, 118.
14. *Life*, I, p. 207. See Psalm 95 in which Jehovah is represented as reproving Israel for its iniquities while passing through the wilderness to the promised land.
15. ibid., I.A., p. 113.
16. ibid., I.A., p. 114.
17. ibid., I, pp. 158-65. The quotations which follow are from this passage.
18. The quoted passage corresponds almost exactly to the text of the *Address* given in ibid., I.A., p. 115, except that the punctuation has been revised to make it more exclamatory.
19. ibid., I.A., pp. 115, 116.
20. ibid., I.A., pp. 120, 121.
21. ibid., I.A., pp. 132-3. The biblical reference is to Micah 4:3,4.
22. ibid., I.A., p. 133.
23. ibid., I.A., p. 133. For the quotations which follow, see ibid., I.A., pp. 133-7.
24. Isaiah 11:6,9. Later, in a rare biblical citation, Owen referred his readers to Isaiah 58, 59 and 65 for more on the calamities of ignorance, the omnipotence of truth, and the changes to take place.
25. *Life*, I.A., pp. iv-v, xvii-xi, xxx-iii, for the quotations which follow.
26. ibid., I.A., pp. xlii-iii.
27. ibid., I, p. 16.
28. ibid., I, p. 36.
29. ibid., I, pp. 100-1. See above pp. 70-71.
30. ibid., I.A., p. xxxvi.

IX: From the Southcottians to Socialism

1. W. A. Smith, whose biography *Shepherd Smith the Universalist*, 1892, contains numerous extracts of letters to and from Smith.
2. ibid., p. 21.
3. Letter of 10 June 1828, ibid., pp. 34-36.
4. Letters of 5 November and 22 December 1828, ibid., pp. 39, 40.
5. Letter of 23 June 1829, ibid., p. 44.
6. Letter of 17 February 1830, ibid., pp. 46-47.
7. *Lion*, I. 78, 99-103; IV. 138-40.
8. n.d. W. A. Smith, p. 53.
9. Letter of 15 June 1831, ibid., p. 54.
10. *Zion's Works*, VI.
11. ibid., VI.
12. W. A. Smith, p. 91.
13. ibid., pp. 61-62. The letter is undated and the recipient is not specified.
14. Letter of 19 November 1833, ibid., pp. 93-94.
15. Letter of 28 March 1834, ibid., pp. 95-96.

16. See Chapter VIII.
17. Two letters from Hibbert and nineteen pages of translation comprise No. 144 of the Owen papers at Holyoake House, Manchester.
18. 'Lettres sur la religion et la politique', *Nouveau Christianisme*, 1832, p. 164.
19. ibid., pp. 174-5.
20. ibid., pp. 203, 280-1.
21. ibid., pp. 228-30, 240, 256.
22. ibid., pp. 260-2.
23. S. C. G. Charléty, *Histoire du Saint-Simonisme*, 1931, p. 64. Charléty does not say which of the Rodrigues brothers.
24. *Pioneer*, 15 March to 28 June 1834. The whole work consists of fourteen letters.
25. Letter III, ibid., 5 April 1834.
26. Letter IV, ibid., 12 April 1834.
27. Letters II and IX, ibid., 22 March and 24 May 1834.
28. Letters XI, XII, XIV, ibid., 7, 14 and 28 June 1834.
29. Letter IX, ibid., 24 May 1834.
30. See reports of his lectures in the *Crisis*, 16 and 30 November 1833 and 4 January 1834.
32. Letter of 28 March 1834, W. A. Smith, p. 98.
33. 'We are trying in the *Pioneer* to bring in the religious world, and we are catching them fast.' ibid.
34. 8 February 1834.

X: The Mormons—Cosmic America

1. B. H. Roberts (ed.), *History of the Church of Jesus Christ of Latter-Day Saints*, 2nd ed., 1957, I, p. xxv.
2. *Evangelical Magazine*, XXX, p. 7-9, 53-56, 98-102.
3. ibid., I (new series), p. 14.
4. *Millenial Harbinger*, I, p. 152; reprinted from Campbell's journal.
5. ibid., I, p. 1.
6. B. H.Roberts (ed.), IV, pp. 222-3.
7. *Millennial Star*, II, p. 77, 126; III, p. 30.
8. B. H. Roberts (ed.), I, p. 492.
9. ibid., I, pp. 4-8, 73-76.
10. T. R. Birks, II, p. 167.
11. *Millennial Star*, I, pp. 30-37; italics added.
12. ibid., II, pp. 105-6.
13. ibid., I, pp. 252-5.
14. ibid., I, pp. 265-74.
15. E. L. Tuveson, *Redeemer Nation: the Idea of America's Millennial Role*, 1968.
16. *Millennial Star*, II, pp. 153-5.
17. ibid., I, p. 84.
18. ibid., II, pp. 21-22.
19. ibid., IV, p. 2.
20. ibid., I, pp. 8-18.
21. ibid., I, pp. 128-9.
22. 'Try the Spirits', ibid., III, pp. 36-43.
23. ibid., II, pp. 49-53.
24. B. H. Roberts (ed.), II, pp. 498-9.
25. *Millennial Star*, II, pp. 54-55.
26. ibid., III, pp. 11-14, 25-28.
27. ibid., II, p. 131.
28. ibid., III, pp. 92-94.

XI: Some Possible Futures

1. *Magic and the Millennium: a Sociological Study of Religious Movements of Protest Among Tribal and Third-World Peoples*, London, 1973.
2. ibid., p. 21.
3. ibid., Ch. 2.
4. ibid., p. 27.

Bibliography

In addition to works cited in the text, a number of sources, both primary and secondary, are listed here because they contributed in some measure to argument and conclusions of this book. In the case of some eighteenth-century English writings, an American publication was used. In some instances a slightly abbreviated title is given below, and no attempt is made to reproduce original capitalization.

I Contemporary Books and Pamphlets.

Aitken, Robert. *The Second Coming of Christ.* London, 1839.

Anon. *Prophecy a Preservative Against Infidelity.* Hackney, 1819.

Anon. *Prophecy of Things that are Fast Approaching, and Which Will Shortly Come to Pass.* London, 1806.

Anon. *A Review of Scripture, in Testimony of the Truth of the Second Advent, the First Resurrection, and the Millennium.* London, 1818.

Benbow, William. *Grand National Holiday and Congress of the Productive Classes.* London, 1832.

Bicheno, James. *The Consequences of Unjust War.* London, 1810.

Bicheno, James. *The Fulfilment of Prophecy Further Illustrated by the Signs of the Times.* London, 1817.

Bicheno, James. *A Glance at the History of Christianity, and of English Non-Conformity.* Newbury, 1798.

Bicheno, James. *The Restoration of the Jews, the Crisis of all Nations.* London, 1800.

Bicheno, James. *The Signs of the Times: or the Overthrow of the Papal Tyranny in France, the Prelude to the Destruction of Popery and Despotism, but of Peace to Mankind,* 4th ed., with large additions. London, 1794.

Bicheno, James. *A Word in Season: or, a Call to the Inhabitants of Great Britain, to Stand Prepared for the Consequences of the Present War.* London, 1795.

Bickersteth, Edward. *Address in Behalf of the London Society for Promoting Christianity amongst the Jews.* London, n.d.

Bickersteth, Edward. *A Help to the Study of the Scriptures . . . by a Churchman.* Norwich, 1815.

Bickersteth, Edward. *A Practical Guide to the Prophecies, with Reference to their Interpretation and Fulfilment, and to Personal Edification,* 4th ed., much enlarged. London, 1835.

Bickersteth, Edward. *A Sermon Preached in the Parish Church of Hatfield, on Monday, June 20, 1831, at the Triennial Visitation of the Lord Bishop of Lincoln.* London, 1831.

Biddulph, Thomas T. *The Prognostics of the Kingdom of God; and the Scriptural Expectations of the Christian Church.* Bristol, 1821.

Birks, T. R. *Memoir of the Rev. Edward Bickersteth.* 2nd ed. London, 1852.

Blunt, John Henry. *Dictionary of Sects, Heresies, Ecclesiastical Parties, and Schools of Religious Thought.* London, 1874.

Bogue, David. *The Diffusion of Divine Truth. A Sermon Preached Before the Religious Tract Society.* London, 1800.

Boone, T. C. *The Book of Churches and Sects.* London, 1825.

Brightman, Thomas. *A Revelation of the Revelation that is. The Revelation of St John Opened Clearly.* Amsterdam, 1615.

Buchanan, Claudius. *Christian Researches in Asia: with Notices of the Translation of the Scriptures into the Oriental Languages,* 2nd ed. enlarged. London, 1811.

Buchanan, Claudius. 'A Sermon Preached . . . Before the Society for Missions to Africa and the East, in *Annual Sermons of the Society.* London, 1810.

Buchanan, Claudius. *Three Sermons on the Jubilee . . . also, The Star in the East,* 2nd and 7th eds. London, 1810.

Carlile, Richard. *An Abstract Embodying the Evidences . . . to Prove that the Bible is not a Book of Historical Record but an Important Mythological Volume.* London, 1837.

Cooper, Edward. *The Crisis; or, an Attempt to Show from Prophecy, Illustrated by the Signs of the Times, the Prospects and Duties of the Church of Christ at the Present Period,* 3rd ed., 'considerably enlarged and altered'. London, 1826.

Cooper, Edward. *A Letter to the Editor of the British Review Occasioned by his Remarks on The Crisis.* London, 1825.

Cooper, Edward. *Letters Addressed to a Serious and Humble Enquirer after Divine Truth.* London, 1817.

Cooper, Edward. *Sermon Preached before the [London Jewish] Society.* London, 1819.

Croly, George. *The Apocalypse of St John, or Prophecy of the Rise, Progress, and Fall of the Church of Rome.* London, 1827.

Croly, George. *The Englishman's Polar Star.* Preston, 1828.

Cuninghame, William. *A Dissertation on the Seals and Trumpets of the Apocalypse, and the Prophetical Period of Twelve Hundred and Sixty Years,* 2nd ed. London, 1817.

Cuninghame, William. *A Letter to . . . Ashley on the Necessity of Immediate Measures for the Jewish Colonisation of Palestine.* London, 1849.

Cuninghame, William. *Letters and Essays, Controversial and Critical, on Subjects Connected with the Conversion and National Restoration of Israel.* London, 1822.

Dealtry, William. *A Sermon Preached . . . Before the London Society.* London, 1815.

Dictionary of Writers on the Prophecies. Compiled by the Editor of the

Investigator on Prophecy. London, 1835.
Drummond, Henry. *A Defence of the Students of Prophecy*. London, 1828.
Drummond, Henry [comp.]. *Dialogues on Prophecy*, 3 v. London, 1828, 1829.
Drummond, Henry. *Social Duties on Christian Principles*. London, 1830.
Drummond, Henry [?]. *Supplement to the Candid Examination of the Controversy . . . Respecting the Human Nature of the Lord Jesus Christ*. London, 1830.
Faber, George Stanley. *The Conversion of the Jews to the Faith of Christ, the True Medium of the Conversion of the Gentile World*. London, 1822.
Faber, George Stanley. *A Dissertation on the Prophecies . . . Relative to the Great Period of 1260 Years*, 2 v. London, 1806; Third Volume (supplementary dissertations). London, 1818.
Faber, George Stanley. *A Dissertation on the Prophecy Contained in Daniel IX. 24-27; Generally Denominated the Prophecy of the Seventy Weeks*. London, 1811.
Faber, George Stanley. *A General and Connected View of the Prophecies, Relative to the Conversion, Restoration, Union, and Future Glory, of the Houses of Judah and Israel*, 2 v. London, 1808.
Faber, George Stanley. *The Many Mansions in the House of the Father*, Prefatory memoir by Francis A. Faber, 2nd ed. London, 1854.
Faber, George Stanley. *Remarks on the Effusion of the Fifth Apocalyptic Vial, and the Late Extraordinary Restoration of the Imperial Revolutionary Government of France*. London, 1815.
Faber, George Stanley. *The Revival of the French Emperorship Anticipated from the Necessity of Prophecy*, 2nd ed. London, 1853.
Faber, George Stanley. *The Sacred Calendar of Prophecy*, 3 v. London, 1828.
Faber, George Stanley. *A Supplement to the Dissertation on the 1260 Years*. Stockton, 1806.
Faber, George Stanley. *Two Sermons Preached Before the University of Oxford Feb. 10, 1799*. Oxford, 1799.
Faber, George Stanley. *A Treatise on the Genius and Object of the Patriarchal, the Levitical and the Christian Dispensations*, 2 v. London, 1823.
Fleming, Robert. *Apocalyptical Key. An Extraordinary Discourse on the Rise and Fall of the Papacy; or the Pouring Out of the Vials . . .* , printed from the original published in the year 1701. London, 1793.
Fleming, Robert (Senior). *The Fulfilling of the Scripture Complete; in Three Parts*. London, 1726.
Frere, James Hatley. *A Combined View of the Prophecies of Daniel, Esdras and St John*. London, 1815.
Frere, James Hatley. *Eight Letters on the Prophecies Relating to the Last Times*. London, 1831.
Frere, James Hatley. *On the General Structure of the Apocalypse*. London, 1826.
Gauntlett, Henry. *An Exposition of the Book of Revelation*, 2nd ed. London, 1821.

Gauntlett, Henry. *Sermons: . . . with a Memoir of the Author*, 2 v. London, 1835.

Gilbee, Earle. *A Sermon, Preached . . . Before the Bedford Auxiliary Society, for Promoting Christianity amongst the Jews*. London, 1812.

Gipps, Henry. *A Treatise on 'The First Resurrection' and 'The Thousand Years' Foretold in the Twentieth Chapter of the Book of Revelations*. London, 1831.

Godwin, B. *A Discourse on the Signs of the Times*. London, 1822.

Goode, William. *Modern Claims to the Possession of Extraordinary Gifts of the Spirit, Stated and Examined*. London, 1833.

Graves, Richard. *A Sermon Preached in . . . Dublin . . . in Aid of the London Society*. Dublin, 1811.

Greenwood, Thomas. *The Latest Heresy: or Modern Pretensions to the Miraculous Gifts of Healing and of Tongues, Condemned by Reason and Scripture*. London, 1832.

Hartley, David. *Observations on Man, his Frame, his Duty, and his Expectations*. London, 1749 (Reprint, 1966).

Henderson, Mrs [?]. *Modern Fanaticism Unveiled*. London, 1831.

Hetherington, Henry. *Cheap Salvation; or, an Antidote to Priestcraft*, 2nd ed. London, 1843.

[Holinsworth, C. B.] *Memoir of John Ward*. Birmingham, 1881.

Holinsworth, C. B. *The Shilohite's Bible, or the Literal 'Bible' as Transformed into Spirit and Life by the Revelation of God to Zion Ward*. n.p., 1901.

Horsley, Samuel. *Biblical Criticism and the First Fourteen Historical Books of the Old Testament; Also on the First Nine Prophetical Books*, 4 v. London, 1820.

Horsley, Samuel. *Critical Disquisitions on the Eighteenth Chapter of Isaiah*. Philadelphia, 1800.

Horsley, Samuel. *The Watchers and the Holy Ones*. London, 1806.

Hunter, Henry. *A Sermon . . . on the Occasion of the Trial, Condemnation, and Execution of Louis XVI . . . To Which is Subjoined . . . a Republication of a Discourse on the Rise and Fall of the Papacy: . . . by Robert Fleming*. London, 1793.

Hurd, Richard. *The Works of R. Hurd*. London, 1811 (Reprint, 1969).

Irving, Edward. *The Coming of the Messiah in Glory and Majesty. By Juan Josafat Ben-Ezra a Converted Jew. Translated from the Spanish, with a Preliminary Discourse, by the Rev. Edward Irving, A.M.* London, 1827.

Irving, Edward. *For Missionaries After the Apostolical School*. London, 1825.

Irving, Edward. *The Prophetical Works of Edward Irving*, 2 v., Ed. Gavin Carlyle. London, 1867-70.

Jones, William. *The Man of Sin*, 3rd ed. London, 1794.

Jurieu, Pierre. *Predictions of the Singular Events Which Have Recently Taken Place in France . . . Extracted from a Work Printed in the Year 1687, written by M. Peter Jurieu . . .* . Bath, 1793.

Jurieu, Pierre. *Remarkable Extracts Selected from a Work Printed in the Year 1687, by Peter Jurieu, Entitled The Accomplishment of the Scripture*

Prophecies etc. Henley, 1793.

Keble, John. *Sermons for the Christian Year*, 11 v. London, 1875-88.

Kett, Henry. *History the Interpreter of Prophecy*, 3 v. Oxford, 1799.

Lacy, John. *The Prophetical Warnings of John Lacy, Esq; Pronounced Under the Operation of the Spirit; and Faithfully Taken in Writing, When They Were Spoken.* London, 1707.

Lead, Jane. *Divine Revelations and Prophecies.* By Mrs Jane Lead. Nottingham, 1830.

Lessing, Gotthold Ephraim. *The Education of the Human Race*, tr. F. W. Robertson, London and New York, n.d.

London Missionary Society. *Four Sermons Preached in London at the 12th Annual Meeting of the Missionary Society . . . 1806, by* [T. Charles, S. Bradley, D. Bogue, R. Whittingham]. London, 1806.

London Missionary Society, *Sermons Preached in London at the Formation of the Missionary Society.* London, 1797.

Love, Christopher. *The Strange and Wonderful Predictions of Mr Christopher Love.* Glasgow, 1783.

McNeile, Hugh. *Letters to a Friend Who Has Felt it His Duty to Secede from the Church of England.* London, 1834.

McNeile, Hugh. *Popular Lectures on the Prophecies Relative to the Jewish Nation.* London, 1830.

McNeile, Hugh. *The Times of the Gentiles.* London, 1828.

Maitland, S. R. *An Attempt to Elucidate the Prophecies Concerning Antichrist*, 2nd ed. London, 1853.

Maitland, S. R. *An Enquiry into the Grounds on Which the Prophetic Period of Daniel and St John has been Supposed to Consist of 1260 Years.* London, 1826.

Maitland, S. R. *A Letter to the Rev. Charles Simeon.* London, 1828.

Maitland, S. R. *A Second Enquiry into the Grounds on Which the Prophetic Period of Daniel and St. John, has been Supposed to Consist of 1260 Years.* London, 1829.

Maitland, S. R. *The Twelve Hundred and Sixty Days. In Reply to a Review in the Morning Watch.* London, 1830.

Maitland, S. R. *The Twelve Hundred and Sixty Days: in Reply to the Strictures of William Cuninghame, Esq.* London, 1834.

Mede, Joseph. *The Apostacy of the Latter Times.* London, 1641.

Mede, Joseph. *Daniel's Weekes: an Interpretation of Part of the Prophecy of Daniel.* London, 1643.

Mede, Joseph. *The Key of the Revelation Searched and Demonstrated.* London, 1643.

Mede, Joseph. *A Paraphrase and Exposition of the Prophecie of Saint Peter.* London, 1642.

Milner, Joseph. *Practical Sermons on the Epistles to the Seven Churches, the Millennium, and the Church Triumphant, and on the CXXXth. Psalm*, with prefatory remarks by Edward Bickersteth. London, 1830.

More, Henry. *Apocalypsis Apocalypseos; or the Revelation of St John the Divine Unveiled.* London, 1680.

More, Henry. *A Plain and Continued Exposition of the Several Prophecies and Divine Visions of the Prophet Daniel.* London, 1681.
Napier, John. *Napier's Narration: or, An Epitome of His Books on the Revelation.* London, 1641.
Napier, John. *A Plaine Discovery of the Whole Revelation of St. John*, 5th ed. Edinburgh, 1645.
Napier, Mark. *Memoirs of John Napier of Merchiston.* London, 1834.
Newman, J. H. *Parochial and Plain Sermons.* London, 1908-16.
Newton, Isaac. *Observations Upon the Prophecies of Daniel and the Apocalypse of St. John.* London, 1733.
Newton, Thomas. *Dissertation on the Prophecies, Which Have Remarkably Been Fulfilled, and at This Time are Fulfilling in the World*, 3 v. London, 1759, 1760.
Noel, Gerald T. *A Brief Enquiry into the Prospects of the Church of Christ, in Connection with the Second Advent of Our Lord Jesus Christ.* London, 1828.
Noel, Gerald T. *A Sermon, Preached . . . Before the London Society.* London, 1820.
Owen, John. *The Shaking and Translating of Heaven and Earth. A Sermon Preached to the Honourable House of Commons . . . on April 19. A Day Set Apart for Extraordinary Humiliation.* London, 1649.
Owen, Robert. *The Life of Robert Owen. Written by Himself. With Selections from His Writings and Correspondence*, v. I. London, 1857.
Owen, Robert. *A Supplementary Appendix to the First Volume of the Life of Robert Owen. Containing a Series of Reports, Addresses, Memorials, and Other Documents Referred to in that Volume. 1808-1820*, v.I.A. London, 1858.
Owen, Robert. *A New View of Society and Other Writings by Robert Owen.* Ed. G. D. H. Cole. London, 1949.
Owen, Robert. *The Signs of the Times; or, the Approach of the Millennium.* London, 1841.
Pastor Fido (pseud.). *Pastorini Proved to be a Bad Prophet, and a Worse Divine; in an Address to the Roman Catholics of Ireland, Earnestly Recommended to Their Serious Perusal. By Pastor Fido.* Dublin, 1823.
Priestley, Joseph. *A Continuation of the Letters to the Philosophers and Politicians of France, on the Subject of Religion.* Northumberland-town, 1794.
Priestley, Joseph. *A Description of a New Chart of History*, 4th ed. London, 1777.
Priestley, Joseph. *An History of the Corruptions of Christianity in Two Volumes*, 2 v. Birmingham, 1782.
Priestley, Joseph. *Institutes of Natural and Revealed Religion*, 2 v. 3rd ed. London, 1794.
Priestley, Joseph. *Letters from Dr. Priestley to the Jews; Inviting Them to an Amiable Discussion of the Evidences of Christianity.* New York, 1794.
Priestley, Joseph. *Letters to the Philosophers and Politicians of France, on the Subject of Religion.* New York, 1794.

Priestley, Joseph. *Two Sermons, viz. I. The Present State of Europe Compared with Ancient Prophecies . . . . II. The Rise of Christianity, Especially in Difficult Times*. Philadelphia, 1794.

Rodrigues, Eugene. *Lettres sur la Religion et la Politique*. Paris, 1829.

Saltmarsh, John. *Sparkles of Glory; or Some Beams of the Morning Star*. London, 1647.

Shand, Alexander [?]. *An Explanation of the Interesting Prophecy Respecting the Two Apocalyptic Witnesses as Fulfilled by the Institution and Progress of the British and Foreign Bible Society*. London, 1817.

Sherlock, Thomas. *The Use and Intent of Prophecy, in the Several Ages of the World*. London, 1749.

Sibthorp, R. Waldo. *The Character of the Prophecy*. London, 1828.

Stewart, James Haldane. *The Cause and Remedy for National Distress*. London, 1826.

Stewart, James Haldane. *A Practical View of the Redeemer's Advent in a Series of Discourses*. London, 1825.

Usher, James. *The Prophecies and Predictions of the Late Learned Rev. James Usher*. London, 1793.

Walmseley, Charles [Pastorini]. *The General History of the Christian Church from Her Birth to Her Final Triumphant State in Heaven: Chiefly Deduced from the Apocalypse of St. John, the Apostle and Evangelist*, 5th ed. Dublin, 1812.

*Ward, John. *Answer to James Smith's Letter of Inquiry*. [Written at Nottingham 4 Dec 1830.] *Works* VI: 90-108.

Ward, John. *Answer to W. Matthews of Glasgow (a Follower of J. Wroe)*. [Written at Nottingham 5 Dec 1831.] *Works* VI: 109-20.

Ward, John. *A Christmas Box for True Reformers*. [Written 1837.] Birmingham 1864.

Ward, John. *The Conduct of Judge Parke, Counsellor Clarke, with Others*. Birmingham, 1834.

Ward, John. *The Creed of the True Believers in Shiloh, the Man of God*. Birmingham, 1832.

Ward, John. *Divine Truth, Being an Explanation of Some Parts of Scripture, Never Before Opened*. Bristol, 1835.

Ward, John. *England Expects Every Man to Do His Duty. Being a Call to Every Englishman to Refuse Complying with the Unjust Demands Made by a Rapacious Clergy*. Birmingham, 1832.

Ward, John. *Epistle Addressed to Mr Harling, Huddersfield*. [Written at Sheffield, 1830.] *Works* I: 118-40.

Ward, John, *Epistle on Carlile*. [Written in 1832.] *Works* II: 280ff.

Ward, John. *Epistle on the Spiritual Alphabet, and 'Reform of the Church,'*

*Ward's pamphlets, as far as possible, were read in their first publication. In some cases, however, subsequent editions were consulted, chiefly those in the twelve-volume *Zion's Works*. In other cases, certain of his writings appear to be available only in these later printings. In both sets of circumstances, reference is made to both the later publication and to the date either of composition or first publication.

as Attempted by R. Carlile. [Written in Derby Gaol, 1832.] *Works* II: 278-375.

Ward, John. *Epistle to John Wroe's Followers, or Modern Jews.* [Written at London, 1829.] *Works* VI: 1-88.

Ward, John. *The Fall of Lucifer, and the Resurrection of Christ.* Bristol, 1836.

Ward, John. *Good and Evil Made One.* [Written 1831.] Birmingham, 1878.

Ward, John. *The Judgement Seat of Christ.* [No 1, 30 May, to No 17, 1 Oct.] London, 1831.

Ward, John. *A Letter Addressed to the Believers in the Kingdom of God, Residing in London.* Birmingham, [1831].

Ward, John. *A Letter Addressed to the True Reformers of Great Britain.* Birmingham, n.d.

Ward, John. *Letters, Epistles and Revelations of Jesus Christ.* [First published, London 1831.] *Works* XI: 183-377.

Ward, John. *The First Part, A Mince Pie for True Reformers and a Christmas Box for All the Parsons. By an Imprisoned Reformer.* Birmingham, n.d.

Ward, John. *The Second Part, A Mince Pie, etc.* Birmingham, [1833].

Ward, John. *The First Part of the Most Important Discovery Ever Made Known to Mankind. By an Imprisoned Reformer.* Birmingham, n.d.

Ward, John. *The Second Part of the Most Important Discovery.* Birmingham, n.d.

Ward, John. *The Third Part of the Most Important Discovery.* Birmingham, n.d.

Ward, John. *New Light on the Bible.* [Written 1835.] Birmingham [?], 1873 or 1874 [?].

Ward, John. *On 2 Esdras VII.28.* [Letter written 28 Oct 1834.] *Works* VI: 265-97.

Ward, John. *The Origin of Evil Discovered.* Birmingham, 1837.

Ward, John. *This Pamphlet Shows that Man is Not an Accountable Being.* [Written at Bristol, 1835.] Birmingham [?], 1870.

Ward, John. *Priestcraft Fairly Exposed, Being First Letter to C. Bradley, Junior.* Birmingham, 1833[?]. *Works* III: 197-217.

Ward, John. *The Rights of Men Explained in a Most Important Letter to Charles Bradley, Jun.* Birmingham, 1833.

Ward, John. *The Standard of Zion. The Valley of Jehoshaphat. The Sword of the Lord, and of Gideon; being the Substance of Two Discourses, Delivered by Zion, at the Rotunda, Black Friar's Road, London.* Birmingham, 1831.

Ward, John. *The Standard of Zion . . . Being the Substance of the Second Discourse.* Birmingham, 1831.

Ward, John. *To Mr. Charles Bradley, Sen. of Birmingham, (This Letter is Addressed) Showing the Creation of Adam etc.* London, 1831.

Ward, John. *The True Fast Explained; or the Patient Turned Doctor.* Birmingham, n.d.

Ward, John. *The Two Prophets.* [Written at Derby, 1833.] Birmingham, 1847.

Ward, John. *The Vision of Judgment; or, the Return of Joanna from Her Trance.* [First published, London 1829.] *Works* XI: 2-78.

Ward, John. *The Vision of Judgment (continued); or, the Trial and Reward of Faith.* [First published London 1829.] *Works* XI: 79-182.

Ward, John. *Wisdom Triumphant Over Philosophy; or, What is Truth?* Birmingham, 1835.

Ward, John. *The Writings of Zion Ward, or Shiloh, the Spiritual Man. Derby County Gaol, August, 1832. The Doctrine of Zion, Derived from Divinity Revealed in Humanity, by Immediate Visitation of God to John Ward, in the Year 1828,* Pt I Birmingham, 1874, Pt II Birmingham & London, 1874, Pt III Birmingham & London, 1875; introductory and concluding notes by C.B.H. [Holinsworth].

Ward, John. *Zion's Works. New Light on the Bible from the Coming of Shiloh, the Spirit of Truth 1828-1837,* 12 v. London, 1889-1901.

Way, Lewis. *The Latter Rain: With Observations on the Importance of General Prayer for the Special Outpouring of the Holy Spirit.* London, 1821.

Way, Lewis. *Millenium. A Reply to the Considerations on this Subject, Contained in the Appendix to the Rev. H. Gauntlett's Exposition of Revelation.* London, 1822.

Way, Lewis. *Reviewers Reviewed: or, Observations on Article II of the British Critic for January, 1819.* London, 1819.

Way, Lewis. *Sermon Preached Before the* [*London Jewish*] *Society.* London, 1817.

Williams, T. *A Dictionary of All Religions, and Religious Denominations,* 3rd ed. London, 1834.

Witherby, William. *Hints Humbly Submitted to Commentators, and More Especially to Such as have Written Elaborate Dissertations on the Prophecies of Daniel and the Revelation of St John.* London, 1821.

Woodd, Basil. *A Sermon Preached . . . Before the Society for Missions to Africa and the East* [in *Annual Sermons of the Society*]. London, 1807.

II Contemporary Journals and Newspapers

The Antichrist; or, Christianity Reformed. London, 1833.

The British Critic, Quarterly Theological Review, and Ecclesiastical Record, v. I to VI. London, 1827-9.

The British Magazine and Monthly Register of Religious and Ecclesiastical Information, v. I to X. London, 1832-6.

The Christian Guardian and Church of England Magazine. Bristol, 1825-30.

The Christian Investigator, no. 1. London, 1833.

The Christian Observer, Conducted by Members of the Established Church, v. XIX to XXXV. London, 1820-35.

The Congregational Magazine, v. IX (New Series). London, 1832.

The Crisis, or the Change from Error and Misery, to Truth and Happiness [v. I no. 1 to v. II no. 15] continued as: *The Crisis and National Co-operative Trades Union and Equitable Labour Exchange Gazette* [v. II no. 16 to v. IV no. 20]. London, 1832-4.

The Derby and Chesterfield Reporter. August, 1832.

The Derby Mercury. August, 1832.

The Derbyshire Courier, Chesterfield Gazette, and General County Advertiser. March, April and August, 1832.

The Eclectic Review, v. XXV to XXX, I to IV (New Series). London, 1826-30.

The Evangelical Magazine and Missionary Chronicle, v. XXVIII to XXX, I to VIII (New Series). London, 1820-30.

The Investigator, v. I to VIII. London, 1820-4.

The Latter-Day Saints Millennial Star, v. I to VII. Manchester, 1840-6.

The Lion, v. I to IV. London, 1828-9.

The Millennial Harbinger and Voluntary Church Advocate, v. I to II. London, 1835-6.

The Morning Watch; or Quarterly Journal on Prophecy, and Theological Review, v. I to VII. London, 1830-3.

The Pioneer, or Trades' Union Magazine [no. 1 to no. 25] continued as: *The Pioneer, or, Grand National Consolidated Trades' Union Magazine* [no. 26 to no. 44]. Birmingham and London, 1833-4.

The Political Soldier. 1833.

The Poor Man's Guardian; a Weekly Newspaper for the People [variant titles from October 1830 to July 1831]. London, 1830-5.

Prophetical Extracts, v. I to IV. London, 1794-5.

The Quarterly Review, v. XXXIII. London, 1826.

Quarterly Theological Review and Ecclesiastical Record, v. I to IV. London, 1825-6.

The Republican, v. XI to XIV. London, 1825-6.

The Shepherd; a London Weekly Periodical, Illustrating the Principles of Universal Science, nos. 1 to 28. London, 1834-5.

The Wesleyan-Methodist Magazine, v. IV to VIII (3rd Series). London, 1825-9.

The Workingman's Friend, and Political Magazine, nos 1-33. London, 1832-3.

III Secondary Books and Articles

Aldred, Guy A. *Richard Carlile, Agitator. His Life and Times*, 3rd ed. Glasgow, 1941.

Armytage, W. H. C. *Heavens Below: Utopian Experiments in England 1560-1960*. London, 1961.

Balleine, G. R. *History of the Evangelical Party in the Church of England*. London, 1908.

Balleine, G. R. *Past Finding Out: the Tragic Story of Joanna Southcott and Her Successors*. London, 1956.

Bett, Henry. *Joachim of Flora*. London, 1931.

Bloomfield, Morton W. 'Joachim of Flora', *Traditio*, 13:249-311 (1957).

Bloomfield, Morton W. & M. A. Reeves. 'The Penetration of Joachism into Northern Europe', *Speculum*, 29:772-93 (1954).

Butler, E. M. *The Saint-Simonian Religion in Germany: the Young German Movement*. Cambridge, 1926.

Canton, William. *A History of the British and Foreign Bible Society*, 2 v. London, 1904.

Capp, B. S. *The Fifth Monarchy Men: A Study in Seventeenth-century English Millenarianism*. London, 1972.

Capp, Bernard. '*Godly Rule* and English Millenarianism', *Past and Present*, 52:106-17 (1971).

Chadwick, Owen. *The Victorian Church*, Pt I. London, 1966.

Charléty, Sébastian. *Histoire du Saint-Simonisme, 1825-1864*. Paris, 1931.

Clouse, Robert G. 'John Napier and Apocalyptic Thought', *The Sixteenth Century Journal*, 5, 1:101-14 (April, 1974).

Cohn, Norman. *The Pursuit of the Millennium: Revolutionary Messianism in Medieval and Reformation Europe and Its Bearing upon Modern Totalitarian Movements*. London, 1962.

Cole, G. D. H. *Richard Carlile*. London, 1943.

Drummond, Andrew L. *Edward Irving and His Circle*. London, 1937.

Elliott-Binns, L. E. *The Early Evangelicals: a Religious and Social Study*. London, 1953.

Evans, D. O. *Social Romanticism in France*. Oxford, 1951.

Flanders, R. B. *Nauvoo, Kingdom on the Mississippi*. Urbana, 1965.

Garrett, Clarke. *Respectable Folly: Millenarians and the French Revolution in France and England*. Baltimore and London, 1975.

Henriques, Ursula. *Religious Toleration in England 1787-1833*. London, 1961.

Hobsbawm, E. J. *Primitive Rebels*. Manchester, 1959.

Hunt, John. *Religious Thought in England from the Reformation to the End of the Last Century*, 3 v. London, 1870-3.

Hunt, John. *Religious Thought in England in the Nineteenth Century*. London, 1896.

Iggers, Georg G. (ed.) *The Doctrine of Saint-Simon: an Exposition. First Year, 1828-1829*, tr. with notes and an introduction by Georg G. Iggers. Boston, 1958.

Jones, Rufus M. *Mysticism and Democracy in the English Commonwealth*. Cambridge, Mass., 1932.

Jones, R. *Studies in Mystical Religion*. London, 1909.

Kubrin, David. 'Newton and the Cyclical Cosmos: Providence and the Mechanical Philosophy', *Journal of the History of Ideas*, 28:325-46 (1967).

Lamont, W. M. *Godly Rule: Politics and Religion, 1603-1660*. London, 1969.

Lamont, W. M. 'Richard Baxter, the Apocalypse and the Mad Major', *Past and Present*, 55:68-90 (1972).

La Piana, George. 'Joachim of Flora: a Critical Survey', *Speculum*, 7:257-82 (1932).

Leff, Gordon. *Heresy in the Later Middle Ages: the Relation of Heterodoxy to Dissent, c.1250-c.1450*. Manchester, 1967.

Lowith, Karl. *Meaning in History: the Theological Implications of the Philosophy of History*. Chicago, 1949.

McCalman, M. 'Popular Radicalism and Freethought in Early Nineteenth Century England', A.N.U. thesis, Canberra, n.d.

Manuel, Frank E. *Isaac Newton Historian*. Cambridge, 1963.

Manuel, Frank E. *The Prophets of Paris*. Cambridge, Mass., 1962.

Manuel, Frank E. *Shapes of Philosophical History*. Stanford, 1965.

Markham, Felix (ed.) *Henri de Saint-Simon: Social Organisation, the Science of Man and Other Writings*. New York, 1964.

Matthews, Ronald. *English Messiahs: Studies of Six English Religious Pretenders*. London, 1936.

Oliphant, Margaret. *The Life of Edward Irving*, 2 v. London, 1862.

Pankhurst, R. K. P. *The Saint Simonians, Mill and Carlyle: a Preface to Modern Thought*. London, n.d.

Reeves, Marjorie. *The Influence of Prophecy in the Later Middle Ages: a Study in Joachimism*. Oxford, 1969.

Reeves, Marjorie. *Joachim of Fiore and the Prophetic Future*. London, 1976.

Reynolds, J. S. *The Evangelicals at Oxford 1735-1871: a Record of an Unchronicled Movement*. Oxford, 1953.

Roberts, B. H. (ed.) *History of the Church of Jesus Christ of the Latter-Day Saints*, 2nd ed. 1957.

Rogers, P. G. *Battle in Bossenden Wood: the Strange Story of Sir William Courtenay*. London, 1961.

Sandeen, Ernest R. *The Roots of Fundamentalism: British and American Millenarianism 1800-1930*. Chicago and London, 1970.

Smith, W. A. *'Shepherd' Smith the Universalist: the Story of a Mind*. London, 1892.

Sykes, Norman. *From Sheldon to Secker; Aspects of English Church History, 1660-1768*. Cambridge, 1959.

Taylor, G. R. *The Angel-Makers: a Study in the Psychological Origins of Historical Change, 1750-1850*. London, 1958.

Thompson, E. P. *The Making of the English Working Class*. London, 1963.

Thrupp, Sylvia L. (ed.) *Millenial Dreams in Action*. The Hague, 1962.

Toon, Peter (ed.) *Puritans, the Millennium and the Future of Israel: Puritan Eschatology 1600 to 1660*. Cambridge and London, 1970.

Tuveson, Ernest Lee. *Millennium and Utopia, a Study in the Background of the Idea of Progress*. 1949.

Tuveson, Ernest Lee. *Redeemer Nation: the Idea of America's Millennial Role*. Chicago, 1968.

Voegelin, Eric. *The New Science of Politics: an Introduction*. Chicago, 1952.

Williams, George H. *The Radical Reformation*. Philadelphia, 1962.

Wilson, Bryan A. *Magic and the Millennium: a Sociological Study of Religious Movements of Protest Among Tribal and Third-World Peoples*. London, 1973.

Wilson, Bryan A. 'Millenialism in Comparative Perspective', *Comparative Studies in Society and History*, VI, 1:93-114 (Oct 1963).

Index

Aitken, Robert, 222
Albury Park conferences, 42, 67, 90, 91, 93, 106-7, 113, 124, 128, 131, 132, 134
Aldred, Guy A., 172
'Allegorical' interpretations, 18-19, 77, 83, 92, 94, 131-2, 135, 139
Allman, Joseph, 155
Almond, Joseph, 177
Antichrist, 22, 31, 32, 33, 34, 35, 37, 38, 39, 42, 47, 48, 50, 51, 52, 53, 54, 55-56, 57, 58, 59, 64, 66, 67, 79, 85, 89, 115, 119, 120, 121, 131, 142, 154, 161, 177, 186, 187-8, 200, 202-3, 219, 220, 233, 235, 240, 241
Antichrist, 201
Augustine, St, 24, 25, 26, 28, 29, 31, 32, 37, 82, 83, 147, 206

Balleine, G. R., 156
Beecher, Lyman, 97, 235
Benbow, William, 171, 174
Bicheno, James, 15, 46-50, 60, 62, 65, 66, 68, 89, 97, 121, 147, 150, 169, 179, 188, 235
Bickersteth, Edward, 22, 90, 124-5, 126, 128, 134, 136-40, 141, 142, 222, 224
Blackwood's Magazine, 217
Bogue, David, 87, 88, 89, 93, 94
Boon, Mary, 155, 157, 158
Bradley, Charles, 153
Brightman, Thomas, 33, 35, 36, 124
British and Foreign Bible Society, 66, 87, 88, 107, 125, 126, 133
British Critic, 50, 91, 93, 125, 232
British Magazine, 51
Brothers, Richard, 173
Buchanan, Claudius, 11, 64-66, 67, 94

Camissards, 33-34, 39, 131, 198, 232
Campbell, Alexander, 219, 235
Campbell, Mary, 130
Campbellites, 220-1
Carlile, Richard, 11, 12, 17, 159, 160, 161-3, 169, 170, 171, 172-4, 193, 199-200, 213
Carlyle, Thomas, 104, 106, 207
Carpenter, Elias, 177
Catholic Apostolic Church, 24, 99, 107, 112, 113, 121, 127, 136
Catholic Emancipation, 42, 67, 100, 108-9, 116, 117-18, 133, 140-1, 142, 152
Christian Guardian, 93
Christian Observer, 36, 71, 73-74, 82, 83-84, 91, 93, 126, 134
Church Missionary Society, 86, 87-88, 97, 136
Clarke, Adam, 98
Cohn, Norman, 13, 15
Cole, G. D. H., 172
Coleridge, Samuel Taylor, 106
Comte, Auguste, 25
Consolidated Union (G.N.C.T.U.), 168, 175, 197, 202, 207, 209, 212, 213, 214
Continental Society, 107, 125
Cooper, Bransby, 152
Cooper, Edward, 64, 66-67, 152
Cousins, B. D., 176
Crisis, 24, 175, 195, 197, 202
Croly, George, 64, 67, 125
Cuninghame, William, 22, 55, 90, 92, 107, 128, 132, 133, 134-6, 142, 150, 222, 239

Davis, Hart, 152
Dawson, Sam, 156
Denman, Thomas, 168
Detrosier, Rowland, 161

Drummond, Henry, 11, 17, 56, 64, 70, 73, 74, 93, 98, 99, 103, 106, 107-13, 114, 116, 117, 120, 121, 123, 124, 125, 126, 127, 128, 130, 131, 132, 133, 134, 135, 136, 137, 138, 139, 140, 141, 142, 145, 150, 152, 169, 193, 198, 207, 210, 215

Emigration, Mormon, 218, 224, 225, 226-9
Enfantin, Barthelemy Prosper, 203, 204
Eschatology, 15, 19, 116, 218, 240, 243
Eusebius, 20, 27, 32, 38
Evangelical Magazine, 93-97, 219
Evangelical Review, 125

Faber, George Stanley, 13, 15, 22, 42, 46, 51, 54-64, 68, 70, 91-92, 93, 119, 120, 129, 134, 136, 141, 142, 147, 150, 179, 239
Fancourt, Miss, 126
Fielding, Joseph, 233-4
Fifth Monarchy, 26, 27, 36, 37, 146
Fleming, Robert (the younger), 37, 39, 43
Fleming, Robert (the elder), 37
Fontana, 203, 216
Foxe, John, 34, 108
Fraticelli, 29
French Revolution, 11, 13, 37, 39, 42-43, 46, 47, 50, 51, 52-3, 58, 64, 97, 119, 120, 134
Frere, James Hatley, 42, 58, 99, 106, 107, 125, 128, 132-4, 135, 136, 141, 142, 179, 222
Fuller, Thomas, 36

Gauntlett, Henry, 128, 140-2, 151
Gipps, Henry, 82
Glossolalia, 34, 71, 126, 132, 231-2
Godwin, Benjamin, 88-89
Goodwin, Christopher, 47
Grand National Consolidated Trades' Union, *see* Consolidated Union
Graves, Richard, 89-90
Greenwood, Thomas, 81
Grotius, Hugo, 82, 83

Hamilton, William, 96, 109
Hartley, David, 12, 34, 36, 38-39, 43, 45
Hegel, G. W. F., 25
Hetherington, Henry, 11, 170-1
Hey, John, 86-87, 88
Hibbert, Julian, 203
Holinsworth, C. B., 156, 157, 159, 200-1
Horsley, Samuel, 12, 50, 51-54, 55, 57, 58, 59, 60, 62, 91, 119, 120
Hume, Joseph, 155, 168
Hunt, Henry, 155, 168
Hurd, Richard, 36, 37, 38, 39, 54, 82

Inglis, R. H., 152
Institution for the Formation of Character, 180
Irving, Edward, 17, 24, 33, 56, 64, 70, 73, 74, 75, 81, 93, 94, 96-97, 98, 99-107, 108, 110, 111, 112, 113, 117, 122, 123, 124, 125, 126, 127, 128, 130, 131, 132, 133, 134, 136, 138, 139, 140, 141, 142, 145, 146, 148, 150, 151, 154, 165, 169, 173, 174, 179, 193, 197, 198, 199, 201, 207, 215, 226, 231, 232, 239
Irvingites, 11, 15, 71, 80, 82, 117, 126, 132, 194, 196, 198-9, 216, 221-2, 230-1, 232, 233, 234, 238

Jefferson, Thomas, 237
'Jesus Movement', 241, 242
Jewish Expositor, 140
Jewish Society, *see* Society for Promoting Christianity among the Jews
Jews, conversion of, 53, 56, 59-60, 62, 76, 89-90, 91, 92-93, 95, 128, 129-30, 131-2, 138, 198, 205
Jews, restoration of, 22, 36, 40, 44-45, 49-50, 51, 56, 59-63, 65, 76, 91-92, 128, 129-30, 131-2, 133-4, 135-6, 138, 223, 224, 225
Joachim of Fiore, 23, 25, 29, 30, 31, 35, 72, 147, 203-4
Jones, William (of Nayland), 50-51
Jones, William, 219
Jurieu, Pierre, 37, 39-40, 43, 44, 46, 47, 71, 169, 235

Keble, John, 11, 113, 114, 117, 128, 142-4, 148, 165
Kett, Henry, 55-56
King, Edward, 51-52

Labour Exchange, 200, 201
Lead, Jane, 157, 160, 177, 200
Lessing, Gotthold Ephraim, 204, 206

'Letters on Associated Labour', 202, 203, 208-15, 217
Lindsay, Alexander, 155
'Literalist' intepretations, 18, 77, 92, 131-2, 139, 143
London Missionary Society, 85-87, 107
Love, Christopher, 43

McNeile, Hugh, 64, 127, 128-32, 133, 135, 136, 141, 142, 222
Maitland, Samuel Roffey, 69, 79-80, 81, 82, 90, 96, 120, 239
Mandeville, Lord, 131
Manuel, F. E., 25, 27
Marx, Karl, 18, 23, 25, 211-12
Mede, Joseph, 13, 33, 35-36, 52, 55, 56
Mill, John Stuart, 207
Millennial Harbinger, 219
Millennial Star, 222, 224, 226, 227, 231, 233, 235
Missionaries, 23, 27, 62-63, 65, 73, 78, 84-98, 107, 129, 133, 135, 136, 138, 176, 243-4
Mitchelson, G., 234
Modern Fanaticism Unveiled, 80-81, 82
Montagu, Basil, 106
Moon, Elder, 226-7
More, Henry, 34, 36, 55
Mormons, 12, 15, 72, 82, 126, 148, 153, 165, 193, 194, 213, 218-38, 239
Morning Watch, 24, 80, 125, 126, 127
Morrison, James, 11, 16, 197, 198, 202, 209, 210, 212, 213, 214, 215, 216, 217
Muggletonians, 160

Napier, James, 198
Napier, John, 33, 34-35
Napoleon Bonaparte, 26, 33, 42, 47, 48, 54, 58, 59, 60, 66, 90, 119, 179
Napoleon, Louis, 64
New Moral World, 24, 176
Newman, John Henry, 11, 20, 50, 117, 128, 129, 142, 144-9, 150, 152, 174, 239
Newsweek, 11
Newton, Isaac, 12, 33, 34, 35, 36, 37, 38, 39, 45, 47, 51, 54, 95
Newton, Thomas, 11, 33, 36, 37-38, 39, 55, 56, 60, 82
Nietzsche, Friedrich, 18
Nixon of Cheshire, 33
Noel, Gerald Thomas, 74-78, 95-96, 126

O'Brien, Bronterre, 171
O'Connell, Daniel, 42
Overall, Bishop, 106, 107
Owen, John (Secretary of Bible Society), 88
Owen, John (Vice-Chancellor of Oxford University), 43, 174
Owen, Robert, 11, 12, 17, 20, 24, 40, 70, 106, 153, 165, 168, 169, 175-96, 197, 198, 201, 203, 207, 209, 210, 212, 213, 215, 216, 222, 223, 235, 238, 239, 242
Owenism, 17, 200, 202, 203, 207, 210, 212, 218

Papacy, 30-32, 36, 37, 42, 43, 47, 52-53, 55, 56, 57, 58, 66, 79, 80, 85, 89, 108-9, 115, 116, 120, 205-6, 235
Perceval, Spencer, 17, 125, 130, 151, 152, 154, 168
Pioneer, 197, 202, 212, 213, 214, 217
Poor Man's Guardian, 169, 170, 212
Post-millennialism, 20-22, 23, 32, 69-70, 78, 83-84, 90, 92-93, 94-96, 97, 127, 136-7, 138, 139, 140, 145, 228
Pratt, Josiah, 97
Pratt, Parley P., 233-4
Pre-millennialism, 20-22, 36, 67, 69-70, 78, 83-84, 90, 91, 92-93, 96, 107, 136-7, 138, 139, 228
Prati, 203, 216
Priestley, Joseph, 11, 12, 15, 33, 34, 36, 39, 43-46, 60, 62, 85, 97, 98, 121, 150, 169, 170, 188, 192, 197, 203, 219, 235, 239
Prophetical Extracts, 33

Radical movements, 17, 151, 163-4, 167, 168, 169, 170-2, 174, 210, 218, 221
Rational Religionists, 178
Reform Bill, 51, 141, 151, 155
Reformation, 25, 29, 30-32, 37, 38, 40, 48, 79, 85, 86, 119
Religious Tract Society, 87
Revivalism, 72, 93, 97, 218, 219
Revue Encyclopedique, 203
Rodrigues, Eugene, 204-6
Roman Empire, 26, 47, 53, 59, 120, 236
Rotunda, Blackfriars, 155, 156, 163, 164
Rymer, Thomas, 33

Sadler, Michael Thomas, 152
St Simon, Henri, 23, 30, 203-4, 205, 206-7, 208, 210, 212, 216
St Simonians, 12, 24, 30, 33, 161, 168, 197, 200, 203-7, 208, 209, 210, 216
Sandemanians, 158
Second Coming, 21-22, 32, 45, 49, 52, 56, 63, 71, 74, 75, 82, 92-93, 101, 102, 103, 121, 122, 129, 131, 134, 135, 137-8, 139, 143, 144, 145-7, 153, 178, 199, 223, 234
Shiloh, 154, 158, 159, 200, 201
Smith, James E., 11, 15, 17, 153, 154, 155, 161, 168, 175, 176-7, 195, 196, 197-217, 235
Smith, Joseph, 222, 224, 226, 227, 232, 236, 237, 238
Society for Promoting Christianity among the Jews, 62, 67, 89-90, 91, 135
Somerville, Alexander, 170
Southcott, Joanna, 81, 147, 153, 154, 157, 158, 159, 160, 173, 182, 195, 197, 198, 199, 221, 234
Southcottians, 15, 33, 148, 153, 154-5, 158, 159, 160, 169, 196, 200, 216, 232
Spiritual Franciscans, 23, 29
Stewart, James Haldane, 70-73, 74, 107, 192
Swedenborg, Emanuel, 160
Sybelline oracles, 33, 35

Taylor, Isaac, 96, 125
Taylor, Robert, 161, 170, 172, 199-200
Terry, G., 33
Thompson, Edward, 17
Tolpuddle Martyrs, 213
Tractarian movement, 112-13, 114, 118, 142, 222, 230
Trade union movement, 17, 168, 170, 193, 194, 197, 208, 213-14
Trinitarian Bible Society, 126
True Believers, 15, 155-7, 166-7
Turner, George, 155
Tuveson, Ernest, 13
Twort, C. W., 156, 167, 168

Usher, James, 43

Venn, John, 87
Voegelin, Eric, 25
Vyvyan, R., 152

Wakefield, Edward Gibbon, 218, 226
Warburton, William, 37
Ward, John, 15, 17, 24, 151, 153-74, 176-7, 179, 193, 195-6, 197, 198, 200-1, 202, 207, 213, 216, 222, 235
Watson, James, 171
Way, Lewis, 64, 83, 91, 92, 107, 128, 130, 131, 135, 136, 140, 142
Wesleyan-Methodist Magazine, 97-98
Whiston, William, 45
Wilkinson, Jemimah, 232
Wilson, Bryan, 243
Wolff, Joseph, 90, 99, 107, 129, 142
Women, 81-82
Wood, James, 234
Woodd, Basil, 87-88
Wroe, John, 155, 199, 200, 201, 234

Zetetic Societies, 161, 172